ANCIENT GREEK TEXTS AND MODERN NARRATIVE THEORY

The taxonomics of narratology have proven valuable tools for the analysis of ancient literature, but, since they were mostly forged in the analysis of modern novels, they have also occluded the distinct quality of ancient narrative and its understanding in antiquity. *Ancient Greek Texts and Modern Narrative Theory* paves the way for a new approach to ancient narrative that investigates its specific logic. Jonas Grethlein's sophisticated discussion of a wide range of literary texts in conjunction with works of criticism sheds new light on such central issues as fictionality, voice, Theory of Mind and narrative motivation. The book provides classicists with an introduction to ancient views of narrative but is also a major contribution to a historically sensitive theory of narrative.

JONAS GRETHLEIN is Professor of Greek at Heidelberg University and a member of the Heidelberger Akademie der Wissenschaften. His most recent books include *Aesthetic Experiences and Classical Antiquity* (Cambridge, 2017) and *The Ancient Aesthetics of Deception* (Cambridge, 2021).

ANCIENT GREEK TEXTS AND MODERN NARRATIVE THEORY

Towards a Critical Dialogue

JONAS GRETHLEIN

Heidelberg University

CAMBRIDGE
UNIVERSITY PRESS

Shaftesbury Road, Cambridge CB2 8EA, United Kingdom

One Liberty Plaza, 20th Floor, New York, NY 10006, USA

477 Williamstown Road, Port Melbourne, VIC 3207, Australia

314–321, 3rd Floor, Plot 3, Splendor Forum, Jasola District Centre, New Delhi – 110025, India

103 Penang Road, #05–06/07, Visioncrest Commercial, Singapore 238467

Cambridge University Press is part of Cambridge University Press & Assessment, a department of the University of Cambridge.

We share the University's mission to contribute to society through the pursuit of education, learning and research at the highest international levels of excellence.

www.cambridge.org
Information on this title: www.cambridge.org/9781009339599

DOI: 10.1017/9781009339605

First published 2023

A catalogue record for this publication is available from the British Library.

A Cataloging-in-Publication data record for this book is available from the Library of Congress

ISBN 978-1-009-33959-9 Hardback

Contents

Figures

vi

Acknowledgements

This book has grown out of three papers that were written separately: one on the significance of the Theory of Mind for responses to narrative in the light of Heliodorus' *Ethiopica* (*Style* 49 (2015): 259–83); one on the motivation of the Penelope scenes in *Odyssey* 18 and 19 (*CCJ* 64 (2018): 70–90); and one on the relation between authors and characters as seen by ancient critics (*CP* 116 (2021): 208–30). Only after writing these papers did I notice the common thread linking them: despite their different foci and objectives, all three papers were motivated by a deeper discomfort with how modern narrative theory, especially structuralist narratology, has made us view ancient narrative. Taken together, the three papers permit us to make a case that is significantly broader than the points for which they argue individually – a case about the study of ancient narrative at large. There can be no doubt about the rich fruits of narratology in Classics, and yet the application of narratological categories, while letting us see the complexity of many texts with fresh eyes, has also occluded the distinct quality of ancient narrative and its understanding in antiquity.

Ancient Greek Texts and Modern Narrative Theory: Towards a Critical Dialogue is the attempt to pave the way for new approaches to ancient narrative beyond narratology. It is an exploration, not a study that exhausts its subject – a book that aspires to be a first step instead of offering the last word. In addition to revising and expanding the original three papers, I wrote three more chapters: one that provides the groundwork by carefully assessing the current state of scholarship on ancient narrative and contemplating alternative approaches to it (Chapter 1); one that discusses the idea of fiction(ality) and the relation between world and words in antiquity (Chapter 2); and one that uses postmodern parallels to throw into relief ancient views of narrative that deviate from modern conventions (Chapter 6).

I thank the editors of *Style*, *CCJ* and *CP* for permitting me to use the material from the articles mentioned above. I have drawn on the following translations, modifying them where necessary:

R. Lattimore (1951)	*The Iliad of Homer*. Chicago
R. Lattimore (1965)	*The Odyssey of Homer*. New York
A. Laks and G. W. Most (2016)	*Early Greek Philosophers*. Cambridge, MA
H. N. Fowler and W. R. M. Lamb (1925)	*Plato. Statesman, Philebus, Ion*. Cambridge, MA
G. M. A. Grube, rev. C. D. C. Reeve (1992)	*Plato. The Republic* . Indianapolis
S. Halliwell (1987)	*The Poetics of Aristotle*. London
W. H. Fyfe (1927)	*'Longinus'. On the Sublime*. Cambridge, MA
J. R. Morgan (1989)	*Heliodorus. An Ethiopian Story*, in *Collected Ancient Greek Novels*, ed. B. P. Reardon. Oakland: 407–686

The names of ancient authors are abbreviated in accordance with the *Oxford Classical Dictionary*; the abbreviations of modern journals follow *L'Année philologique*.

My debts are significant – many friends and colleagues have enlightened my thinking about ancient narrative in one way or another. I will not be able to list all of them here, but I wish to thank at least Markus Asper, Jaš Elsner, Renaud Gagné, Simon Goldhill, Stephen Halliwell, Luuk Huitink, Richard Hunter, Benedek Kruchió, Chris Pelling, Jim Porter, Michael Squire, Aldo Tagliabue, Stefan Tilg, Athanassios Vergados, Gregor Vogt-Spira and Tim Whitmarsh. I am particularly grateful to Monika Fludernik for numerous discussions about narratological issues and to Eva von Contzen for her insights into medieval narrative. Benjamin Allgaier, Emma Burton and Thomas Kuhn-Treichel have as circumspectly as kindly read a first draft of the book. Isabel Caspar, Leonhard Gerke and Sabine Hug were an indispensable help in preparing the manuscript. I am also grateful to Cambridge University Press's two anonymous readers for their instructive comments and to Kathleen Fearn for her excellent copy-editing. As in the past, it has been a privilege to work with Michael Sharp.

I dedicate the book to my daughters, Antonia and Klara – it has been a highlight of my life in the past years to tell them stories and to watch their responses as well as to follow their own beginnings as narrators.

CHAPTER I

Narratology and Classics

I The Success and Critique of Narratology in Classics

Classics is a demanding discipline. Before being able to read ancient texts, students have to learn Greek and Latin.[1] They have to memorize various declensions and conjugations, drill into their heads numerous irregular verb forms, acquaint themselves with a third voice in addition to the active and passive voices, master the uses of tense and mode in conditional clauses and so on. Once they have achieved this, Classicists face a long history of scholarship; when trying to come up with something new about Homer, Tacitus and Augustine, they have to plough through shelves of books and articles discussing these authors. Little surprise, then, that not all scholars in Classics delve enthusiastically into theory – the days when traditional philologists were in irreconcilable opposition to the disciples of Roland Barthes, Mikhail Bakhtin and Jacques Derrida are over, and yet there is still a considerable faction that avowedly uses their time for reading ancient texts rather than books on postcolonialism, new materialism and cognitivism.

There is, however, one approach that even conservative Classicists have gratefully embraced, and this is narratology, more specifically structuralist narratology.[2] Key to the dissemination of narratological analysis in Classics

---

[1] There is currently a lively debate on whether Classics departments should give up their language requirements. The main reason for such a change is the wish to be more inclusive – in some countries, Greek and Latin is taught chiefly at expensive private schools (on England, see https://cucd .blogs.sas.ac.uk/files/2021/02/Holmes-Henderson-and-Hunt-Classics-Poverty.docx.pdf), and therefore Classics departments tend to recruit their students from a small and ethnically as well as socially exclusive group. For discussions of the situations in the United States, UK and Italy, see the essays in *QUCC* 129/3 (2021). While I hope that there will be room for different tracks, some involving the languages, others doing without them, I do not dare to predict what Classics will look like in twenty-five years. At the moment, however, its scholarly practice is still premised on the knowledge of Greek and Latin.

[2] Fowler 2001: 68: 'It is an approach which has been taken up and adapted even by classicists relatively hostile to theory'.

was Irene de Jong's dissertation on *Narrators and Focalizers in the* Iliad (1987), but other pioneering works ought not to be forgotten. While de Jong utilized Mieke Bal's system, John Winkler's *Auctor & Actor. A Narratological Reading of Apuleius'* Golden Ass (1985) was inspired chiefly by Barthes, and Massimo Fusillo marshalled Gérard Genette's taxonomy for his examinations of Apollonius' *Argonautica* (1985) and the ancient novel (1989).[3] In the introductory chapter to a volume geared to bringing together theory and philology in Classics, Stephen Harrison parades narratology as an approach that illustrates the potential of this endeavour: 'The application of narratology to classical texts has been a success story.'[4]

One of the reasons for the popularity of narratology is 'its technical and descriptive nature', which 'is non-threatening to conventional models of interpretation'.[5] The classification of a narrator as extradiegetic or intradiegetic, heterodiegetic or homodiegetic is, after all, not that different from identifying the forms ῇ or *missum iri*. However, what is appraised in Oxford is not necessarily *le dernier cri* at Cambridge. The formalism that renders Bal's and Genette's taxonomies so attractive to Harrison and many other scholars is a major weakness in the eyes of others. In his review of de Jong's *Narratology & Classics. A Guide to Narratology*, Simon Goldhill contends that the kind of analysis presented in this book 'is bound to seem like no more than a rather trivial formal observation'.[6] If narratology wants to cut some ice, it needs to confront semantic issues in the manner of Barthes' *S/Z*. From a slightly different angle, but also taking issue with narratology's formalism, Tim Whitmarsh notes: 'Like many readers, I suspect, I have long found the antiseptic formulae of narratologists incompatible with my experience of reading.'[7] The criticism of narratology is not confined to Cambridge – the US scholar William Thalmann exacerbates a feeling of discomfort shared by others when he chastises 'an often rebarbative jargon . . . that at best helps systematize features common to a great many narratives and at worst mystifies simple concepts'.[8]

And, in fact, narratology is best seen as a tool, not an end in itself. Narratological analysis becomes fruitful when it is used for interpretation.[9] De Jong's analysis of focalization in the *Iliad*, for example, has significantly improved our understanding of Homer's way of presenting his story.[10] Generations of scholars had called Homer's style 'objective'. However, de

---

[3] Scodel 2014a: 4 ignores these works preceding de Jong's landmark study.   [4] Harrison 2001: 13.
[5] Schmitz 2015: 707.   [6] Goldhill 2015: 328.   [7] Whitmarsh 2013: 244.
[8] Thalmann 2014: 176.   [9] For this point, see Grethlein and Rengakos 2009.
[10] See also, however, the critical discussion of Bal's concept of focalizers deployed and made popular in Classics by de Jong in Rood 1998: 294–6. It has already been criticized by Genette 1983: 48.

Jong showed that in Homer's narrator text, adjectives can be focalized by characters. When, for example, Homer reports that Priam 'kissed the hands/ that were dangerous and man-slaughtering and had killed so many of his sons' (24.478–9), the hands, de Jong suggests, are described through the lens of Priam. Far from objective, the account is emotionally charged through the perspective of the character. Now, de Jong was not the first to observe the emotional quality of such passages – Jasper Griffin had followed up comments on *pathos* in ancient scholia[11] – and yet her narratological examination put such interpretations on a new footing. De Jong's argument was corroborated not least by the observation that many of the adjectives deployed in embedded focalization were elsewhere confined to character speech.[12]

Another example illustrates that, whereas most narratological models were developed for fiction, our understanding of factual texts can also benefit from their deployment. In a pioneering chapter, Simon Hornblower considered anachronies in Thucydides.[13] The *History of the Peloponnesian War* is chronological and follows the course of the war from season to season, but some events are displaced in the narrative. As Hornblower shows, some of these displacements help downplay Athens' aggressiveness before the outbreak of the war. The narratological analysis thus backs up Ernst Badian's thesis about Thucydides' minimization of Athens' share in the escalation leading to the Peloponnesian War.[14] In itself, the examination of anachronies is worth little, but as part of an interpretation it can become powerful – in our example it sheds light on the bias of a putatively objective historian.[15]

It would be easy but also boring to fill pages with references to further studies that have deepened our understanding of a long list of Greek and Roman authors with the help of narratology. At the same time, it needs to be admitted that narratological analysis is less exciting when it is done for its own sake; the purposeless parsing of narrators and mere tracing of anachronies quickly become tedious. A case in point is the volumes of

---

[11] Griffin 1980: 103–43.

[12] The potential of the notion of embedded focalization is further illustrated by Fowler 1990, who gives it a different twist by calling it 'deviant focalisation' and uses it to reassess the *Aeneid*'s stance on power.

[13] Hornblower 1994: 139–45. His examination of the 'self-conscious narrator' in the *History of the Peloponnesian War* is also noteworthy, as it shows that the expression of doubts about particulars is a means of strengthening the credibility of the overall presentation or other details (149–52).

[14] Badian 1993.

[15] The fruitfulness of a narratological analysis for the interpretation of Thucydides is further proven by Rood 1998.

the *Studies in Ancient Greek Narrative*, a large-scale project spearheaded by de Jong.[16] The first volume examines narrators and narratees, the second time, the third space, the fourth characterization, each pursuing Greek literature chronologically from Homer to the Imperial era. By no means are the volumes without value – each of them contains chapters with intriguing observations, and yet, on the whole, the enterprise falls flat. None of the narratological categories yields an interesting trajectory for the history of Greek literature. We do not gain a better understanding of it by analysing the narratorial position or temporal orchestration diachronically. Interesting points often emerge when the different narratological categories are viewed in conjunction. Most importantly, the chapters that are rewarding to read illustrate that narratology ought to have an ancillary status – they illuminate Greek texts by using the narratological analysis for interpretation and combining it with other approaches.

2   The Priz/ce of the Modern Lens of Narratology

There is another issue with narratology in Classics that has not received much attention but is, I think, equally serious as the formalism decried by Goldhill and Whitmarsh and ultimately more challenging. Narratologists present their taxonomies as transhistorical tools, and, indeed, any narrative can be dissected with regard to voice, time and perspective (just as any flower can be classified as a daisy or a non-daisy). However, the categories of narratology were coined in readings chiefly of modern realist novels.[17] Genette, to name arguably the most influential proponent in the field, developed his taxonomy in a reading of Proust's *À la recherche du temps perdu*. More recent approaches in narrative theory, including cognitive narratology, also tend to privilege modern texts as their basis. This does not undermine their applicability to premodern texts – such a claim would be hermeneutically naive – and yet it raises the question of how far it gets us.

At first sight, there seems to be no doubt about the fruitfulness of the endeavour, as 'classical texts themselves display the kind of narrative complexities which narratology can help to unravel and categorize'.[18] Indeed, as de Jong's investigation has shown, there are complex instances of focalization in Homer, just as the condensation of the action in both

---

[16] See, for example, the critical comments in Scodel 2005; Feeney 2008; Grethlein 2012a.

[17] The idea of realism is contested, and there are of course other novels in the nineteenth and twentieth centuries that challenge realist conventions, but the very existence of these conventions attests to a mainstream – a mainstream that forms the material basis of many narratological studies.

[18] Harrison 2001: 14.

Iliad and *Odyssey* is premised on a complex temporal orchestration that can be captured through Genette's categories of order, duration and frequency. One of the reasons for the fruitfulness of analysing ancient texts with the help of narratological categories forged for modern novels is the genealogical links between ancient and modern literature. It is not always acknowledged in literary histories, but the ancient tradition had a significant impact on the rise of the modern novel. To mention just one strand, the ancient Greek novels were translated into the vernacular languages in the sixteenth century, and Longus' *Daphnis and Chloe* and Heliodorus' *Ethiopica* especially served as models for Baroque novels, which influenced the novels emerging in the eighteenth and nineteenth centuries.[19] In an important monograph, Nick Lowe traced the emergence of 'the classical plot and the invention of Western narrative' in ancient literature.[20]

There are also strategic reasons for the infatuation of Classicists with narratology – the application of categories forged for the analysis of modern texts allows Classicists to prove the complexity and, closely linked to it, quality of their material.[21] The inclination of classical narratologists to demonstrate through their investigations that their authors compare to the likes of Henry James is tangible in the rhetoric of 'Homer first' pervading the works of de Jong. In *Narrators and Focalizers in the* Iliad, she triumphantly declares: 'Despite the uniformity bestowed upon the Iliadic text by the unity of metre . . . the formulas and the typical scenes, the narrative has more variety of presentation than many a modern novel.'[22] Besides the notorious NF1, the primary narrator-focalizer, the *Iliad* also features tertiary focalizers and hypothetical speakers! The same argumentative strategy can be found in all volumes of *Studies in Ancient Greek Narrative*. In the first volume, *Narrators, Narratees, and Narratives in Ancient Greek Literature*, de Jong proudly announces: 'The first texts we have, the Homeric epics, display much of the narratorial repertoire and handle it in a virtuoso manner.'[23] In the second volume, which focuses upon time in narrative, we read: 'This chapter has shown that just about the whole

---

[19] Pavel 2003 is a historical account of the modern novel that acknowledges the role of the reception of Heliodorus especially.
[20] Lowe 2000.
[21] The notion of complexity in scholarship would be worth investigating. It is, I suspect, a highly charged category through which scholars who have been trained not to call their texts 'great' implicitly convey judgements. Complexity as a value term is firmly embedded in the hermeneutics of suspicion, which attempts to uncover the deeper meaning hidden in texts. See below, p. 119.
[22] De Jong 1987: 227.   [23] De Jong, Nünlist and Bowie 2004: 552.

arsenal of time-related narrative devices which modern narratology has identified is to be found in Homer.'[24]

The appeal of this rhetoric of 'Homer first' to Classicists is admittedly hard to resist. It shows that the texts we work on are far from primitive – they even rival the experiments of William Faulkner and other modern authors. In proving the sophistication of ancient authors, we can also showcase our own cleverness. Our colleagues in the English and Comparative Literature departments may ignore our texts and consider us brutish philologists, but with the help of their tools we can finally get the better of them. To a certain extent, this strategy works, because many of the features of modern novels can be found in ancient genres. At the same time, it comes at a considerable price. While permitting us to identify putatively modern features in ancient narratives, narratology has been less helpful for elucidating what renders them specific and different from modern literature. The taxonomies derived from the study of modern realist novels have let us see in ancient narratives primarily elements that these narratives share with modern texts. The victory march of narratology in Classics has thus had the unfortunate side effect of detracting from what distinguishes ancient from modern literature. The focus on continuity at the expense of alterity has seriously impaired our understanding of ancient narrative.

The problem we encounter here is not limited to structuralist narratology and has deep hermeneutic roots. Structuralist narratology is not alone in having been developed with an eye to modern novels; many other approaches in the broader field of narrative studies and literary theories in general were forged or at least tested in readings of novels of the nineteenth and twentieth centuries. Our reading expectations in general are shaped not exclusively but chiefly by modern texts. More profoundly, we always understand texts from other periods and cultures in the horizon of our present. Hans-Georg Gadamer envisaged this understanding as the melting of the horizons of author and reader, but this view has been criticized as overly optimistic.[25] Even if we do not subscribe to a radical scepticism that challenges the possibility of understanding what others mean in general, the gaps separating cultures ought not to be underestimated. The coining of narratological categories in readings of modern novels epitomizes our general tendency to view texts through the lens of our own time.

---

[24] De Jong and Nünlist 2007: 36.
[25] Gadamer 2013 [1960]: 263–4. For the controversy, see, for example, Derrida and Gadamer 1989. For an emphasis on the 'inter' of interpretation as marking an unbridgeable gap, see Grethlein 2022.

3 Alternative Approaches

If we wish to highlight the gap between ancient and modern texts and the understanding of narrative in antiquity and today, we can take different routes. First, Classicists have drawn on narratology mostly to show the complexity of ancient texts and to emphasize their similarity to modern literature, but narratological analysis can also be harnessed to spotlight differences. This is the goal of the diachronic narrative called for by Monika Fludernik in an influential article from 2003.[26] The examination of the history of narrative forms and functions, she argues, opens up a huge new field for narratological investigations. The *Studies of Ancient Greek Narrative*, however, reveal that a diachronic survey of major narratological categories can be unrewarding. Even if done differently, an examination of anachronies or pacing from Homer to Handke is unlikely to enhance our understanding of where ancient narratives deviate from modern ones.

Fludernik's case study illustrates that diachronic narratology has to proceed more subtly and circumspectly. She explores scene shifts from Middle English literature to modern texts in relation to larger narrative patterns and to their functions. In the oral delivery of episodic narrative, scene shifts had an important structuring function. They lost this function with the introduction of chapters in texts written to be read, notably the novel, and were refunctionalized as meta-narrative comments. The case of scene shifts reveals that it may be heuristically fruitful to focus on more specific narrative elements instead of the major narratological categories. Perhaps even more importantly, it shows that it will not do to survey the transformation of narrative forms – the forms need to be examined in conjunction with their functions. Such an examination may also lead to extratextual aspects, such as medium in Fludernik's discussion, which help to explain differences.

An article by de Jong throws into relief how important the consideration of the function of narrative forms is for diachronic narratology in delivering interesting results. In her contribution to Douglas Cairns and Ruth Scodel's *Defining Greek Narrative*, de Jong investigates the motif of the anonymous traveller in European literature.[27] After introducing the motif, she starts from an example in Proust, gives further instances from Flaubert and Stendhal, makes a huge jump to Procopius and works her way back through ancient literature until she arrives at Homer. She then raises the question of whether the anonymous traveller is a universal or a distinctly Greek device with an impressive reception history. Instead of doing the

---

[26] Fludernik 2003b.   [27] De Jong 2014a.

work necessary to prove or disprove the existence of a literary tradition, however, she hijacks a concept of Richard Dawkins and declares the anonymous traveller 'an originally Greek meme that has proved to be an extremely fit survivalist'.[28] But even more disappointing than this conclusion is the diachronic survey itself. Where Fludernik considers the form in light of the functions it plays in different genres and cultures, de Jong merely lists examples and perfunctorily surveys the narrative contexts – all that we can note after her inquiry is that the anonymous traveller can be traced back to antiquity. Done in this way, diachronic narratology will certainly not help elucidate the distinctiveness of ancient narrative.

By no means do I wish to belittle the value of de Jong's article. The identification of the motif of the anonymous traveller in ancient literature is full of merit, and the juxtaposition of its occurrences in ancient and modern texts is interesting even without further analysis. This said, the article shows what is required if diachronic narratology is to shed light on the specific character of ancient literature. If we only trace forms back to antiquity without carefully scrutinizing their use and exploring the contexts of production, circulation and reception, all we learn is that ancient authors already deployed them. Another major challenge consists in identifying narrative forms that are specific enough to be analysed across a wide range of texts and nonetheless sufficiently significant to grant insights into different conceptions of narrative. Diachronic narratology can grasp only such differences as are related to narrative forms surfacing across epochs and cultures.

Pertinent to my discussion is a distinction that has recently been proposed. While many scholars use 'diachronic narratology' and 'historical narratology' indistinctly, some differentiate between them: in a programmatic article that advances the term 'chrononarratology' as an umbrella term for approaches that pay attention to the historical dimension of narrative, Dorothee Birke, Eva von Contzen and Karin Kukkonen envisage the diachronic approach as including 'texts from different periods' and aiming to 'trace developments across these periods, while the historical approach foregrounds a corpus of texts from a single historical period'.[29] In a survey of recent contributions, they note that diachronic studies tend to emphasize continuity, whereas the investigations of historical narratology rather come down on the side of alterity.[30] There are, however, also

---

[28] De Jong 2014a: 333.
[29] Birke, von Contzen and Kukkonen 2022: 30. See also von Contzen 2018: 23–8.
[30] In addition to diachronic versus historical and continuity versus alterity, Birke, von Contzen and Kukkonen 2022 propose the third axis of universalist versus particularist: whether scholars use terms that can be applied to narratives of all epochs or prefer epoch-specific terminology.

exceptions, as the authors duly note – the article of Fludernik just mentioned (n. 26), for example, is sensitive to the differences between historical epochs. De Jong's influential work, on the other hand, illustrates the inclination of diachronic analysis to stress continuity.

The distinction made by Birke, von Contzen and Kukkonen leads us to another way of approaching the distinct quality of ancient narrative, namely, turning directly to ancient texts. The careful scrutiny of ancient narrative is, of course, essential to all the approaches outlined here, but whereas diachronic narratology is premised on identifying narrative forms and tracing them across epochs, other scholars prefer simply to take a close look at ancient texts themselves. Ancient criticism in particular gives us glimpses of how ancient readers viewed their texts. While Aristotle's *Poetics*, Pseudo-Longinus' *de sublimitate* and Horace's *Ars poetica* have occupied scholars for a long time, recent work has done much to chart the scholia, using them to give us an idea of what questions were asked and which answers were given in the numerous critical treatises that have not been preserved.[31] For attempts to identify the ancient logic of narrative, the scholia are a priceless treasure.

Here too, however, we can see the tendency to view the ancient material either explicitly as prefiguring modern standards or at least through the lens of modern categories. Even René Nünlist, who considers a vast amount of ancient material and takes care not to present it as narratology *avant la lettre*, draws partly on major narratological categories such as plot, time and focalization to structure his foray into the field of Greek scholia.[32] The alternative of taking Greek terms as organizing principles would only conceal this tendency and is also rendered impractical by the lack of a coherent critical terminology in antiquity.

Stefan Feddern's *Elemente der antiken Erzähltheorie* illustrates how easy it is to slide from the inevitable process of translation to a view of ancient criticism as a prefiguration of modern narratology: 'In my investigation of ancient narrative theory, modern narrative theory serves chiefly to systematize the discursive field, in which – this is a second step – individual ancient positions can be distinguished from one another.'[33] Modern

---

[31] For example, Dickey 2007; Nünlist 2009; Montanari 2015; 2020. Richardson 1980 and Meijering 1987 remain important points of reference. Much attention has been given to the Roman grammarian Servius, whose commentaries on Virgil provide rich material, see, for example, Santini and Stok 2004; Casali and Stok 2008; Bouquet-Méniel 2011; Garcea, Lhommé and Vallat 2016.

[32] Nünlist 2009.

[33] Feddern 2021: 3: 'Die moderne Erzähltheorie dient in dieser Untersuchung der antiken Erzähltheorie vordringlich dazu, das diskursive Feld zu systematisieren, innerhalb dessen sich in einem zweiten Schritt die antiken Positionen ausdifferenzieren lassen.'

narratology seems to be the innocent grid through which ancient narrative theory is assessed; that this, however, implies reducing ancient views to anticipating modern categories is evident in the preceding sentence: 'In fact, the ancient narrative theory presented here consists of the most important reflections on narration, many of which, *mutatis mutandis*, correspond to those categories that modern narratologists such as Genette have coined and/or compiled (the adherence to them in this monograph will not be slavish).'[34] Genette's use of Greek terms makes it easy to use them for charting ancient theoretical reflections but should not detract from the fact that these are categories forged in the analysis of Proust. Looking only at reflections that correspond to modern categories risks losing sight of aspects that are different from what we encounter in modern literature.

I also wonder what justifies Feddern's notion of 'the ancient narrative theory'. One of the strengths of his study is its breadth – Feddern takes into account far more texts than other studies of ancient criticism, drawing attention to some that are relevant but rarely discussed. But 'the ancient narrative theory' suggests a unitary entity and veils the very different contexts from which the references stem. I do not take issue with the theory of *narrative*. There are several terms in Greek and Latin that we translate as 'narrative', and ancient authors often focus on specific forms of narrative – for example, song, tragedy or speeches – but if we take into account their focus, it is legitimate to explore their discussions as reflections on what we call narrative. It is *the theory* of narrative that is problematic, as it downplays the disagreements and the variety of genres in which narrative is addressed.

Another recent book, Genevieve Liveley's *Narratology*, circumvents this danger of claiming a single ancient theory by discussing author by author (at the price of a much smaller breadth than Feddern's study) but also reveals the pull to view ancient critics as the predecessors of modern narratologists.[35] Liveley advances an account of the history of narrative theory from Plato to Post-classicism. Her study is illuminating in many regards, not least because it lets us see the presence and transformation of ancient ideas in modern theory. At the same time, the teleological structure makes Liveley's history less apt at spotlighting the peculiarities

---

[34] Feddern 2021: 2–3: 'Vielmehr besteht die hier präsentierte antike Erzähltheorie aus den wichtigsten Reflexionen über das Erzählen, von denen viele *mutatis mutandis* denjenigen Kategorien entsprechen, die moderne Narratologen wie Genette konzipiert und/oder kompiliert haben, ohne dass sich diese Monographie sklavisch an dieser Norm orientiert.'

[35] Liveley 2019.

of ancient views on narrative. Teleologies inevitably direct us to points that will turn out to be significant for the outcome, while neglecting others that were significant in their own time without, however, leaving noteworthy traces.

The danger of falling back onto modern categories is equally present in studies that concentrate on ancient narrative instead of criticism. Scodel's own contribution to *Defining Greek Narrative* is a case in point.[36] The chapter examines shifts of focus, the management of gaps and the characters' mind reading in Homer. Scodel contends that Homer takes pains to engage us with his heroes' consciousness processes, whether they are described explicitly or need to be conjectured. His ways of making recipients mind read are fundamental for later ancient literature: 'The Homeric narrative thereby provides a basis for drama, in which the audience must make sense of the action without a narrator's help ... it shows narrative possibilities that were to be developed by tragedy, Virgil and the realist novel.'[37] Scodel explicitly rejects the narratological category of focalization as a frame for her analysis, and yet, as I will argue in one of this book's chapters, her argument fails to capture the logic of Homeric narrative because it is premised on reading expectations generated by modern realist novels.[38] As readers of Henry James, Ford Maddox Ford and Jonathan Franzen, we are trained to concentrate on the characters' mind – there are of course fictional minds also in ancient narratives, but other aspects are more important for enticing the recipients.

As this survey reveals, in Classics not only diachronic investigations, but also studies that through their focus on ancient texts rather fall under the category of historical narratology, tend to stress the continuities with modern literature. In this regard, scholarship in Classics is different from the strong tradition of historical narratology in Medievalist Studies, which elaborates on the alterity of medieval texts.[39] One reason for this may be the claims still inherent in a discipline called 'Classics', another is certainly the greater conspicuousness of the clash of medieval narrative conventions with modern expectations. This said, as I hope to show in this book, there are also flagrant discrepancies in what is still seen as the continuum linking modern to ancient literature.

---

[36] Scodel 2014b. [37] Scodel 2014b: 56.

[38] See Chapter 4, esp. 108-110 for a critical discussion of one of Scodel's cases.

[39] Historical narratology is particularly prominent in scholarship on German literature from the Middle Ages (e.g., Haferland and Meyer 2010; Schulz 2012; Plotke 2017) but can also be found elsewhere, for example, in the works of Spearing 2005; 2012. On historical narratology in general, see also von Contzen 2014 and von Contzen and Tilg 2019.

The paper by Scodel just mentioned also touches on a third way of identifying what is Greek about Greek narrative, namely the comparison with other ancient literatures. While Scodel refers only in passing to Erich Auerbach's juxtaposition of Homer with the Hebrew Bible, the comparative approach forms the core of two other contributions to the volume. Johannes Haubold also starts from the first chapter of *Mimesis* but goes on to replace the Hebrew Bible with the *Gilgamesh* epic.[40] His comparison yields a similar result though: 'Auerbach was right: the Homer who emerges from my discussion is still a master of immediacy.' However, Haubold finds the differences 'aesthetically meaningful rather than merely betraying different mentalities'.[41] What renders Haubold's chapter particularly thought-provoking is its reflection on the politics of comparisons. It is not incidental that the Jewish exile Auerbach compared the Hebrew Bible with 'the Homer of Schiller and Goethe', just as Haubold's own probing into the differences between Homer and *Gilgamesh* is firmly situated in the current urge to delimit the Western canon. Haubold's reflections underline that comparisons are never innocent operations – they are always imbued with political agendas.

Adrien Kelly compares the battle scenes in Homer with those in texts of the Ancient Near East, notably the Hebrew Bible and Akkadian as well as Egyptian epics.[42] His conclusion is that Homeric epic is distinct in its narrativization and aestheticization of the happenings on the battlefield. Kelly's inquiry is simultaneously impressive on account of the wide range of Near Eastern texts it discusses and precise by virtue of the focus on battle scenes. This focus, however, also limits insights into the narrative techniques, as only a very special type of scene is examined, which may determine some of the findings. Here, we touch on a general problem of the comparative approach. The more specific the comparison is, the more precise the results can be, but the narrowing of the focus, just like the exclusion of other potential material, may reduce the significance of the comparison.

4 Approaching the Fault Lines

All three approaches mentioned have their merits: a close engagement with ancient texts is indispensable, and comparisons can be immensely illuminating, whether synchronically in a juxtaposition of ancient cultures or as

---

[40] Haubold 2014. See also Haubold 2013 for his comparative approach to Greek and Mesopotamian literature and Clarke 2019 for an instructive juxtaposition of the *Iliad* with the *Gilgamesh* epic.
[41] Haubold 2014: 27.   [42] Kelly 2014.

a part of a diachronic narratology that traces the development of narrative forms through epochs. In this book, though, I will try another route: each of the following chapters takes a central concept of modern narrative theory and investigates how ancient texts relate to it. However, instead of striving to prove the existence or prefiguration of these concepts in antiquity and thereby to prove ancient literature to be modern *avant la lettre*, I will zero in on the fault lines, where the ancient sense of narrative does not map onto our categories. This inquiry will alert us not only to the limits of modern narrative theory with regard to antiquity. It also prepares the ground for probing into what renders the ancient understanding of narrative unique.

A possible objection to my approach is that, not unlike narrative theory, the target of its criticism, it uses the filter of modern narrative, as it starts from concepts and categories derived from its examination. However, to take modern concepts as a starting point is part of a hermeneutic exercise. We inevitably view antiquity through the lens of our time. Even where we do not explicitly invoke theory, our viewpoint is, more or less strongly, shaped by assumptions premised either on theory or on our reading experiences (where, in most cases, modern novels will dominate). The strategy of simply looking closely enough at the ancient material without the use of theory bypasses this to its own detriment – the modernizing interpretations that its advocates set out to avoid frequently return in the unreflected premises of their readings. By taking my cue from modern concepts that guide our approaches to literature, I try to make explicit our hermeneutic horizon; this, I hope, will make it easier to tease out where the ancient understanding of narrative deviates from it.

My approach not only opposes the tendency of classical narratologists to pinpoint the modern features of ancient narrative, but it also differs from the diachronic narratology envisaged by Fludernik. Instead of tracing the transformation of narrative forms, I look at major narrative concepts. My inquiry is concerned not only with ancient narrative, but more broadly with the ancient sense of narrative. In order to elucidate this sense, I will discuss ancient criticism alongside ancient narratives. What I consider the distinctly ancient understanding of narrative manifests itself both in narrative texts and in critical reflections on these texts.[43] By no means do

---

[43] It is, I think, not a mistake to view ancient literature and criticism in conjunction. On the one hand, many literary texts are highly reflexive and are therefore discussed in studies of ancient poetics and aesthetics, for example, the *Odyssey* in Peponi 2012 and Halliwell 2011. On the other hand, at least some ancient critical treatises are highly rhetorical themselves and have a literary quality that merits our attention, Pseudo-Longinus being an obvious example. In addition, criticism influenced later

narrative practice and the concepts of critics always coincide. Nor is there a single view to which all authors unanimously subscribe – on the contrary, ancient writers not only contemplated various narrative forms that only partly map onto each other, such as *logos, mythos, aoidē, poiēsis*; they also indulged in disagreements and advanced a significant number of rival concepts. At the same time, ancient narratives and the various comments of critics belong to a gravitational field. When I refer to the ancient sense or understanding of narrative, it is not a unified theory but a question of certain premises shared by a wide range of positions expressed in different contexts and forms.

This book thus triangulates modern narrative theory, ancient narrative and ancient criticism.[44] Its title has only two parts, because 'ancient texts' encompass criticism as well as narrative. Only studied in conjunction with and thrown into relief by modern approaches do narrative practice and criticism permit us to capture the distinct sense of narrative in antiquity. 'Practice', here, is not a mere *façon de parler*; in some cases, it will not suffice to consider textual features, but it will be necessary also to take into account the production, circulation and reception of texts. This context, so different from ours, can help explain some of what strikes us as the peculiarities of ancient literature. For the reasons already stated, the third part of the triangulation is modern narrative theory, which, however, in some ways reflects the practice of modern narrative, as many of its categories derive from the examination of modern literature. At the same time, modern narrative theory, besides itself encompassing various approaches, is far from fully mapping onto ancient criticism. Greek and Roman critics not only had their own objectives, but a significant part of their work is only accessible in the truncated form of scholia. This said, it is the asymmetries between the corpora involved – the tensions between narrative practice and narrative theory as well as the gap between ancient and modern views – that renders the triangulation, on which this inquiry is premised, productive.

Let me add a comment on the use of theory in literary studies in order to avoid misunderstanding. By no means am I opposed to the deployment of modern concepts in the interpretation of ancient texts. On the contrary, I am convinced that the application of modern theories to Greek and Roman literature can be extremely useful and that it is also, in some ways, inevitable. As I have pointed out, we cannot but understand texts against

literary texts, as argued, for example, by Schlunk 1974 for the Homeric scholia and Virgil's *Aeneid* and by Farrell 2016 for commentaries on Theocritus and Virgil's *Eclogues*.

[44] This triangulation has already proven fruitful for the exploration of the experiential quality of ancient narrative in Grethlein, Huitink and Tagliabue 2020.

the horizon of our own time. It is preferable to reflect on the parameters of one's readings than to mistake them for an objective frame. Theories are neither legitimate nor illegitimate per se; they serve heuristic functions – their value depends on the questions raised and the texts to which they are applied.

There is a considerable pay-off in the application of structuralist narratology and other more recent approaches in narrative theory to all sorts of texts, including ancient ones. But they are less than helpful for the purposes of this study – in fact, they have generated a one-sided view of ancient literature that I wish to complement. Shaped by readings mostly of modern realist novels, narratological approaches have drawn our attention to features that ancient texts share with modern ones, making us neglect aspects that jar with the conventions of the works of Gustave Flaubert, Charles Dickens and other modern authors. In this book, I am not distancing myself from structuralist narratology and other approaches of narrative theory because it is anachronistic to apply their taxonomies and concepts to Greek and Latin texts, but because they are not the right tool for the purpose of appreciating what renders ancient literature distinct.

Needless to say, given the vastness of the material, my readings will be highly selective. Neither in the material covered nor in the topics tackled is exhaustiveness possible, nor would it be desirable. However, even if my samples are only halfway representative, as I hope they are, they will give us insights into the ancient sense of narrative. While the texts that I discuss range from the Archaic to the Imperial eras, most of them are Greek – this is due to my expertise and does not mean that my argument works only for Greek literature. Occasional references to Latin material will at least suggest its applicability to Latin literature as well.

The goals of this book are far more modest than the 'defining Greek narrative' advertised by the volume that emerged from the 7th Leventis Conference at Edinburgh.[45] Not only does Greek narrative seem, at least to me, too protean to become the object of a definition, but it is also beyond the scope of this book to capture fully the ancient logic of narrative. As the subtitle *Towards a Critical Dialogue* indicates, *Ancient Greek Texts and Modern Narrative Theory* aims to stimulate scholars, inviting them to view ancient narrative and criticism along new lines. Not only, but especially, narratology has let Classicists detect modern features in ancient literature.

---

[45] Commenting on Scodel's hope 'that we will someday achieve a general view of the history of ancient Greek narrative', Rood 2015: 329 notes: 'It is an ambitious hope, and it is not to detract from the generally very high standard of the pieces to say that the volume as a whole still leaves the prospect of attaining that hope as distant as ever.'

As instructive as this has been, it is, I think, equally important to account for other aspects. After having learned to analyse the complexities reminiscent of modern novels, it would be beneficial at this stage also to explore what renders ancient narrative and its understanding in antiquity distinctive. It bears repeating that I am far from arguing against the narratological analysis of ancient literature – it has been immensely fruitful and will, I have no doubt, continue to be an important tool for Classicists. What I wish to do is to direct the attention of Classicists also to aspects of ancient narrative that the application of Bal's and Genette's taxonomies and of other concepts of narrative theory has occluded in the past decades. My goal is not to replace narratology but to complement the view of ancient narrative that we have gained with its help.

By no means is this book the first and only attempt at teasing out peculiarities of ancient literature. In the course of this introduction, I have had the chance to refer to several illuminating inquiries, and there are others that could be mentioned.[46] The oralist tradition in Homeric scholarship deserves singling out as a major endeavour to approach early Greek epic on its own terms. And yet, on the whole our perspective on ancient narrative is dominated by the logic encapsulated in de Jong's claim that 'Classical scholars can now lay bare the literary DNA of the most popular literary form of our times, the novel, in ancient narrative texts'.[47] If my attempt at teasing out ancient views of narrative prompts Classicists to view Greek and Latin literature not chiefly as the DNA of the modern novel or even induces them to take the exploration of its peculiarities further, this book will have succeeded.

While *Ancient Greek Texts and Modern Narrative Theory* primarily addresses Classicists, it also reaches out to scholars of narrative theory. In a famous sentence of his first Critique, Kant states that 'thoughts without content are empty, intuitions without concepts are blind'.[48] Literary theory needs literature to have substance, just as readings without reflection risk falling flat. Most theoreticians continue to focus on modern literature, understandably, as it is more accessible to us. But premodern texts not only pose a special challenge to modern readers, they also have the potential to redirect theory. In another book, I exploited ancient reflections to reconsider our ideas of aesthetic experience:[49] ancient authors, I contended,

---

[46] For example, Halliwell 2002; 2011; Hunter 2009; Peponi 2012; Gurd 2016; Liebert 2017.
[47] De Jong 2014b: 11.
[48] Kant (1929 [1781/7]) A48/B75: 'Gedanken ohne Inhalt sind leer, Anschauungen ohne Begriffe sind blind.'
[49] Grethlein 2017b. For a programmatic article also addressing scholars outside Classics, see Grethlein 2015.

draw our attention to the affective dimension and long-lasting effects of aesthetic experiences that have been sidelined by many theoreticians and at the same time contemplate the ambiguity between immersion and reflection with great nuance.

The chapters of this book invite scholars of narrative to reconsider some of their concepts in the light of ancient material. For example, as I hope to show, Greek literature makes it difficult to maintain claims about the Theory of Mind being the essential mode of engaging with narrative. Ancient views of narration will also turn out to be cognitively more realist than the structuralist model of narration. In this respect, *Ancient Texts and Modern Narrative Theory* goes beyond the goals of a historical narratology that tries to chart the specific gestalt of narrative in an epoch – it also aims to unlock the potential of ancient narrative to shape theoretical concepts.

5 Synopsis

As starting points for the chapters, I have chosen concepts and categories that stem from different fields of narrative studies and allow us to tackle core aspects of narrative. Fiction(ality) is a key concept in literary theory and has come to attract considerable attention from narratologists in the past two decades. No surprise, then, that it also looms large in Classics. However, a brief look at the discussion indicates that there must be something wrong. Classicists have made numerous cases for the birth of fiction – the texts credited with it range from the Homeric epics to the Imperial novel. Most of these cases flagrantly contradict each other – if Hesiod invented fictionality, how can it have been discovered by Menander or Theocritus? It has also been argued that fictionality is a core concern of Greek literature from its beginnings to the Imperial era. In Chapter 2, I agree with the idea that fictionality did not have to be discovered at some point but then proceed to argue that it never played an important role either. After presenting evidence for the familiarity of fictionality in antiquity, I reconsider two authors who often appear as cornerstones in histories of fictionality, Gorgias and Aristotle. A closer look at their reflections draws our attention to two dimensions of ancient narrative that were deemed far more important than its referentiality, namely its immersive quality and its moral thrust.

Chapter 3 turns to a key category of structuralist narratology that is not unrelated to the issue of fictionality, voice. The narrator as an entity independent of the author owes its prominence in modern criticism, it has been suggested, ultimately to the concept of fictionality – the narrator helps suspend referentiality in fictional texts. In ancient criticism, however, the idea of a narrator independent of the author is absent. What is more, ancient critics tended to ascribe utterances of characters in general to authors. This, I argue, is not a deficiency, but the expression of a distinctly ancient view of voice, which I reconstruct on the basis of a wide array of texts. Where we see several narrative levels nested into each other, ancient authors and readers envisaged narration as an act of impersonation. One of the upshots of my analysis is that, while it may be intriguing to explore *metalepseis* in ancient literature, the very idea of *metalepsis* conflicts with the premises of narrative as it was understood in antiquity. The ancient view of narration can be linked at least partly to the prominence of performance and therefore reveals the impact of socio-cultural factors; at the same time, it resonates with recent cognitive theory, notably embodied and enactive models of cognition.

That it would be wrong to consider all strands of cognitivism an apt framework for the investigation of ancient narrative emerges from Chapter 4. Perhaps the most prominent cognitivist concept in recent narratology is the Theory of Mind. Alan Palmer, Lisa Zunshine and others have been highly influential with their claim that mind reading is at the core of our engagement with narrative in general. However, not only have these scholars ignored how controversial the idea of the Theory of Mind is in psychology, but ancient literature, I believe, also belies their argument about narrative at large. Mind reading is certainly central to our responses to modern realist novels, but ancient narratives – as my test case, Heliodorus' *Ethiopica*, illustrates – were more invested in the reconfiguration of time than in individualized minds. Plot was crucial for the experiential quality of narrative hailed by critics, as shown in Chapter 2. This prominence of plot is reflected in Aristotle's *Poetics* and other critical works. In order not to play off plot against character, I propose experience as a category that integrates cognitive processes as well as matters of plot.

Chapter 5 touches on some of the points brought up in Chapter 3, notably ancient views of character, but has a different focus – narrative motivation, a category prominent particularly in story-oriented narratology. The *Odyssey* is the origin of the classical Western plot, and yet, the motivation of the Penelope scenes in books 18 and 19 does not follow the logic that modern realist novels have made our default model. Instead, I suggest, *Odyssey* 18 and 19 have a design premised on features that we encounter in medieval narratives, notably retroactive motivation, thematic isolation and suspense about how. The reason why Penelope has provoked innumerable psychologizing interpretations in modern scholarship is that her comportment is not psychologically motivated by Homer. Similar cases of motivation that are bound to strike the reader of modern novels as peculiar can be found in Homer and also in later literature. At first sight, these cases may seem to conflict with the emphasis on motivation in Aristotle and the scholia, but in viewing motivation rather in terms of plot than psychology, the critics share common ground with the texts discussed.

To round up and sharpen the critical dialogue of ancient Greek texts with modern narrative theory, the final chapter compares the ancient sense of narrative as explored in the course of this study with what we find in postmodern literature. At first sight, the similarities are striking: postmodern narratives challenge the distinction between fact and fiction, ignore the boundaries between narrative levels, play with character presentation and forgo motivation in psychological terms. However, whereas postmodern authors consciously undercut the conventions of modern realist novels, ancient authors follow their own, independent logic. The parallels between pre- and postmodern narratives belong to utterly different frameworks, which endow them with different significances. Cast as a challenge, postmodern texts remain fixated on modernism. Ancient texts, on the other hand, while having influenced the rise of the modern novel, are premised on their own distinct view of narrative. Teasing out some features of this view is the objective of the following chapters.

CHAPTER 2

Word and World: Fiction(ality)

1   Modern Theories of Fiction(ality)

Fiction is a term with a rich history, having different meanings in various contexts. David Hume, for example, called causality, the unified self and similar concepts 'fictions'. Today, scientists sometimes speak of fiction when they refer to atoms – elementary particles that are postulated to explain observations but whose existence remains indeterminate. Philosophers, on the other hand, refer to Putnam's 'Brain in a Vat or Twin Earth' and other thought experiments as fictions, defined by them as counterfactual deductive devices from which valid conclusions about the real world are derived. More mundanely, someone who enters a bookstore and looks for a novel will turn to the fiction section; until the eighteenth century, however, fiction signified chiefly poetry. Yet another sense of fiction is on display in an example sentence offered by the Cambridge English Dictionary: 'At work she kept up the fiction that she had a university degree.' Here, it is a wilful act of deception that is called fiction. Simultaneously and crucially for this chapter, fiction is also one of the most prominent categories of literary theoreticians, who oppose fictional texts to factual texts.

The prominence of fictionality, the quality that makes texts fiction, in literary theory is attested by the attempts to deconstruct it. Post-structuralists in particular contended that every representation is a construction and therefore fiction. This argument had special poignancy for the assessment of historiography. Hayden White, for instance, explored the emplotment used by historians and philosophers of history to show that their narratives shared much common ground with novels.[1] The post-structuralist attack on the distinction between fact and fiction was countered by the objection, among others, that the construction of a representation has no implications

---

[1] White 1975.

for its ontological status. In the terms of Werner Wolf, *fictio*, something that is made by an author, is not necessarily *fictum*, something that is made up.[2]

Interestingly, fictionality did not play a major role in the beginnings of narratology. This marks a fissure: while developing their taxonomies for narrative at large, Gérard Genette, Franz Karl Stanzel, Mieke Bal and other pioneers exclusively discussed examples from fiction. It was only later that Genette, joined by others like Dorrit Cohn, discussed in what way narratological categories also applied to factual texts.[3] More recently, the fact/fiction divide has become a hot spot of narratological and literary scholarship in various languages. Just a few examples: Frank Zipfel's analytical examination of fictionality has engendered a rich German tradition in the field.[4] Richard Walsh's *The Rhetoric of Fictionality*, introducing a distinction between generic fictions such as the novel and fictionality as a discourse mode present across genres and media, paved the way for a mostly anglophone rhetorical narrative approach.[5] In France, Françoise Lavocat provided a broad study of fictionality, making a case that it is a historically variable and institutionally based practice.[6] Monika Fludernik and others have come to broach narrative factuality as opposed to narrative fictionality.[7]

While narratologists have developed a keen interest in fictionality and factuality, it deserves pointing out that the fields of narratology and the theory of fiction do not fully map onto each other. In the past decades, both fields have been enlarged; many theoreticians nowadays confine neither narrative nor fiction to texts but include also, for example, visual representations.[8] However, whereas any representation can be assessed as either fictional or factual, not every representation is narrative. A portrait of a king as well as a description of his looks, for example, can refer to a historical person or not, but neither of them qualifies as narrative. Fiction and narrative are categories whose fields intersect without being identical.

It is a widespread but far from universal assumption that fiction is a product of the modern age. Many scholars tie its emergence to the rise of the modern realist novel in the eighteenth century.[9] It is therefore not surprising that this view, in combination with the prominence of the notion

---

[2] Wolf 1993: 38–9.   [3] Genette 1993; Cohn 1999.   [4] Zipfel 2001; Klauk and Köppe 2014.

[5] Walsh 2007. See, for example, Nielsen, Phelan and Walsh 2015.   [6] Lavocat 2016.

[7] Fludernik, Falkenhayner and Steiner 2015; Fludernik and Ryan 2020. Other approaches to fictionality include possible worlds theories (Ryan 1991; Doležel 1998), the theory of make-believe (Walton 1990; Bareis 2008) and the analytical approach of Lamarque and Olsen 1994. For a survey, see Klauk and Köppe 2014.

[8] For example, Walton 1990; Schaeffer 1999; Ryan 2001.

[9] See especially the influential argument by Gallagher 2006; 2011. Paige 2011 sees a paradigm shift from pseudo-factual to fictional narrative in the late eighteenth century.

of fictionality for our understanding of literature, has prompted scholars of premodern literatures to make cases for its existence before the eighteenth century. While Medievalists have taken pains to detect fiction in the Middle Ages,[10] Classicists have claimed that the idea of fiction emerged in antiquity. In an influential paper, Wolfgang Rösler tried to show that, building on ideas of Gorgias, Aristotle in his *Poetics* advanced a theory of fictionality.[11] Fiction as a distinct textual category, he contended, could only arise when the oral performance culture ceded to a literate culture. Other Classicists identified other authors and texts as the birthplace of fiction: in addition to Gorgias and Aristotle, Homer, Hesiod, Pindar, the Platonic dialogue, Old and New Comedy, Theocritus, the Greek novel and Augustine have all been credited with the discovery of fiction.[12]

Even without going into details, one can note that the wide range of texts from Archaic poetry to late antique literature adduced as the beginning of fiction instils little confidence in the attempt to pinpoint the birth of fiction. One scholar who consciously eschewed the logic of discovery narratives is Stephen Halliwell, a prominent advocate of a universalist position in Classics. In his eyes, authors from Homer to the Imperial critics meditated intensely on fictionality. Halliwell distinguishes four broad stages: 'the complex poetic self-consciousness of the Archaic period'; 'a phase of more explicit theorization in a group of Classical thinkers which includes Gorgias, Plato, Aristotle, and Isocrates'; 'formalized Hellenistic and Imperial typologies of discourse'; and 'Greek and Latin categorizations' involving the vocabulary of fiction that would ultimately lead to the modern term 'fiction'.[13]

While Halliwell's departure from the discovery narratives is praise-worthy, his sketch has problems of its own: basically the entire history of implicit poetics and explicit criticism has become a multifaceted reflection on fictionality. This view is the upshot of Halliwell's definition of fictionality. Observing that there is no 'completely agreed modern concept', he understands fiction as 'an inherently complex zone of discourse, thought, and imagination which cuts across a strict dichotomy of truth and falsehood and intrinsically complicates both halves of that division'.[14]

---

[10] Recently, see Orlemanski 2019; Karnes 2020 and the forum on medieval fictionalities in *NLH* 51/1 (2020).

[11] Rösler 1980.

[12] See the list in Halliwell 2011: 10 n. 19 and the survey in Feddern 2018: 8–35, which concentrates on German scholarship. Feddern's wide-ranging study is useful in its broad coverage of ancient material, but see also the critical comments of Vogt-Spira 2020 on a range of issues, including an unclear concept of fictionality.

[13] Halliwell 2015: 343.   [14] Halliwell 2015: 342.

The capacity to subsume Hesiod as well as Asclepiades of Myrlea and Longinus together with Isocrates illustrates the alarming vagueness of this definition.[15]

There is in fact extensive discussion about fictionality, but most scholars of narrative would, I think, agree on a rough definition. Semantic models of fictionality, it is safe to claim, have lost their appeal. Gottlob Frege and Bertrand Russell bound fictionality to the ontological status of narrative entities and the truth-value status of propositions about these entities.[16] However, texts that are unanimously agreed to be fictional are populated with real-world entities. Napoleon surfaces in *War and Peace*, and the action of *Ulysses* unfolds in historical Dublin. Counterfactual stories pose particular challenges for semantic definitions of fictionality – what exactly is the status of a Lord Nelson who loses the battle of Trafalgar? By no means are semantic criteria irrelevant, but they are obviously not apt to define fictionality.

Likewise, syntactic approaches to fictionality, while generating important insights, have not yielded the wished-for results.[17] Käte Hamburger and Ann Banfield tried to identify syntactic features that are constitutive of fiction.[18] These features, notably free indirect discourse and anomalies of spatial and temporal deixis, all use a grammatically third-person perspective to present the perception and mental processes of a first-person. This definition, however, would exclude first-person narrative and also third-person narratives that do not centre on internal focalization. The linguistic analysis of the classical modern consciousness novel does not provide a viable definition of fiction.

Given the shortcomings of semantic and syntactic approaches, most scholars today opt for a pragmatic definition of fictionality.[19] John Searle's paper on 'The logical status of fictional discourse' remains a landmark contribution.[20] For Searle, fiction consists of pretended

---

[15] Orlemanski's approach to fiction(ality) in medieval literature (2019) is similar to Halliwell's as she stretches 'fiction' to encompass 'such diverse medieval phenomena as imagination, mimesis, pagan myth, virtuality, counterfactuality, example, ideal, lie, trope, experiment, romance, *fabula*, *argumentum*, phantasm, *engin*, allegory, invention, and dream' (163). While the confrontation of modern concepts with a wide range of premodern material gives us a chance to reassess the concepts themselves, the broadening of concepts by Halliwell and Orlemanski ultimately occludes distinctions.

[16] Frege 1960; Russell 2005 [1905].   [17] Schaeffer 2014.

[18] Hamburger 1993 [1957]; Banfield 1982.

[19] This includes the 'Institutionenmodell', which focuses on the institutional framework for the production and reception of fiction, for example, Köppe 2014, building especially on Lamarque and Olson 1994.

[20] Searle 1979.

speech-acts: neither the ontological status of the narrative's elements nor its syntactic features are decisive, but the intention with which it is presented and received. Searle's definition has not been impervious to criticism,[21] and yet a majority of scholars would agree that fictionality is best understood as the suspension of the claim to referentiality. Instead of being void of referentiality, fictional texts are texts that bracket off the question of whether they refer to reality or not. Fictionality involves the levels of author, text and reader; the author's suspension of the claim to referentiality manifests itself in textual and paratextual signs that are to be recognized by the reader. Needless to say, this process can be dismantled: the signs which express the fictional status of the text can be ignored by the reader or lose their significance across different epochs and interpretive communities. This explains why texts can change their status. While most ancient audiences considered the *Iliad* and the *Odyssey* accounts of historical events (I will return to this point), most readers today approach them as fictional. The example of Homer alerts us to the interplay of author, text and audience – all of them are involved in establishing the framework of fictionality.

In German scholarship, the pragmatic definition has crystallized in a simple and helpful distinction:[22] while 'fictional' describes the status of a text, 'fictive' refers to the status of textual elements. There can be 'non-fictive' elements in 'fictional' accounts, for example, Napoleon in *War and Peace* and, inversely, 'fictive' elements in 'non-fictional' reports, when someone consciously reports something that did not take place or a historian unknowingly makes a claim that is wrong. The general use of 'fictive', 'fictional' and 'fictitious' in English is more liberal, but in the following discussions I will use 'fictional' for the status of the text and 'fictive' for the status of textual elements. This will make it easier to stick to a pragmatic definition of fictionality and to avoid the traps of the semantic model in particular that, while rejected by most theoreticians, is quick to return through the back door.

Let me illustrate the relevance of the fictional–fictive distinction by a brief look at a famous passage that in the eyes of many critics involves a reference to fictionality. At the beginning of the *Theogony*, Hesiod narrates his initiation as a poet. The Muses presented themselves to him

---

[21] For example, Walton 1990; Hempfer 1990. For a defence of central points of Searle's argument, see Onea 2014.

[22] On the terminology in different languages, see the survey by Rajewsky 2020: 33–43.

on Mount Helicon; before they gave Hesiod a staff and 'breathed into him divine song', they emphasized their powers and teased him (26–8):

ποιμένες ἄγραυλοι, κάκ' ἐλέγχεα, γαστέρες οἶον,
ἴδμεν ψεύδεα πολλὰ λέγειν ἐτύμοισιν ὁμοῖα,
ἴδμεν δ' εὖτ' ἐθέλωμεν ἀληθέα γηρύσασθαι.

You shepherds who sleep in fields, lowest of the low, mere bellies,
We know how to tell many falsehoods that seem like true things,
And we know, when we wish, how to utter the truth.

The 'falsehoods that seem like true things' are generally interpreted as a first explicit reflection on fictionality.[23] However, as we have just noticed, fictive elements, claims or entities which do not refer to real things do not necessarily constitute fiction. Just as factual entities can surface in fiction, fictive elements can form part of factual narrative. Fictionality, the quality that defines texts as fictional, does not hinge on the ontological status of its elements – it is a framework that suspends the question of whether or not a narrative is referential.

The teasing tone of the Muses, who put Hesiod in his place before elevating him, further suggests that the resemblance of the falsehoods to truth is so close that it deceives their human recipients.[24] Creeping on the ground and mostly concerned with the daily search for food, humans are incapable of distinguishing between the truths and falsehoods with which the Muses humour them. Just as Odysseus' listeners are taken in by his liar stories and believe that they are facing a Cretan, the poets and their audiences are incapable of detecting whether or not the Muses have passed on the truth. This reinforces the argument that the passage does not involve the idea of fictionality. While fictive elements do not suffice to establish a fictional narrative, the recipient's understanding that referential claims are suspended is indispensable to fictionality. The Muses, however, mock humans, who are concerned with the truth status but incapable of assessing it.

The issue of fictionality offers us a first point of entry for the endeavour to capture the specific ancient understanding of narrative instead of detecting features derived from the study of modern realist novels. In the bulk of

---

[23] For example, Havelock 1963: 105; West 1966: 162; Puelma 1989: 75; Bowie 1993: 21–2; Halliwell 2011: 15 with further literature in n. 31. The interpretation is marred further when the possible quote of *Od.* 19.203 is interpreted as Hesiod's pitting of his poetry, which offers the 'truth', against Homer's fictional narrative. For example, Kannicht 1980: 15–20; Finkelberg 1998: 157. An extensive doxography can be found in Feddern 2018: 119 n. 5.

[24] *Pace* Halliwell 2011: 15, who contends that 'it is crucial to distinguish ... between the Muses' dramatic tone ... and the symbolic import of their words, namely that song itself stands in a shifting relationship to truth and reality'.

investigations of fiction in antiquity, the agenda that has dominated scholarship over the past decades is visible: scholars have tried to identify the notion of fictionality in ancient literature and criticism. While letting us appreciate the modern quality of ancient texts, this procedure has detracted from features that are distinctive about ancient literature and ancient views on it. In this chapter, I will argue that, while antiquity was familiar with the notion of fictionality and produced fictional literature, the idea of fiction was far less prominent than it is for us. It will emerge that ancient authors and readers were more concerned with other aspects of narrative than with its suspension of referentiality. Given the vastness of pertinent material, my discussion will have to be highly selective, but I hope that, despite or rather thanks to the lack of exhaustiveness, my argument will highlight the outlines of ancient narrative and its conception that are easily buried under the wealth of material.

In a first step, I will consider evidence for the familiarity of fictionality right from the beginning of Greek literature and then briefly assess the weight that fictional texts had in the ancient hierarchy of genres (§2 Fiction in Ancient Narrative). I will then move on to criticism and have a look at Aristotle's *Poetics*, widely hailed as the first theory of fiction. And in fact, Aristotle addresses the suspension of referential claims when he juxtaposes poetry with historiography in chapter 9, but a closer look at this juxtaposition and its argumentative context will caution us against the common assumption that Aristotle provides us with a theory of fiction (§3 Aristotle's Poetics: A Theory of Fiction). After this, I will discuss a famous fragment of Gorgias about tragedy that is often quoted as an acknowledgement of fictionality (§4 Gorgias and the Deception of Tragedy). Instead of focusing on the suspension of referential claims, however, the fragment incites reflection on two aspects that loom large and outshine the issue of fictionality in ancient criticism. One is the immersive capacity of narrative, the other its moral dimension, both to be discussed in subsequent sections (§5 Immersion in Ancient Criticism and §6 The Morals of Truth). Nonetheless, there were also reflections on fictionality – their survey will however reveal that the suspension of referentiality, which is constitutive of fictionality, rarely took centre stage in ancient criticism (§7 Ancient Discussions of Referentiality).

2 Fiction in Ancient Narrative

It has been argued that the engagement with fiction is a transcultural ability that humans develop in early childhood. Kendall Walton, for example, envisages fiction as a form of make-believe and aligns it with children's games.[25] Just as children who play may imagine a tree trunk to be a bear, novels, like other forms of representation, prompt us to engage our fantasy. Both the children's games and the perusal of fiction are predicated on an 'as-if': we immerse ourselves in something that is represented with a residual awareness of the representation. The children may scream, but they do not actually believe that they are facing a bear. Likewise, readers may be transfixed by the adventures of James Bond without, however, forgetting that they are merely reading a narrative.

Now Walton's comparison of children's games and fiction is not without problems, some of which I have discussed elsewhere.[26] Most important for my argument here is that the response described by Walton is elicited by representations by and large independently of their referential status: a historical account as well as a novel can transport us to the world and action it narrates. Attending to a representation in the form of make-believe and suspending the question of its referentiality are two distinct processes. Nonetheless, the mental simulation explored by Walton is an important part of our engagement with fiction, without, however, being exclusive to it; it can also be triggered by non-fictional representations. Walton's argument therefore suggests that our responses to fiction centrally involve a transcultural capacity. If young children acquire the cognitive ability necessary to play the games of fiction, why should the idea of fiction have to be discovered at some point in Greek history?

But is it possible to prove the presence of the idea of fiction in Archaic Greece? Most narratives of this epoch retell myths, and it is well known that the Greeks, while granting their authors a certain degree of poetic freedom, considered their myths historical events.[27] Nonetheless, we can, I think, with due caution detect traces of a sense of fictionality already at the beginning of Greek literature. In her study *Lying and Poetry from Homer to Pindar*, Louise Pratt identifies a 'model of fiction' in a scene from *Odyssey* 13. Odysseus has just returned to Ithaca and encounters Athena in the disguise of a young shepherd. In the first of his Cretan liar stories, Odysseus pretends to be from Crete and invents a fictive biography. Athena is not angry about being lied to but amused and, once she has disclosed her own identity, lavishly praises Odysseus' verbal skills. In Pratt's eyes:

> Athena's response to Odysseus' lie provides one model for an intelligent response to fiction: a failure to believe it, but amusement and even pleasure

---

[25] Walton 1990.　　[26] Grethlein 2017b: 25–9.
[27] For some of the intricacies of the ancient understanding of myths, see Veyne 1988.

at the cleverness of the author . . . Athena is a model for the least involved type of audience to fiction, an audience that appreciates a work as the creation of the poet's intelligence but nonetheless sees through it entirely.[28]

Indeed, a sense of fictionality can be detected in this passage, but not where Pratt sees it. Athena's reaction is certainly not a 'model for an intelligent response to fiction' – she does not appreciate the story independently of its truth value but indulges in Odysseus' witty lie (13.291–5):

κερδαλέος κ' εἴη καὶ ἐπίκλοπος, ὅς σε παρέλθοι
ἐν πάντεσσι δόλοισι, καὶ εἰ θεὸς ἀντιάσειε.
σχέτλιε, ποικιλομῆτα, δόλων ἆατ', οὐκ ἄρ' ἔμελλες,
οὐδ' ἐν σῇ περ ἐὼν γαίῃ, λήξειν ἀπατάων
μύθων τε κλοπίων, οἵ τοι πεδόθεν φίλοι εἰσίν.

It would be a sharp one, and a stealthy one, who would ever get past you
in any contriving; even if it were a god against you.
You wretch, so devious, never weary of tricks, then you would not
even in your own country give over your ways of deceiving
and your thievish tales. They are near to you in your very nature.

If, as Pratts asserts, Athena approached Odysseus' story as fictional, she would comment on, say, its plot, the exquisite diction or the powerful effect it has had on her, but, as it stands, she hones in on the fact that the story is a lie. Athena's response thus concentrates on the very question that is suspended in fiction.

There is a response to another of Odysseus' liar stories that is closer to proving Pratt's claim. After Athena has disguised Odysseus as a beggar, he first arrives at the hut of the swineherd Eumaeus. Eumaeus welcomes and generously hosts the beggar, but when night falls Odysseus starts to shiver. In order to elicit a cloak from Eumaeus, the beggar alias Odysseus invents a story from the Trojan War and narrates how he, together with Odysseus, was lying in ambush and freezing. In this situation, Odysseus came up with a ruse: he sent one of the messengers back to the camp of the Greeks and the beggar could cover himself with the cloak that the messenger left. Eumaeus immediately understands the point of the story and gives Odysseus a thick cloak and fleeces of wool: 'Old sir, that was a blameless fable the way you told it;/ and you have made no unprofitable speech, nor one that/ missed the point, so you shall not lack for clothes' (ὦ γέρον, αἶνος μέν τοι ἀμύμων, ὃν κατέλεξας,/ οὐδέ τί πω παρὰ μοῖραν ἔπος νηκερδὲς ἔειπες·/ τῷ οὔτ' ἐσθῆτος δευήσεαι, 14.508–10). Whereas Athena sees through Odysseus' lie and indulges in his deceitfulness, Eumaeus' response focuses not on the referential status of the story but on the message it conveys. That said, even this does not constitute a full-blown case of fiction: Odysseus narrates the story as something that actually took place, and Eumaeus, while not concentrating on its referential status, shows no sign of doubting it.

Nevertheless, a case can be made that fictionality is somehow at stake in Odysseus' liar stories. Central to this argument is the fact that embedded narratives partake of two different levels of communication. Embedded narratives are intradiegetically told by one character to another and simultaneously form part of the narrative with which the author addresses us, his audience. Now, as we have seen, fictionality does not surface at the intradiegetic level: Odysseus deceptively presents his story as truthful, and Athena considers it as a lie. The very aspect that is bracketed in fiction, referentiality, thus defines both speech-act and reception. It is at the extradiegetic level, in the communication between the author and his recipients, where fictionality comes into place. We can read the story not only as a speech-act in which Odysseus engages, but also as a story that Homer conveys to us. Thus seen, the story is freed from the referential status that it has intradiegetically; simultaneously, it is not subject to the truth claim with which Homer narrates the primary story – it can be received as fiction.

If we read Odysseus' liar stories like this and put their referential status in brackets, then these stories illustrate a feature of many fictional narratives, namely the blend of fictive with factual elements. Whereas, for example, the French Revolution is a fact, Frédéric Moreau is a fictive person, and his experiences in post-revolutionary France are Gustave Flaubert's invention. In the same vein, the Cretan who Odysseus pretends to be is fictive, but the Trojan War – within the world of the *Odyssey* – is a real event. One could thus say that Odysseus' Cretan stories are obliquely fictional: as speeches in the intradiegetic world, they are of course lies and non-fictional, but as stories that Homer tells us they are fictional. Homeric epic comes with a pronounced truth claim and was received as historical throughout antiquity, and yet the liar stories suggest that this status of epic is not owed to the absence of a notion of fictionality.

Admittedly, this argument involves a sleight of hand: we have to extricate the embedded stories from their narrative context and ascribe them to the author, who conveys them to us without vouching for or denying their veracity. However, the story that Odysseus tells Eumaeus directs us to further proof that the idea of fictionality was not unknown in early Greece.

Eumaeus calls the beggar's Trojan anecdote an *ainos*. Other than 'praise', *ainos* signifies a tale with a moral, a story with a message. This is not only the meaning active in Eumaeus' speech, but also the meaning that led to the use of *ainos* as name for the fable. Fables are fictional stories that drive home a message, which is often pinpointed in an explicit conclusion.

Now, the fable can be traced back to the very beginning of Greek literature.[29] Hesiod's *Works and Days* contain the fable of the hawk and the nightingale (202–11): when the nightingale starts to mourn in the claws of the hawk, the hawk rebukes the nightingale that its mourning is useless, for the victim is fully at the mercy of the victor. The fragments of Archilochus, who composed his poems roughly at the same time in the middle of the seventh century BCE, feature further fables, one about the eagle's punishment after he betrayed his compact with the fox (fr. 172–81 W), and another about the ape who tried to establish himself as the king of the beasts (fr. 185–7 W). Both Hesiod and Archilochus narrate these fables in order to buttress points, Hesiod to deepen his reflection on injustice in the Age of Iron, Archilochus to enrich his polemics against Lycambes.

The fable is a special type of narrative. It often, but not necessarily, features animals or even plants who act and speak like humans. This idiosyncrasy notwithstanding, there can be no doubt that fables qualify as fiction. We would not wonder about the historicity of fables, nor is the fact that speaking animals are obviously impossible held against them. The fictional character of the fable is explicit in the definition of the genre by the Imperial rhetorician Theon, which is still unsuperseded in its conciseness: 'A fable is an untrue narrative which illustrates reality' (μῦθός ἐστι λόγος ψευδὴς εἰκονίζων ἀλήθειαν, *progymn*. 3).[30] Special as it is, the genre of the fable thus highlights that fictionality was not something that had to be discovered. In the genre of the fable, Eumaeus' indifference to the referential status of the beggar's tale and his focus on its message has evolved into a full fictional framework. Being part of Greek literature from its very beginning, fables drive home that Greeks were familiar with stories and the suspension of referentiality.

However, as I wish to show in this chapter, fictionality played, on the whole, a marginal role in antiquity. A brief and far from complete survey of fictional genres will give us a first hint at this. The genre that Hellenistic and Imperial critics usually adduce as an example of *plasma/argumentum* – that narrative which is only likely but not true – is comedy; in some cases,

---

[29] For a survey of the ancient fable, see Grethlein 2011a.   [30] Cf. Feddern 2018: 412–25.

drama/dramatikon is even used synonymously with *plasma/plasmatikon*. Old Comedy features historical persons such as Cleon and Socrates as well as freely invented characters but involves them in obviously invented plots.[31] While preferring tightly structured plots over the exuberance of Aristophanes, Menander and the other authors of New Comedy maintain the fictional frame. Another fictional dramatic form is the *mimos*, defined in antiquity as 'a representation of life which embraces the morally proper and improper' (μῖμός ἐστιν μίμησις βίου τά τε συγκεχωρημένα καὶ ἀσυγχώρητα περιέχων, Diomedes, *GL* 1 p. 491). This popular form of theatre has roots in the Archaic age, was practised beside the institutionalized dramatic performances in the Classical age and was made artsy by such Hellenistic poets as Herodas and Theocritus.

Theocritus, best known as a pastoral poet, leads us to another fictional poetic genre. The setting of bucolic poetry is a highly artificial world in which the shepherds are at ease to meditate on their lives and to recite poetry.[32] The poetic contest between two poets is a fixed form that recurs time and again. While Theocritus' bucolic poems are located in Sicily and other places, Virgil, the most important Roman pastoral poet, made Arcadia the country of shepherds. Just as Virgil's shepherds are highly idealized, his Arcadia has little to do with the geographical region but is an elaborate poetic topos. Virgil may allude to real political events or circumstances, but this does not detract from the fictional frame of bucolic poetry. It is not incidental that in the eras of the Renaissance and Baroque, the pastoral romance was a favourite genre for intricate plays with fictionality. Such works as Jacopo Sannazaro's *Arcadia* and Honoré d'Urfé's *L'Astrée* artfully exploit the juxtaposition of bucolic and urban worlds to reflect on the relation between fiction and reality.[33]

Yet another genre of fiction is fictional dialogue.[34] After the death of Socrates, several of his disciples, most prominently Plato and Socrates the Younger, started to write conversations of Socrates. In these dialogues, Socrates converses with other historical persons. And yet, the multiple framings of such dialogues as the *Symposium* and *Menexenus* signal that the conversations reported are not to be read as factual. At the same time, the *Sokratikoi logoi* are not entirely non-referential. The portrayal of characters is, as far as we can tell, closely modelled on the historical persons, and more generally the dialogues can be seen as the attempt to be true to the spirit of

[31] On comedy as fiction, see Lowe 2000; Ruffell 2011.
[32] Compare Payne 2007 on Theocritus as 'fully fictional fiction'.
[33] Compare Iser 1991, who uses the pastoral romance to elaborate on his theory of fiction.
[34] On the fictionality of Platonic dialogue, see Gill 1993: 66–9.

Socrates and to reproduce his style of inquiry. One of the intriguing questions that, alas, I cannot discuss here is how the fictional status of Platonic dialogue relates to the reflections on discourse and falsehood in the *Republic* and other dialogues.

A major difference between ancient and modern literature is that the genre which for us is the paradigm of fiction seems to have risen late in antiquity and failed to attract attention from critics. Earlier generations of scholars speculated about the Hellenistic origins of the novel, but the fully preserved ancient novels all stem from the Imperial period and have been shown to be firmly embedded in the world of that period.[35] The sophistication of such works as Apuleius' *Golden Ass* and Heliodorus' *Ethiopica* rules out the possibility that they were trivial literature for the masses. The high degree of intertextuality and the deft use of such forms as *ekphrasis* clearly address a well-educated reader. Nonetheless, it is striking that we can find only very few references to novels in criticism. There was not even a distinct name for the genre; *faute de mieux*, Byzantine readers such as Photius refer to the ancient novel as *drama*. A possible reason is that the concepts and taxonomies of criticism had already been fully developed when the novel emerged.[36] Whether or not this is true, the unconcern of ancient criticism with the novel illustrates the marginal role of fictionality in antiquity. It is not incidental that for us the novel is not only the paradigm of fiction, but also the genre that arguably receives most attention from literary critics and general readers alike. The minor position of the novel in ancient literature highlights that fictionality, while not unknown, was far less prominent.

That said, it seems that fiction became more important and fictionality the object of sophisticated literary reflections in the Imperial era.[37] The romance-novel genre to which the five fully preserved ancient Greek novels belong is only a tiny part of the prose fiction produced by Imperial authors. There were also such fantastical novels as Antonius Diogenes' *The Wonders Beyond Thule*, for which we have to rely on papyri and the summary of the Byzantine bishop Photius: the core of this multiply layered story is the adventures of a sister and a brother, who travel to the outermost edges of the world.[38] The Latin novels of Petronius and Apuleius seem to be indebted to Greek traditions that are mostly lost, but there are traces of satirical ass novels in Greek and of the *Milesian Stories* which seem to have treated frivolous subjects.

---

[35] For a survey, see Whitmarsh 2011: 5–12.   [36] For example, Bowie 1994: 442.
[37] Bowersock 1994.   [38] For a new edition and commentary, see Schmedt 2020.

Some Imperial authors used Homer and the Trojan War to engage playfully with the idea of fictionality.[39] Dio's *Trojan Oration* claims that Homer lied and that the Trojan War had actually been won by the Trojans. In Philostratus' *Heroicus*, a vine dresser offers new information that the ghost of the Greek hero Protesilaus passed on to him. Both Dio and Philostratus refute previous accounts as *pseudea* and present their own versions emphatically as the truth; they thereby spotlight the issue of historical reference, which is put into brackets in fiction. But unlike Eratosthenes and Strabo, these authors are not really concerned with the value of Homeric epic as a historical source and rather reflect critically on the authority of Homer in Imperial culture. While invoking the dichotomy of truth versus falsehood, they implicitly use the topic of the Trojan War as a field for fictional experimentation.

Lucian is another author who reflects on fictionality.[40] The *True Stories* shrewdly satirize the genre of travel narrative. Lucian autobiographically narrates such adventures as an encounter with Vine-Women and Ass-legs, a trip to the Moon and an extended stay inside the belly of a whale. Like Dio and Philostratus, Lucian invokes the truth–falsehood dichotomy. In fact, one of the major comic effects of *True Stories* is the constant deployment of all sorts of authentication devices for such obviously impossible stories – a fierce stab at the historiographic and ethnographic tradition enamoured with the marvellous. At the beginning, however, Lucian explicitly refers to the fictional framework of his own work when he states that he 'turned to lying ... My readers, therefore should definitely not believe these things' (ἐπὶ τὸ ψεῦδος ἐτραπόμην ... διὸ δεῖ τοὺς ἐντυγχάνοντας μηδαμῶς πιστεύειν αὐτοῖς, 1.4). As Lawrence Kim notes, 'this frank admission of his forthcoming narrative's falsity is widely recognized as a humorous "concretization" of the normally implicit fictional contract between author and reader, which carves out a space for storytelling that need not be assessed on the basis of its relation to "reality"'.[41]

As this superficial glance reveals, fictionality did not have to be discovered but was present in various genres. Fable, comedy, Platonic dialogue, bucolic poetry and novel illustrate the familiarity of the notion of fiction to which Imperial authors such as Philostratus and Lucian applied their sharp intellects. At the same time, it is noteworthy that the weightiest

---

[39] Kim 2010.

[40] See especially Ní Mheallaigh 2014. However, I disagree with her on *Philopseudes*, which, as I argue in Grethlein 2021: 168–80, is concerned not so much with the suspension of reference as with the allure of obviously fake stories.

[41] Kim 2010: 154.

genres, notably epic and tragedy, were in general not seen as fictional.[42]
The place of the novel in ancient literature illustrates the minor role of
fictionality. The most important genre and the incarnation of fiction for
us, the novel, seems to have developed only in the Imperial age and, despite
its sophistication and various forms, got short shrift from critics.

3   Aristotle's *Poetics*: A Theory of Fiction?

It is now time to examine how much attention fictionality received in
ancient criticism.[43] Theoreticians as well as Classicists credit Aristotle with
a or even the first theory of fiction in the history of criticism.[44] In chapter 9
of the *Poetics*, Aristotle writes: 'It is a further clear implication of what has
been said that the poet's task is to speak not of events which have occurred,
but of the kind of events which could occur, and are possible by the
standards of probability or necessity' (φανερὸν δὲ ἐκ τῶν εἰρημένων καὶ
ὅτι οὐ τὸ τὰ γενόμενα λέγειν, τοῦτο ποιητοῦ ἔργον ἐστίν, ἀλλ' οἶα ἂν
γένοιτο καὶ τὰ δυνατὰ κατὰ τὸ εἰκὸς ἢ τὸ ἀναγκαῖον, 1451a36–8). The
poet is distinguished from the historian not through his use of metrical
form: 'The difference lies in the fact that the one speaks of events which
have occurred, the other of the sort of events which could occur' (ἀλλὰ
τούτῳ διαφέρει, τῷ τὸν μὲν τὰ γενόμενα λέγειν, τὸν δὲ οἶα ἂν γένοιτο,
1451b4–5). There can be no doubt that Aristotle's juxtaposition of poetry
with historiography encapsulates a view of poetry as free from the obligation to referentiality.

That said, what is widely assumed to be Aristotle's theory of fiction
needs to be qualified in two important regards. We first have to consider
the place of Aristotle's claims about poetry as fictional in the context of the
argument of the *Poetics*. Scholars tend to speak of Aristotle's theory of
fiction as if he had identified fictionality as constitutive of poetry and fully
analysed it in its own right. However, chapter 9 of the *Poetics* forms part of
a larger argument. Aristotle does not introduce fictionality as the core
aspect of poetry but only touches on it in order to elaborate on what in his
eyes is essential: plot. Chapters 7 to 14 are devoted to plot, for Aristotle the
most important category of poetry. In chapters 7 and 8, Aristotle emphasizes the need for coherence and unity. As spelled out in chapter 8, 'plot
does not possess unity (as some believe) by virtue of centring on an

---

[42] For a qualification about tragedy, see below at n. 91.
[43] In this section, I draw on material from Grethlein 2021: 47–9.
[44] For example, Puelma 1989; Fuhrmann 1992: 7; Nightingale 2006: 40; Janko 2011: 233; Lavocat 2016:
   20; Feddern 2018: 212–58 with doxography on 216 n. 386.

individual' (μῦθος δ' ἐστὶν εἷς οὐχ ὥσπερ τινὲς οἴονται ἐὰν περὶ ἕνα ᾖ, 1451a16–17). Instead, plot needs to be about a single action which forms an organic unity : 'Its parts, consisting of the events, should be so constructed that the displacement or removal of any of them will disturb and disjoint the work's wholeness' (τὰ μέρη συνεστάναι τῶν πραγμάτων οὕτως ὥστε μετατιθεμένου τινὸς μέρους ἢ ἀφαιρουμένου διαφέρεσθαι καὶ κινεῖσθαι τὸ ὅλον, 1451a32–4).

From this requirement follows the assertion of chapter 9 that poetry treats not what happened but what might happen. In order to be able to produce unitary and coherent plots, poems need to be free from the obligation to report everything that happened to a person or in a given period. If, however, poetry tackles 'not events which have occurred, but the kind of events which could occur' (οὐ τὸ τὰ γενόμενα λέγειν, τοῦτο ποιητοῦ ἔργον ἐστίν, ἀλλ' οἷα ἂν γένοιτο, 1451a36–7), then it can bestow on a plot coherence and unity. The striking juxtaposition of poetry with historiography makes it easy to assume that in chapter 9 Aristotle addresses a key aspect of poetry or even advances a basic definition, but, as a closer look at the argumentative context reveals, he introduces fictionality only as a means to show how a unitary and coherent plot can be achieved.

The second point concerns Aristotle's notion of fictionality. One could say that he softens the juxtaposition of poetry with historiography when he notes that tragedians often use the names of historical figures and, we may add, draw on stories that were considered historical. Further along, Aristotle explicitly admits that poets can even represent historical events, for there is historical material that fulfils the requirements of poetry (1451b29–32). The use of historical figures or even historical events, however, does not undermine the idea of fictionality. It bears repeating that fiction can feature factual elements; what is decisive is its framework, which suspends referentiality.

At the same time, Aristotle's definition of poetry goes beyond this suspension. It is first more specific, insofar as Aristotle limits the content of poetry to 'the kind of events which could occur, and are possible by the standards of probability or necessity'. The realm of fiction harbours all sorts of stories – possible and impossible stories alike. Later in chapter 25, Aristotle elaborates on different forms of impossibility that poets ought to avoid and only deploy in special cases. These qualifications notwithstanding, it is noteworthy that Aristotle's focus on possible events deviates from the breadth of stories under the umbrella of fiction. He juxtaposes the reference to past events in historiography with a specific modality that defines poetry.

There is another important regard in which Aristotle's reflection on the content of poetry does not map onto the idea of fictionality (1451b5–11):

> διὸ καὶ φιλοσοφώτερον καὶ σπουδαιότερον ποίησις ἱστορίας ἐστίν· ἡ μὲν γὰρ ποίησις μᾶλλον τὰ καθόλου, ἡ δ᾽ ἱστορία τὰ καθ᾽ ἕκαστον λέγει. ἔστιν δὲ καθόλου μέν, τῷ ποίῳ τὰ ποῖα ἄττα συμβαίνει λέγειν ἢ πράττειν κατὰ τὸ εἰκὸς ἢ τὸ ἀναγκαῖον, οὗ στοχάζεται ἡ ποίησις ὀνόματα ἐπιτιθεμένη· τὸ δὲ καθ᾽ ἕκαστον, τί Ἀλκιβιάδης ἔπραξεν ἢ τί ἔπαθεν.

> It is for this reason that poetry is both more philosophical and more serious than history, since poetry speaks more of universals, history of particulars. A 'universal' comprises the kind of speech or action which belongs by probability or necessity to a certain kind of character – something which poetry aims at despite its addition of particular names. A 'particular', by contrast, is (for example) what Alcibiades did or experienced.

For Aristotle, poetry reveals universals. What these universals are that render poetry distinct from historiography and similar to philosophy is controversial. While the significance that Aristotle ascribes to the vividness of poetic representation (1455a22–6) speaks against identifying these universals with abstract entities such as Platonic ideas, the context and a later discussion in chapter 17 indicate that the universals are related to plot. As Halliwell notes, they concern 'causes, reasons, motives, and intelligible patterns of human life in the structure of a dramatic poem as a whole'.[45] Crucial for my argument here is the impact that the universals have on Aristotle's understanding of poetry's referentiality. They show that Aristotle not so much suspends referentiality as replaces factualness with a deeper sort of reference, a reference to the general logic of human action.

It has, I hope, become clear why I am hesitant to call the *Poetics* a theory of fiction. Certainly, in juxtaposing poetry with historiography and assigning to it subjects 'which could occur', Aristotle thinks about poetry in terms of fictionality. This reflection, however, does not stand alone but is part of an exploration of plot; Aristotle muses on the subjects of poetry in order to show how coherent and unitary plots can be achieved. Moreover, he stipulates the topics of poetry beyond the suspension of referentiality when he restricts them to possible events and relates them to universals. In the *Poetics*, the suspension of referentiality only appears as a part of a theory of plot and is combined with a more profound sort of reference, a reference to the universals of human action.

---

[45] Halliwell 2002: 195. On the notion of universals in *Poetics* 9, see Halliwell 2002: 193–206; Schmitt 2008: 372–426 with further literature.

4   Gorgias and the Deception of Tragedy

My reading of Aristotle's *Poetics* illustrates that fictionality, which is so central to our understanding of literature, was less significant in antiquity. In order to grasp what attracted the attention of ancient critics instead, I will now turn to a fragment that is often seen as paving the way to Aristotle's idea of fiction but that rather highlights why ancient critics were less concerned with fictionality.[46] Gorgias was one of the major sophists, a teacher of rhetoric with far-reaching interests in physiology, ontology, epistemology and poetics. In one of his most famous fragments, he claims that tragedy generates 'a deception, in which the one who deceives is more just than the one who does not deceive, and the one who is deceived is more intelligent than the one who is not deceived' (ἀπάτην ... ἣν ὅ τ᾽ ἀπατήσας δικαιότερος τοῦ μὴ ἀπατήσαντος καὶ ὁ ἀπατηθεὶς σοφώτερος τοῦ μὴ ἀπατηθέντος, fr. B 23 DK).

We do not know whether this statement was an isolated quip or belonged to an extended discussion, perhaps even a poetological treatise, but it wittily engages with the traditional view of poetry as *pseudos*, better translated as 'falsehood' than as 'lie'. Yes, Gorgias admits, tragedians deceive; and yet their deception is just, and it is a sign of intelligence to succumb to it. Another text illustrates what Gorgias means by deception in fr. 23 DK. In *Helen*, Gorgias sets out to clear Helen from the charge of having caused the Trojan War. He develops four lines of defence. Besides divine will, physical power and love, speech is one of the forces that Helen would not have been able to resist. The power of speech receives significantly more attention than the other three reasons; its discussion is the centrepiece of the text. To illustrate the capacity of speech, Gorgias also comments on poetry: 'Those who hear it are penetrated by a terribly fearful shuddering, a much-weeping pity and a yearning that desires grief, and on the basis of the fortunes and misfortunes of other people's actions and bodies, their soul is affected, by an affection of its own, by the medium of words' (ἧς τοὺς ἀκούοντας εἰσῆλθε καὶ φρίκη περίφοβος καὶ ἔλεος πολύδακρυς καὶ πόθος φιλοπενθής, ἐπ᾽ ἀλλοτρίων τε πραγμάτων καὶ σωμάτων εὐτυχίαις καὶ δυσπραγίαις ἴδιόν τι πάθημα διὰ τῶν λόγων ἔπαθεν ἡ ψυχή, fr. B 11.9 DK).

The description of audience response in *Helen* spells out the deception of fr. 23 DK: tragedy and also other forms of poetry trigger strong emotions

---

[46] For Gorgias fr. 23 DK as a reflection on fictionality, see Finkelberg 1998: 177; Rösler 1980: 311–12; Halliwell 1986: 12–13; Franz 1991; Wardy 1996: 36–7; Primavesi 2009: 119; von Contzen and Tilg 2020: 94. For a reconsideration of the fragment along different lines, see Grethlein 2021, chapter 1.

and put listeners into the shoes of characters.[47] Poetry 'deceives' by transporting its recipients, by, as we would say today, immersing them in represented worlds.[48] The reference to the listeners' intelligence gestures to their contribution to the success of aesthetic illusion. Aesthetic illusion is premised on an 'as-if' response – while recipients remain aware of attending to a representation, they enter into the represented world. The basic pun of fr. 23 DK is premised on the word that Gorgias uses for aesthetic illusion: *apatē*, an ethical term, traditionally harnessed to criticize poetry. In deploying *apatē* to signify the aesthetic effect of poetry, namely immersion, Gorgias deflates the charge against the poets.

The transportation of the audience, whether it is called immersion, absorption or experience, is often confused with fictionality.[49] We have, however, already seen that it is a distinct phenomenon. Immersing oneself in the represented world while maintaining an awareness of its representational character is different from the suspension of referentiality. The former describes a specific mode of attention to the represented, the latter the assessment of the representation's truth status. A recipient's absorption in the represented world is largely independent of whether they deem the representation fictional or factual. The difference between aesthetic illusion and fictionality is tangible in that not only fictional but also factual narratives can absorb us:[50] we may follow a historian's narrative and have the sense of being conveyed right to the scene without losing the awareness that our attention is being directed towards a text.

5   Immersion in Ancient Criticism

While the highly rhetorical play with paradox in fr. 23 DK is typically Gorgianic, the focus on immersion is representative of a broader concern in antiquity. Numerous reflections embedded in poetry and prose texts as well as comments of critics highlight the capacity of narrators to enthral their audiences and readers.[51] The bards and narrators in the *Odyssey*, for

---

[47] Segal 1962 remains a key analysis of the role of poetry in *Helen*. Most recently, see Schollmeyer 2021.

[48] There are, however, also differences between the modern concept of immersion and ancient concepts that seem to anticipate it: see below, pp. 41-2.

[49] In Classics, for example, Feeney 1993; Morgan 1993; Ioli 2018.

[50] As Schaeffer 2009 notes, this has been proven by cognitive experiments. Compare Ryan 2001: 93. On the difference between aesthetic illusion and fictionality, see Wolf 2008.

[51] Surveys can be found in Walsh 1984; Halliwell 2011; Peponi 2012; Grethlein 2017b. Focusing on Hellenistic and Imperial rhetorical and poetological concepts, Vogt-Spira 2022: 116 makes the important observation: 'An evaluation of the reference is not a criterion for the mechanism of making something present.' ('Kriterium für den Mechanismus der Vergegenwärtigung bildet nicht

example, are capable of 'delighting' (*terpein*) and 'bewitching' (*kēlein*) their listeners. Their songs and narrations elicit strong affective responses, as when Odysseus, listening to Demodocus' recital of Troy's fall, bursts into tears.[52] The immersive power of song is exacerbated and gains an uncanny dimension in the Sirens. The aesthetic experience triggered by the Sirens' song is so powerful that it even eclipses real-life experiences.

The pervasiveness of poetic enchantment also comes to the fore in Plato's *Ion*.[53] In this dialogue, Socrates inquires whether the rhapsode Ion owes his brilliance to art or to divine inspiration. The divine mania, as described by Socrates and Ion, triggers an immersion – Ion answers in the positive when Socrates asks him if 'your soul in an ecstasy supposes herself to be among the scenes you are describing, whether they be in Ithaca, or in Troy, or as the poems may chance to place them' (παρὰ τοῖς πράγμασιν οἴεταί σου εἶναι ἡ ψυχὴ οἷς λέγεις ἐνθουσιάζουσα, ἢ ἐν Ἰθάκῃ οὖσιν ἢ ἐν Τροίᾳ ἢ ὅπως ἂν καὶ τὰ ἔπη ἔχῃ, 535c1–3). In addition to claiming that his soul is transported to the place of the action he narrates, Ion emphasizes his emotional involvement: 'When I relate a tale of woe, my eyes are filled with tears; and when it is of fear or awe, my hair stands on end with terror, and my heart leaps' (ἐγὼ γὰρ ὅταν ἐλεινόν τι λέγω, δακρύων ἐμπίμπλανταί μου οἱ ὀφθαλμοί· ὅταν τε φοβερὸν ἢ δεινόν, ὀρθαὶ αἱ τρίχες ἵστανται ὑπὸ φόβου καὶ ἡ καρδία πηδᾷ, 535c5–8).[54] The immersion pertains not only to the performer, but also to the audience. Earlier in the dialogue, Socrates adduced the image of a magnet to illustrate how the inspiration of the poet is carried over first to the reciter, then to the listeners. Author, speaker and audience alike are captivated and conveyed to the scene of the action, be it the camp of Troy or Odysseus' palace on Ithaca.

Ion's description of his art is only the view of a character in a dialogue, and it is contrasted with an understanding of rhapsodic performance as a *technē*. And yet, it reflects a broad cultural consensus about the spell of narrative to which Plato himself seems to have subscribed. The capacity of poets to enchant audiences is one of the main reasons for their ban from the ideal city in the *Republic*.[55] In the first discussion of poetry in books 2 and 3,

die Überprüfung der Referenz.') However, he still subsumes the ancient concepts of *enargeia* and *phantasia* under the idea of fictionality.

[52] For a discussion, see Grethlein 2015: 313–16.

[53] For a recent discussion with bibliography, see Halliwell 2011: 166–79.

[54] Plato has Ion also gesture to the reflection that balances the immersion when he states that, while reciting, he keeps a close eye on the audience to monitor the success of his performance (535e1–6).

[55] For this argument, see Grethlein 2020; 2021, chapter 4.

Socrates is particularly concerned with *mimēsis*, direct speech, as it makes reciters and listeners impersonate questionable characters. When Socrates returns to poetry in the *Republic*'s final book, he identifies as the 'greatest charge' against poetry the fact that it makes audiences indulge in affects such as grief, lust and laughter and thereby strengthens the weak part of the soul. Socrates does not ignore the 'as-if' of aesthetic experience; in fact, it is the recipient's awareness of attending to a representation that renders poetry so dangerous. Knowing that they are attending only to a representation of the experiences of others, they give in to affects they are otherwise eager to suppress, while ignoring the lasting impact of their response on their souls. Immersion is key to the poetic corruption of the soul that gave Plato such a headache.

When Archaic and Classical authors highlight the arresting force of poetry, they refer to the performances in which poems mainly circulated until the fourth century. The ritual context of the symposium and polis festivals, the joint experience in a crowd and the presentation through skilled speakers, who reinforced their recitation through mimics and gestures, rendered poetry particularly captivating. That said, the establishment of a reading culture and its refinement in the Hellenistic age did not lessen the emphasis on immersion. On the one hand, performances continued and gained particular importance in the epideictic rhetorical culture of the Imperial era. On the other hand, the power to transport was also valued in texts that were written to be read.

The salience of immersion is evident in its presence in such different critical treatises as Pseudo-Longinus' *de sublimitate* and Plutarch's *de audiendis poetis*. Pseudo-Longinus juxtaposes the capacity of rhetoric and poetry to enthral audiences (15). In a famous passage, he quotes from Euripides' *Phaethon*: 'Would you not say that the writer's feelings are aboard the car, sharing the perilous flight of those winged horses? Never could he have shown such imagination, had he not run neck and neck with those celestial doings' (ἆρ' οὐκ ἂν εἴποις, ὅτι ἡ ψυχὴ τοῦ γράφοντος συνεπιβαίνει τοῦ ἅρματος καὶ συγκινδυνεύουσα τοῖς ἵπποις συνεπτέρωται; οὐ γὰρ ἄν, εἰ μὴ τοῖς οὐρανίοις ἐκείνοις ἔργοις ἰσοδρομοῦσα ἐφέρετο, τοιαῦτ' ἄν ποτε ἐφαντάσθη, 15.4). Immersing himself, the author is capable of immersing his audience.[56] While for Pseudo-Longinus the intense effect attests to the author's abilities,

---

[56] Pseudo-Longinus' use of the concept of *phantasia*, the blurring of the boundary between oratory and poetry and the examples he quotes make chapter 15 a particularly rich and challenging object of inquiry. See, for example, Halliwell 2011: 347–50 for some of the intricacies.

Plutarch in *de audiendis poetis* provides young readers with reading strategies that prevent them from succumbing to the spell of stories.[57] Before giving his instructions, Plutarch references drugs, erotic desire and the Sirens to illustrate the absorption that narrative can instil in readers (15b–f). Despite the glaring difference, he converges with Pseudo-Longinus in his belief in the immersive power of narrative.

The prominence of immersion for the ancient understanding of literature is illustrated by a key category of Hellenistic and Imperial rhetoric: *enargeia*.[58] While the *progymnasmata*, Imperial rhetorical handbooks, define *enargeia* as the capacity to (nearly) transform listeners into viewers, the discussions of ancient critics imply that it also involves other senses and signifies the 'presence' of the narrated world more broadly.[59] In their rhetorical training, students learned how to describe actions, places and objects vividly. Such *ekphraseis* were an important element in various rhetorical genres, in fictional judicial and deliberative speeches as well as in *encomia* and other epideictic speeches. Since rhetorical competence was crucial to the identity of elite Greeks in the Roman Empire, *enargeia* was a highly charged capacity.[60]

Enargeia is also a quality that is praised in poetry. Homer in particular was seen as a master of vivid narration. A scholion on the beginning of the chariot race in *Iliad* 23, for example, notes: 'He [i.e. Homer] has projected the entire mental image in a vivid way so that the listeners [i.e. Homer's readers] are captured no less than the spectators [i.e. the intradiegetic audience of the chariot race]' (πᾶσαν φαντασίαν ἐναργῶς προβέβληται ὡς μηδὲν ἧττον τῶν θεατῶν ἐσχηκέναι τοὺς ἀκροατάς, scholion bT *Il.* 23.363–72). While ancient critics single out various narrative and linguistic features that create *enargeia*, it is striking that many of the passages they discuss are enactive and embodied accounts that fulfil the criteria for immersive narrative identified in cognitive scholarship.[61] One difference, however, is also noteworthy: our concept of immersion has the recipient dive into the narrated world, just as Plato has Ion claim that when he recites Homer, his soul feels like it is at Troy or Ithaca and Pseudo-Longinus describes Euripides on Phaethon's chariot. *Enargeia*, on the other hand, is

---

[57] For this argument, see Grethlein 2021, chapter 6.
[58] The bibliography on *enargeia* is vast. See, among others, Zanker 1981; Manieri 1998; Otto 2009; Webb 2009: 87–130.
[59] Webb 2016: 211–13.
[60] On the role of *ekphrasis* in rhetorical training, see especially Webb 2009; on the significance of rhetorical competence for the Greek elite in the Roman Empire, see Swain 1996; Schmitz 1997; Whitmarsh 2001.
[61] Grethlein and Huitink 2017.

the power to bring the narrated world close to the recipient. While the two concepts envision opposite movements, they converge in the idea of the recipient's 'presence' at the represented events.[62]

I will return to *enargeia* when I challenge claims about the relevance of mind reading in Chapter 4. For my argument here, it is particularly intriguing that *enargeia* is also a virtue to which historians aspired.[63] Plutarch, for example, praises Thucydides' ability to transport his readers: 'Thucydides is always striving for this vividness in his writing, since it is his desire to make the listener a spectator, as it were, and to instil in readers the emotions of amazement and consternation felt by eyewitnesses' (ὁ γοῦν Θουκυδίδης ἀεὶ τῷ λόγῳ πρὸς ταύτην ἁμιλλᾶται τὴν ἐνάργειαν, οἷον θεατὴν ποιῆσαι τὸν ἀκροατὴν καὶ τὰ γινόμενα περὶ τοὺς ὁρῶντας ἐκπληκτικὰ καὶ ταρακτικὰ πάθη τοῖς ἀναγινώσκουσιν ἐνεργάσασθαι λιχνευόμενος, *de gloria Atheniensium* 347a). The salience of *enargeia* as a quality of historiography highlights that immersion as a textual effect cuts across the fact–fiction divide. As chapter 9 of Aristotle's *Poetics* underscores, the idea of fictionality was not unknown in antiquity. And yet ancient readers were far more concerned with the capacity of performances and texts to transport readers than with their suspension of referential claims.

6   The Morals of Truth

Gorgias' comment on tragedy as a form of deception also reflects a second point that looms large in ancient criticism and outranks the issue of fictionality, namely the moral dimension of literature. By deploying the word *apatē* and making it signify aesthetic illusion, Gorgias evokes and discharges the claim that poets tell falsehoods. This claim is a staple especially, but not only, in Archaic and Classical reflections on poetry.[64] *Pseudos*, which is used more often than *apatē* in such discussions, can signify various matters, but, by and large, authors levelling accusations against poets tend to target morally questionable stories rather than deviations from what actually happened.

A few examples will illustrate this inclination to charge *pseudos* ethically. Xenophanes, a poet and philosopher of the sixth century BCE, is on record in histories of religion as one of the first critics of the anthropomorphic gods. His polemics against traditional religion have a strong moral

---

[62] Compare Allan, de Jong and de Jonge 2017: 36–7.   [63] Walker 1993; Grethlein 2013b.
[64] See, for example, Puelma 1989; Pratt 1993; Finkelberg 1998; Ford 2002; Ioli 2018.

dimension: he blames Homer and Hesiod for attributing to the gods all 'what among humans brings rebuke and blame, stealing, committing adultery and deceiving one another' (ὅσσα παρ' ἀνθρώποισιν ὀνείδεα καὶ ψόγος ἐστίν, κλέπτειν μοιχεύειν τε καὶ ἀλλήλους ἀπατεύειν, fr. B 11 DK; cf. fr. B 12 DK).[65] The ethical thrust of Xenophanes' criticism is also on display in a poem that describes an ideal symposium.[66] After laying out the setting and ritual procedure, Xenophanes specifies the topics that must not be addressed in sympotic conversation (fr. B 1.21–4):

> οὔ τι μάχας διέπειν Τιτήνων οὐδὲ Γιγάντων
> οὐδὲ < > Κενταύρων, πλάσμα<τα> τῶν προτέρων,
> ἢ στάσιας σφεδανάς· τοῖς οὐδὲν χρηστὸν ἔνεστιν·
> θεῶν <δὲ> προμηθείην αἰὲν ἔχειν ἀγαθήν.

> and not to narrate the battles of the Titans and of the Giants,
> or of the Centaurs, the inventions of our ancestors,
> or violent civil strifes. In these tales there is nothing useful.
> But always to have respect for the gods, that is good.

Xenophanes takes issue with these tales not so much on account of their being invented as on the grounds that they cast the gods as unethical models.

Pindar's first *Olympian* provides another much-discussed rejection of what is considered a false account.[67] In this epinician, Pindar questions the traditional account of Pelops, whom, the story goes, his father Tantalus cooked and served to the gods. Demeter, still in mourning over the theft of her daughter, failed to recognize Tantalus' ruse and ate Pelops' shoulder, which after his resuscitation was replaced by an ivory prosthesis. Pindar criticizes that 'in men's talk stories are embroidered beyond the truth, and so deceive us with their elaborate lies' (καί πού τι καὶ βροτῶν φάτις ὑπὲρ τὸν ἀλαθῆ λόγον/ δεδαιδαλμένοι ψεύδεσι ποικίλοις ἐξαπατῶντι μῦθοι, *Ol.* 1.28–9). The poetological meditation in *Olympian* 1 is complex and involves the allure of poetry as well as the juxtaposition of praise with blame, both highly pertinent to the epinician itself;[68] and yet it can be noted that it is not so much the referential deficiency that exasperates Pindar as the presentation of the gods as engaging in such a transgression: 'but it is seemly for a man to say good things about the gods' (ἔστι δ' ἀνδρὶ φάμεν ἐοικὸς ἀμφὶ δαι/μόνων καλά, 1.35).

---

[65] See, however, Schein 2019 with references to earlier literature, on the moral and didactic dimensions of Homeric epic.

[66] Compare Babut 1974; Pratt 1993: 138–40; Ford 2002: 53–8; Feddern 2018: 101–4.

[67] For example, Howie 1984; Richardson 1986; Köhnken 1974; Grethlein 2019.

[68] Cf. Pratt 1993: 123–6.

Plato's anxiety about immersion is entwined with his attacks against the 'falsehoods' of poetry. On the whole, he seems to equate 'false' with 'bad' and to blend together ontological categories with ethical categories.[69] However, some arguments reveal that for Plato ontology and ethics do not necessarily coincide and that his primary concern is with the latter.[70] He has Socrates state not only that falsehoods are to be condemned especially if they spread wrong values (*Resp.* 377d8–9), but also, in commenting on the story about the conflict between Uranus and Cronus, that 'even if it were true, it should be passed over in silence, not told to foolish young people' (οὐδ᾽ ἂν εἰ ἦν ἀληθῆ ᾤμην δεῖν ῥᾳδίως οὕτω λέγεσθαι πρὸς ἄφρονάς τε καὶ νέους, ἀλλὰ μάλιστα μὲν σιγᾶσθαι, 378a2–4). On the other hand, there is even place in the ideal city for lies that are useful (382d1–4; see also 414b8–415d4; 522a6–8).

The moral dimension of literature is a prominent feature from the Archaic era to the Imperial.[71] Admittedly, some critics tried to absolve poetry from its instructional task.[72] Eratosthenes, for example, director of the Alexandrian library in the third century BCE, claimed that 'every poet aims at enchantment, not instruction' (ποιητὴς πᾶς στοχάζεται ψυχαγωγίας, οὐ διδασκαλίας). However, the fact that we owe this fragment to an author, Strabo, who vehemently disagrees with its content (1.1.10) makes it evident that poetry was widely credited with an instructional function not only, but especially, on moral matters.[73] Aristophanes' *Frogs*, written at the end of the fifth century, drives home the fact that ancient audiences expected moral instruction from tragedy: Aeschylus wins the contest with Euripides because of the benefits that his poetry can offer to the polis. The contest is by no means straightforward, and Dionysus' verdict raises more questions than it answers; nonetheless, it reflects the general assumption that it is the task of tragedy to teach the citizens. In the Imperial era, Plutarch's *de audiendis poetis*, one of the few critical treatises from antiquity that have been preserved, elaborates on the edification that students can receive from reading poetry, just as the primary goal of Plutarch's *Lives* is to refine the moral sensitivity of the readers.[74] Plutarch is indebted to Plato in his moralist view of poetry as well as his awareness of its immersive capacity, but unlike Plato

[69] This is emphasized, for example, by Gill 1993.   [70] See also Halliwell 2015: 345–6.
[71] For a brief and helpful survey, see Russell 1981: 84–98. For careful qualifications of influential emphasis on the didactic and moralizing character of Archaic poetry in Jaeger 1943 and Havelock 1963, see, for example, Heath 1987: 5–7; Ford 2002: 197–202 and Liebert 2017: 16–18.
[72] On the juxtaposition of enchantment and instruction as goals of literature in Hellenistic criticism, see Gutzwiller 2010: 339–64.
[73] Compare Nünlist 2009: 180.   [74] For example, Duff 2005.

he is confident that students are able to resist the spell of stories and instead identify their moral lessons – if they follow his instructions in *de audiendis poetis*.[75] Basil's *ad adulescentes* illustrates that the long tradition of reflections on the moral impact of poetry also fed into the negotiations of Christian authors on how to deal with the heritage of pagan literature.[76]

The importance of the moral dimension of literature is also on display in historiography, which is by definition factual and, in Aristotle's words, narrates 'events which have occurred'.[77] The accurate record that Thucydides strives to give is not an aim in itself but serves to be 'useful' for those 'who wish to look at the plain truth about both past events and those at some future time that, in accordance with human nature will recur in similar or comparable ways' (ὅσοι δὲ βουλήσονται τῶν τε γενομένων τὸ σαφὲς σκοπεῖν καὶ τῶν μελλόντων ποτὲ αὖθις κατὰ τὸ ἀνθρώπινον τοιούτων καὶ παραπλησίων ἔσεσθαι, ὠφέλιμα, 1.22.4). Like most other ancient historians after him, Thucydides considers usefulness his central goal.[78] The truth is the means of providing useful knowledge and, in offering insights into human nature, goes beyond the factual rendering of what happened. Concerning power, greed and fear, the insights furnished by the *History of the Peloponnesian War* have a strong moral dimension.

In a different way, Herodotus also aims at something that deviates from the factual truth that many modern historians consider their main goal.[79] Besides often providing us with alternative versions, sometimes without signalling his preference, Herodotus also fully narrates stories that he condemns as non-credible.[80] For example, after recounting Xerxes' retreat to Asia by land, he adds another version that has Xerxes sail on from Eion. When a storm comes up, the helmsman urges the reduction of the number of passengers. Upon arrival in Asia, Xerxes awards a garland of gold to the helmsman for saving him 'and then cuts off his head for causing the deaths of so many Persians' (ὅτι δὲ Περσέων πολλοὺς ἀπώλεσε, ἀποταμεῖν τὴν κεφαλὴν αὐτοῦ, 8.118.4). Herodotus marshals various arguments to prove that this account cannot be true. Why does he nonetheless bother to tell it in full detail? The anecdote, I suggest, nicely captures the character of

---

[75] On *de audiendis poetis* as an implicit engagement with Plato's critique of poetry, see Schlemm 1893; Hunter 2009: 169–201; Grethlein 2021, chapter 6.

[76] On Basil's debts to Plutarch and Plato, see Sandnes 2009: 172–85 and Stenger 2016: 91–6.

[77] Hau 2016.   [78] Compare Raaflaub 2010.

[79] While Hayden White's (e.g., 1975) emphasis on the fictional quality of historiography had wide repercussions in the theory of history, it was rejected or ignored by most historians.

[80] For example, Lateiner 1989: 76–90; Baragwanath 2008: 122–59.

Xerxes and Persian mores. The truth at which Herodotus aims lies beyond the reproduction of what happened; it is, as this example illustrates, closely bound up with ethical questions.

Some critics challenged the poets' instructional claims, but on the whole the moral dimension of literature was a central concern of ancient audiences and readers. Edification was an important task attributed to authors from Homer to the Imperial era. The fact that it equally applied to fictional and factual texts underlines that the fact–fiction divide was less significant than it is for us. Seen against the backdrop of the lessons to be learnt from all sorts of texts, their referential status paled into insignificance.

7   Ancient Discussions of Referentiality

Ancient narrative and criticism encompass a wide range of ideas and positions. Taking my cue from Gorgias fr. 23 DK, I have tried to identify two hubs around which reflections cluster: first, the strong effect of narrative on listeners and readers, particularly its capacity to immerse them; second, its moral dimension, which comes to the fore in invectives against falsehood and is also felt in factual genres. Both points were more important than the idea of fictionality. It is now time to show that the issue of referentiality and its suspension, while not taking centre stage, was not absent from ancient criticism.

I have already mentioned Eratosthenes' claim that poets aim at enchantment instead of instruction. In another fragment, Eratosthenes asserts that poetry is 'free to invent what seems to it conducive to entertain' (δέδοται πλάττειν ... ὃ ἂν αὐτῇ φαίνηται ψυχαγωγίας οἰκεῖον, I A 19 Berger). Therefore, we cannot 'judge poems with reference to their meaning and seek history from them' (μὴ κρίνειν πρὸς τὴν διάνοιαν τὰ ποιήματα, μηδ' ἱστορίαν ἀπ' αὐτῶν ζητεῖν, I A 17 Berger). Homer, Eratosthenes seems to have argued, for example, had intended to place Odysseus' wanderings in the western part of the Mediterranean but gave up this plan because he lacked reliable information and wanted to lead his narrative 'towards the more awe-inspiring and the more marvellous' (ἐπὶ τὸ δεινότερον καὶ τὸ τερατωδέστερον, I A 14 Berger). At the same time, Eratosthenes was ready to acknowledge that Homer embedded in his account numerous details that he knew about Greece and exotic countries such as Egypt and Ethiopia (I A 4 Berger).[81]

---

[81] On Eratosthenes' reading of Homer, see Meijering 1987: 58–61; Kim 2010: 56–60.

We also find statements on poetic licence in scholia that comment on deviations from mythical traditions.[82] A scholion on a Pindaric ode, for example, claims that 'the poets are at liberty to invent what they want' (ἀλλ᾽ ἔξεστι πλάττειν τοῖς ποιηταῖς ἃ βούλονται, on *O.* 4.31b). The idea of poetic licence was also marshalled by critics grappling with unnatural elements and minor contradictions in poetry. None other than Aristarchus, one of Eratosthenes' successors as director of the Alexandrian library, demanded 'that what is said by the poet [i.e. Homer] be taken as more mythical in accordance with poetic licence, and we ought not to busy ourselves with anything beyond what is said by the poet' (τὰ φραζόμενα ὑπὸ τοῦ ποιητοῦ μυθικώτερον ἐκδέχεσθαι, κατὰ τὴν ποιητικὴν ἐξουσίαν, μηδὲν ἔξω τῶν φραζομένων ὑπὸ τοῦ ποιητοῦ περιεργαζομένους, scholion D on *Il.* 5.385). Besides voicing the famous principle of 'explaining Homer out of Homer', this comment allows for unrealistic and fantastic elements in epic poetry, in this specific case the tale that gods were hurt by mortals. In another note, Aristarchus relies on the same principle when he comments on two different descriptions of Agamemnon's sword, in one case as silver, in other cases as golden (A on 2.45a). Such cases of incoherence ought not to be taken 'literally' (*kyriōs*) but reveal the poet's liberty to write 'on impulse' (*kat' epiphoran*).

While there are such comments that grant poetry the status of fiction, another view is more pervasive: that poets recounted past events with a certain degree of freedom in the shaping of details. A scholion on Sophocles' *Electra*, for example, notes that the circumstances in which Agamemnon is murdered differ from the Homeric version. There is, however, no reason to criticize Sophocles on account of this (on 446): 'It was sufficient that the whole agrees with the fact. For everybody has the licence to arrange the details as he fancies, as long as he does not affect the whole of the plot' (ἤρκει γὰρ τὰ ὅλα συμφωνεῖν τῷ πράγματι· τὰ γὰρ κατὰ μέρος ἐξουσίαν ἔχει ἕκαστος ὡς βούλεται πραγματεύσασθαι, εἰ μὴ τὸ πᾶν βλάπτῃ τῆς ὑποθέσεως).

This is also the position advocated by Strabo in his polemics against Eratosthenes. In Strabo's view, Homer offers history coated with mythical elements. When he discusses the placing of Odysseus' wanderings in the area of Italy and Sicily, for instance, he argues: 'Convinced that Odysseus' wandering took place there, he took this true foundation and elaborated it poetically' (πεισθεὶς ἐκεῖ τὴν πλάνην τῷ Ὀδυσσεῖ γενέσθαι, λαβὼν ἀληθῆ ταύτην τὴν ὑπόθεσιν ποιητικῶς διεσκεύασε, 1.2.11). Besides taking pains

---

[82] Compare Meijering 1987: 63–70; Nünlist 2009: 174–84; Feddern 2018: 518–28.

to defend the traditional idea of Homer as a universal teacher, Strabo believes that historical core and poetic embellishment can be neatly separated (1.2.9):

Ἄτε δὴ πρὸς τὸ παιδευτικὸν εἶδος τοὺς μύθους ἀναφέρων ὁ ποιητὴς ἐφρόντισε πολὺ μέρος τἀληθοῦς, ἐν δ' ἐτίθει καὶ ψεῦδος, τὸ μὲν ἀποδεχόμενος τῷ δὲ δημαγωγῶν καὶ στρατηγῶν τὰ πλήθη. „ὡς δ' ὅτε τις χρυσὸν περιχεύεται ἀργύρῳ ἀνήρ," οὕτως ἐκεῖνος ταῖς ἀληθέσι περιπετείαις προσεπετίθει μῦθον, ἡδύνων καὶ κοσμῶν τὴν φράσιν, πρὸς δὲ τὸ αὐτὸ τέλος τοῦ ἱστορικοῦ καὶ τοῦ τὰ ὄντα λέγοντος βλέπων.

Since he lifted the myths to an instructive form, the poet [i.e. Homer] cared much about the truth. He placed in it falsehood, accepting the former [i.e. the truth], and using the other [i.e. falsehood] to lead and marshal the masses. 'Like a man, who covers silver with gold', Homer added myth to the true events, sweetening and adorning his diction, but still aiming at the goal of the historian and of one who tells facts.[83]

Like Strabo, the majority of ancient critics continued to read Homeric epic and other poetry as, on the whole, factual. For them, fictive elements and embellishments contributed to the enchanting effect but did not detract from the overall factualness. The mainstream of ancient criticism thus appears as complementary to the modern understanding of epic: where we see fictional poems that are interspersed with factual elements, ancient readers tended to see factual narratives enriched by fictive elements. The place that the suspension of referentiality occupies today was held by the poet's freedom to embellish the record of the past in antiquity.

Let me finally mention a concept that seems to have emerged in the Hellenistic era, a threefold taxonomy of narrative.[84] In *Against the Grammarians*, Sextus Empiricus, writing in the second century CE, distinguishes between three forms of the substance of narrative, namely *historia*, the account of things that occurred; *plasma*, the account of things that did not happen but are narrated in a similar way as those that happened; and *mythos*, the account of events that did not happen and could not happen, such as the birth of the race of spiders and snakes from the blood of the Titans. In one of his two discussions of this taxonomy,[85] Sextus credits Asclepiades of Myrlea, a philosopher of the first century BCE, as his source.

---

[83] On this passage, see Kim 2010: 68–70; on Strabo and poetry, see Feddern 2018: 280–97 with further literature.

[84] Cf. Feddern 2018: 297–379.

[85] On the tensions between the two accounts (252–3; 263–4) and a third reference in passing (93), see Blank 2007: 266–70 on 252–3. On Asclepiades and his threefold taxonomy of narrative, see also Rispoli 1988: 170–204; Schirren 2005: 15–22.

While we do not know whether or not Asclepiades coined the threefold taxonomy of *historia–plasma–mythos*, it is likely that it emerged in Greek criticism of the Hellenistic period.[86]

Similar if not entirely identical taxonomies can be found in three prominent Latin texts of the first centuries BCE and CE: Cicero's early handbook for orators *de inventione* (1.27), the anonymous *Rhetorica ad Herennium* (1.13) and Quintilian's *Institutio oratoria* (2.4.2), as well as in a number of minor rhetorical manuals and works on rhetorical instruction.[87] The differences that are partly owed to the respective contexts need not concern us here;[88] the basic distinction between *historia*, *argumentum* and *fabula* remains the same. Quintilian, for example, writes:

> et quia narrationum, excepta qua in causis utimur, tris accepimus species, fabulam, quae uersatur in tragoediis atque carminibus non a ueritate modo sed etiam a forma ueritatis remota, argumentum, quod falsum sed uero simile comoediae fingunt, historiam, in qua est gestae rei expositio.

> We are told that there are three species of narrative, apart from those used in actual causes. One is *fabula*, found in tragedies and poems, and remote not only from truth but from the appearance of truth. The second is *argumentum*, which is the false but probable fiction of comedy. The third is *historia*, which contains the narration of actual events.

Particularly striking about this passage is that Quintilian adduces tragedies and poems as examples of *fabula*. This designation demonstrates not only that new concepts emerged in the course of antiquity but that the assessment of individual genres also changed or was controversial. Tragedians were traditionally granted poetic licence, but it had been agreed that their subjects were historical. Even Aristotle, who contended that poetry dealt with what could occur, noted that tragedy mostly used historical figures as its characters. Some later critics continued with the traditional view and assigned tragedy to the field of *historia*.[89] The majority however subsumed tragedy under *mythos/fabula* or, more rarely, under *plasma/argumentum*.[90] Figures and actions that originally had been deemed historical, if poetically

---

[86] Hose 1996 claims that the taxonomy is a Roman coinage. Oddly, he only refers to *Against the Grammarians* 263–4 and disproves the obviously untenable claim that it can be traced back to the Pergamenian philosopher Krates but ignores *Against the Grammarians* 252–3, where Sextus ascribes the distinction to the Greek philosopher Asclepiades. Asclepiades seems to have written before Cicero and the author of the *Rhetorica ad Herennium*, and even if he wrote at the same time, he certainly wrote independently of them.

[87] Compare Barwick 1928: 264–6; Meijering 1987: 72–87.   [88] For example, Calboli 1993: 214–17.

[89] For example, scholion on Dionysios Thrax 173.3–4 discussed by Meijering 1987: 88.

[90] Compare Barwick 1928: 273–4; Meijering 1987: 87–90; Rispoli 1988: 24. For tragedy as *plasmatikon*, see, for example, *Hermog.* 4.17.

embellished, came to be seen as unhistorical and even defying the laws of verisimilitude.

Put forward in canonical texts, the tripartite taxonomy of *historia–argumentum–fabula* not only exerted massive influence on Imperial criticism but was also received in the Middle Ages through Isidor of Seville.[91] It is tempting to see in the category of *argumentum*, finally, a clear concept of fiction, as it seems to give a distinct name to literature which does not claim referential status.[92] However, the ancient triad differs from the modern dichotomy: it combines the criterion of reference with the criterion of verisimilitude, a category that Aristotle's *Poetics* had made prominent. The taxonomy relies on an internal factor, the plausibility of the plot, as well as on an external factor, the relation to reality. Whereas the absence of reference distinguishes *argumentum* from *historia*, its verisimilitude sets it off from *fabula*. On the other hand, fiction in the modern sense would encompass *fabula* as well as *argumentum*. While overcoming the implicit ethical evaluation of the traditional juxtaposition of truth with falsehood, the triad *historia–argumentum–fabula* does not map onto our dichotomy of fact versus fiction. This observation is further evidence for my argument that the idea of fictionality was known in antiquity, but far from playing a central role.

8   Conclusion

This chapter has touched on a wide range of texts and has taken the liberty of ignoring an even wider range:[93] much more could be said about the passages quoted, and numerous other ancient authors could be brought in. I have referred only in passing to the diachronic dimension, noting that important concepts such as *enargeia* or the triad *historia–plasma–mythos* were coined in the Hellenistic era and that the Imperial era seems to have seen an increase in fictional writing. A much closer look would be necessary to trace the development of ancient views of fictionality and to assess its relation to the institutional settings of literature. That said, I hope that the broad brushstrokes of this chapters are justified by its purposes, namely to show a crucial difference between our and ancient approaches to literature. For our understanding of literature, fictionality is a key concept – even those trying to blur the boundary between fact and fiction remain concerned with referentiality and its intricacies.[94] This salience of fictionality is

---

[91] Green 2002: 3–13.   [92] For example, Rispoli 1988; Hose 1996; Tilg 2017: 98.
[93] More relevant texts are discussed in Feddern 2018.   [94] I return to this point below in chapter 6.

manifest in the numerous attempts to pinpoint its discovery in antiquity, which bespeak a pervasive tendency in Classics – the use of categories established in the analysis of modern realist novels and the desire to apply them to ancient literature and to detect them in one form or another in ancient criticism. This strategy is not only understandable as it helps prove the modernity of ancient literature – a highly coveted quality in an era in which Classics is badly in need of legitimization – it has also yielded important insights; at the same time, it has detracted from what renders ancient texts and their understanding distinctive.

As I have argued in this chapter, we find reflections on fictionality as well as fictional texts right from the beginning of ancient literature, and yet the suspension of reference did not command the same attention as it does today. It was in the shadow of two other concerns that envision the relation between text and world along different lines. On the one hand, ancient critics took a strong interest in the enticing quality of texts, especially their immersive dimension. The visceral responses elicited by poetry and prose were assessed differently – they could be praised as an expression of an author's brilliance as well as condemned on the charge of threatening the good order of the soul. But in both cases, the recipient's absorption was deemed more important than the referential status of the text. On the other hand, despite some attempts to ascribe to poetry in particular the function of entertaining, the moral dimension of literature looms large throughout antiquity. Like the immersive effect, moral significance cuts across the fact–fiction divide; historiography as well as poetry was credited with the power of edifying readers and audiences. Antiquity was not an age before the birth of fiction, nor was fictionality discovered at a specific point in antiquity; it was an epoch that was familiar with the idea of fictionality and produced fiction but preferred to approach narrative through other frameworks.

CHAPTER 3

Voice(s): Author/Narrator/Character

1   Apuleius: Author and Ass?

The distinction of different narrative levels is a basic tenet of narratology and has become a general premise of literary scholarship.[1] Scholars working in English, Romanic, Germanic and Comparative Literature departments all assume that the author installs a narrator who resides on a different ontological plane. Regardless of whether the narrator is also a character in the story, they belong to the world of fiction and address not the reader but the narratee. The characters of the story-world inhabit yet another level, interacting with each other but incapable of reaching out to either narrator or author. We thus have three separate levels that are nested within each other like Russian dolls. Some theoreticians add a fourth level, the implied author, the author-image evoked by a work, who, squeezed between the (real) author and the narrator, addresses the implied reader.[2] Further narrative levels emerge when a character is an embedded narrator telling stories about characters in an embedded story-world, who can themselves be narrators and so on.

However, the assumption that all fictional narratives have a narrator distinct from the author has not remained unchallenged. Ann Banfield, an adherent of generative grammar, rejects the idea that narrative is an act of communication and therefore requires a narrator.[3] Simple narration, she argues, is neither an act of communication nor an expression of subjectivity. Represented speech and thought expresses the subjectivity of a character, but without the present tense and first- and second-person pronouns that distinguish direct speech; it is therefore, like narration, non-communicative and narrator-less. Coming from a different angle, Richard Walsh makes the case that what underlies the narratological paradigm of

---

[1] See, for example, Chatman 1978; Genette 1980; Rimmon-Kenan 1983; Bal 1985; Schmid 2010.
[2] The implied author was introduced by Booth 1961.
[3] Banfield 1982. For a critique of Banfield's approach, see, for example, McHale 1983.

the narrator is the attempt to cope with the idea of fictionality.[4] The assumption of a narrator different from the author provides us with a representational frame within which fictional accounts can be read as reports rather than invention. It is, however, not necessary to make the narrator a distinct and inherent instance of narrative. Walsh argues that the narrator is either a character or the author. While there are further scholars who have questioned the idea that narrative requires a narrator distinct from the author, the vast majority of scholars continue to subscribe to what Tilmann Köppe and Jan Stühring label 'pan-narrator theories'.[5]

Classicists are no exception. They have wholeheartedly embraced the narratological model of distinct levels and assign distinct narrators to all texts. Speaking of the Hesiodic narrator or the narrator of a poem of Sappho has helped to avoid the biographic readings so popular in earlier scholarship. Analysed as the utterance of a narrator, Archilochus fr. 5 W does not necessarily imply that Archilochus himself threw away his shield in battle. For some texts, the distinction between narrative levels has proven particularly useful, for instance for Xenophon's *Anabasis*. Xenophon narrates his own experiences as a member of the expedition of the Ten Thousand; in fact, from book 3 onwards, he is a prominent character in the action. However, Xenophon does not present the march through Asia *as* his own experience – at least formally, Xenophon is treated like the other characters in the *Anabasis*.[6] Perhaps the *Anabasis* was even published anonymously; this is at least what Plutarch, followed by many modern scholars, concluded from the reference to an account of the march by a man called Themistogenes in the *Hellenica*.[7] Here, the narratological distinctions are illuminating – they permit us to speak of the narrator, who is distinct from Xenophon the character and who was perhaps not intended to be identified with the author.

As useful as the category of the narrator can be, there are no signs of it in ancient criticism.[8] The general identification of the speaking voice with the

---

[4] Walsh 1997; 2007.

[5] Köppe and Stühring 2011. Further opponents to the general assumptions about narrators include Hamburger (1993 [1957]); Kania 2005; Kablitz 2008; Patron 2009; Currie 2010: 76–85; Boyd 2017.

[6] See, however, Grethlein 2012b for the argument that, just as Xenophon the narrator tends to adopt the perspective of Xenophon the character, the character appropriates narratorial functions. On the intricacies of Xenophon's voice in the *Anabasis*, see also Pelling 2013, who compares it with Caesar's voice in his *Commentarii*.

[7] Plut. *De gloria Atheniensium* 345e. For a survey of modern positions, see Pitcher 2012.

[8] Compare Nünlist 2009: 132–3; Whitmarsh 2013: 235; Tilg 2019: 69–70; Feddern 2021: 5. It has been argued, esp. by de Jong 1987: 5–8 and Rabel 1997: 8–21, that Aristotle anticipates the notion of an independent narrator when he praises Homer as knowing that 'the poet should speak as little as possible. For in this way he is not a *mimetes*' (*poet.* 1460a7–8). The majority of scholars, however,

author manifests itself visually, for example, in the so-called Roman Vergil in the Vatican library (Ms. Vat. Lat. 3867), a grand and richly illustrated codex from the fifth century CE containing the *Eclogues*, *Georgics* and *Aeneid*. The odd-numbered *Eclogues*, which feature dialogues, are preceded by a picture showing the dialoguing parties; in front of the even-numbered *Eclogues*, we find a portrait of Vergil, who is thereby presented as the speaker, just as the rubric heading features 'poeta' in addition to the figures appearing in the poem.[9] Where modern critics refer to an *Eclogue*'s narrator, ancient readers heard Vergil speak.

The absence of the notion of a narrator distinct from the author is also tangible in the persistent tendency to read texts biographically in antiquity.[10] As Mary Lefkowitz showed, most of the data in the *Lives* of ancient poets are derived from their works – ancient readers did not hesitate to identify the poetic 'I' with the author. Critias, for example, 'blamed Archilochus for being very critical of himself', referring to such poems as fr. 5 W (88 B 44 DK = Ael. *VH* 10.13).[11] And Pindar reads Archilochus' iambic invectives as assaults against personal enemies when he expresses his disdain for slander: 'For I have seen, long before me, abusive Archilochus often in a helpless state, fattening himself with strong words and hatred' (εἶδον γὰρ ἑκὰς ἐὼν τὰ πόλλ' ἐν ἀμαχανίᾳ/ ψογερὸν Ἀρχίλοχον βαρυλόγοις ἔχθεσιν/ πιαινόμενον, *Pyth.* 2.54–6). It is noteworthy that writers themselves read poems of others biographically, as it reveals their expectation about how their own works were to be approached.

A particularly perplexing comment can be found in *de civitate dei*. When Augustine mentions Italian landladies who put drugs into cheese and thereby transformed unsuspecting wayfarers into pack animals, he adds that the metamorphosis did not affect the minds of the wayfarers, which

---

assumes that Homer is praised since he prefers direct speech over authorial narrative, for example, Lucas 1968: 226–7; Fuhrmann 1976: 101 n. 10; Halliwell 1986: 126–7. For a survey with more literature, see de Jong 2005, who recants her earlier position and argues that Aristotle praises Homer for the tendency to show instead of telling. Moreover, see Lattmann 2005: 39–40, who, in my eyes unconvincingly, tries to show that Aristotle introduces the idea of an independent narrator in *poet.* 1448a20–4.

[9] See Wright 1993 and, most recently, Elsner 2023, who interprets these illustrations as visual epitomes.

[10] Especially in Latin poetry, there are some passages such as Catullus 16.5-6 that separate the persona in poems from the author. While Clay 1998 highlights this use of separate personae by poets, Mayer 2003 is more skeptical and emphasizes the specific contexts of such claims that ought not to be generalized. Both, however, concur in the conclusion that ancient criticism did not produce the idea of the literary persona of which modern criticism is so fond.

[11] On this fragment, see, for example Rosen 2007: 243-68. On the case of Archilochus and the ancient reception of his poems in general, see Dover 1964 with the critical remarks by Rösler 1985: 136.

remained 'rational and human, in the same way as Apuleius, in his book bearing the title of *The Golden Ass*, reported or affected to have been the case for him, when after taking a potion, he became an ass, while still retaining his human mind' (*sed rationalem humanamque seruari, sicut Apuleius in libris, quos asini aurei titulo inscripsit, sibi ipsi accidisse, ut accepto ueneno humano animo permanente asinus fieret, aut indicauit aut finxit,* 18.18).

Augustine is one of antiquity's smartest minds and readers, and yet he turns out to be oblivious to one of the most basic distinctions of narratology and literary studies at large. Even the most naive undergraduate has no difficulty understanding that Apuleius is the author of *The Golden Ass* and Lucius its hero and narrator. Augustine may prefer to believe that Apuleius only pretends to have experienced Lucius' fate, but this does not alleviate the disturbing assumption that the author Apuleius is identical with the narrator and main character of his story.[12] Augustine's reference to Apuleius also highlights that ancient authors and readers did not anticipate the criticism of the instance of the narrator by some scholars today. For Banfield, Walsh and others, heterodiegetic narrators are the most questionable case. If narrative is not presented by a character and does not 'authorize ... imaginings about a fictional narrator',[13] then, they contend, it is safe to claim that it is voiced by the author. The *Golden Ass*, however, has a homodiegetic narrator, and, what is more, Augustine identifies Apuleius not only with Lucius the narrator, but also with Lucius the experiencing character.

Is the absence of the notion of the narrator as a distinct instance of narrative a major deficiency of ancient criticism? A brief look at medieval studies rather suggests that the narrator is a category that narratologists found helpful, perhaps even indispensable for the study of their material – mostly modern novels – and then proclaimed a universal entity of narrative, but that the category may have been far less significant in premodern literatures. Not only is there no sign of the narrator in medieval criticism either, it has also been argued that the narrator is a category that warps the analysis of most medieval narratives. Spearing, for example, made a case that the bulk of medieval narrative does not have a distinct narrator, that 'whereas the modern assumption has been that consciousness precedes narrative, the medieval assumption appears to have been that narrative

[12] For discussions of Augustine's reference to Apuleius, see Mayer 2003: 65 and Whitmarsh 2013, a stimulating discussion of the ancient first-person narrative, to which I will return at the end of this chapter.
[13] Köppe and Stühring 2011: 74.

preceded consciousness'.[14] Even 'behind the "I" of a medieval text there may be no narrator or speaker, no represented fictional person, and in the commonest kinds of Middle English poem, especially up to the middle of the fourteenth century, there is usually none'.[15]

What at first glance appears as a major deficiency of ancient criticism can be shown to be part of a view of narrative that is distinct from the modern model. In this chapter, I will try to sketch the outline of this view, which, despite the differences, was shared by readers from the Archaic to the Imperial eras. I will first advance the thesis that the identification of the narrating 'I' with the author is part of a broader phenomenon: ancient critics tended to ascribe utterances of characters in general to authors. At the same time, their comments attest a full aware-ness of the difference between authors and characters (§2 Authors and Characters in Ancient Literature and Criticism). By no means due to the inability to distinguish author from characters, the tendency to take utterances of characters as statements of their authors is tied to an understanding of direct speech that is markedly different from that on which modern narratology is premised. I will discuss two famous passages in Plato and Aristotle and adduce later criticism to demonstrate that ancient readers envisioned direct speech as the author's impersonation of a character (§3 Authorial Impersonation). This concept of direct speech can be linked to the salience of auditory reception in antiquity and forms part of a broader view of poetic composition, which has the author enact the narrative in their imagination (§4 Oral Performance and Literary Composition). This broader view will allow us to reconsider the idea of metalepsis in antiquity. I will not take issue with the application of this category to ancient texts – recent scholarship has impressively demon-strated how fruitful this can be – but I will argue that the ancient understanding of authorial voice is decisively unmetaleptic. At the same time, it resonates with embodied and enactive models of cognition. This resonance demonstrates what can be gained from studies inspired by cognitive approaches for our understanding of ancient criticism and literature (§5 From Metalepsis to Immersion).

---

[14] Spearing 2005: 26. He suspects that the idea of the narrator emerges with Descartes' epistemology of *cogito*. For an alternative thesis, see Jajdelska 2007, who contends that the narrator comes into life together with the practice of silent reading in English literature of the late seventeenth and early eighteenth centuries (11).

[15] Spearing 2012: 16. Plotke 2017 is another thought-provoking study that contemplates how the medieval sense of voice and authorship was shaped by the design of manuscripts. For bibliography on the narrator in medieval literature, see Plotke 2017: 1 n. 12; Kragl 2019.

2 Authors and Characters in Ancient Literature and Criticism

It has been duly acknowledged in scholarship that ancient readers are inclined to see the author behind the narratorial 'I'. In this section, I will argue that this inclination is part of a general willingness to hear the author's voice in utterances of characters. The understanding of first-person narrative is a special case of how character speech was conceptualized in general.

The tendency of ancient readers to ascribe utterances of characters to authors is particularly blatant in drama where only characters and the chorus speak.[16] A spectacular case are the references to a memorable verse in Euripides' *Hippolytus*: 'My tongue has sworn an oath, but my mind is free of it' (ἡ γλῶσσ' ὀμώμοχ', ἡ δὲ φρὴν ἀνώμοτος, 612). Whilst without greater significance in the play – Hippolytus does not break the promise of secrecy – the line was widely quoted in antiquity.[17] In *Thesmophoriazusae*, Aristophanes has the in-law reference it when he reminds Euripides of his promise to help him, should something go wrong on his expedition to the women: 'So now remember this, that your mind swore, but your tongue didn't swear, and I didn't swear.' (μέμνησο τοίνυν ταῦθ', ὅτι ἡ φρὴν ὤμοσεν,/ ἡ γλῶττα δ' οὐκ ὀμώμοκ', οὐδ' ὤρκωσ' ἐγώ, 275–6). The joke, it seems, is premised on the idea that Hippolytus' statement reflects Euripides' readiness to embark on perjury. Aristophanes has the in-law wittily invert the statement that reveals Euripides' as well as Hippolytus' questionable attitude to oaths in order to oblige him in his current predicament.

Now one could say that we should not press this passage too much, as Aristophanes follows his own agenda and may blur the boundaries between character and author for comic purposes. Aristotle's *Rhetoric*, however, supplies us with a parallel quotation of Hippolytus' statement in a far more serious context, namely the dealings of a law court (*rhet.* 1416a28–31). In an antidosis trial, a man named Hygiaenus accused Euripides of impiety and quoted Hippolytus' very statement as evidence that Euripides was an endorser of perjury. Euripides' answer, as recorded by Aristotle, is somewhat enigmatic: 'He said he was wrong to bring trials into the law courts that belonged in the Dionysiac contest; for he had given or would give an account of the words there if anyone wanted to bring a complaint.' (ἔφη γὰρ αὐτὸν ἀδικεῖν τὰς ἐκ τοῦ Διονυσιακοῦ ἀγῶνος κρίσεις εἰς τὰ

---

[16] Compare Nünlist 2009: 131–2.

[17] For example, Ar. *Ran.* 101–2; 1471; *com. fr.* 832; Plat. *Theaet.* 154d; *Symp.* 199a and further references in Austin and Olson on Ar. *Thesm.* 275–6.

δικαστήρια ἄγοντα· ἐκεῖ γὰρ αὐτῶν δεδωκέναι λόγον, ἢ δώσειν εἰ βούλεται κατηγορεῖν). Euripides objects to using evidence from a play in the court, but interestingly he does not point out, as we would, that the line was uttered by a character in a play: 'It is ironic and most unfair that this line spoken by a character proven, in all of tragedy, most loyal to oaths in the most trying and tragic circumstances, should have laid Euripides open to ancient and modern charges of impiety, promoting perjury, and hostility.'[18] Even if we doubt the historicity of the anecdote, it reveals the general plausibility of blaming an author for statements voiced by his characters.

The reception of Hippolytus' comment on perjury is emblematic of a general inclination of ancient readers to find the author's view in statements made by his characters. Scholia not rarely assign gnomic utterances of the chorus directly to the author. When for example in *Hippolytus* the chorus remarks that the divine helps them to temper their anxiety, a scholion notes: 'The poet transfers the role to himself, leaving behind the role of the chorus' (μεταφέρει δὲ τὸ πρόσωπον ἐφ' ἑαυτοῦ ὁ ποιητής, καταλιπὼν τὰ χορικὰ πρόσωπα, scholion on Eur. *Hipp.* 1102). The position of the chorus, which has a specific identity in the play, but which also taps into the tradition of independent choral song,[19] lends itself to such readings, but they can also be found in comments on character speech. In *Andromache*, for instance, the eponymous heroine curses the Spartans as the worst enemies of all humans. The scholion claims: 'Euripides is saying this in the disguise of Andromache, scolding the Spartans on account of the current war' (ταῦτα ἐπὶ τῷ Ἀνδρομάχης προσχήματί φησιν Εὐριπίδης λοιδορούμενος τοῖς Σπαρτιάταις διὰ τὸν ἐνεστῶτα πόλεμον, scholion on Eur. *Andr.* 445). Again, this comment is not predicated on an arbitrary conflation of a character with the author; it is the resonance of the verses within the historical context of the Peloponnesian War that prompts the scholiast to detect the author's voice in the utterance of a character. And yet, if we leave the proponents of the infamous *interprétation historique* aside, modern interpreters would be hesitant to advance such an interpretation.

In the cases mentioned, it is the content of an utterance that prompted the ancient critic to ascribe it to the author. In other cases, however, ancient readers refer to authors as voicing the comments of their characters without such a reason. In the *Life of Pericles*, for instance, Plutarch writes: 'And Eupolis, in his *Demes*, having made inquiries about each one of the

---

[18] Mikalson 1991: 86. Compare Avery 1968: 19–24; Dillon 1995: 141–4.
[19] Compare Calame 1999; Gagné and Hopman 2013.

demagogues as they come up from Hades, says, when Pericles is called out last: "The very head of those below have you now brought".' (ὁ δ' Εὔπολις ἐν τοῖς Δήμοις πυνθανόμενος περὶ ἑκάστου τῶν ἀναβεβηκότων ἐξ Ἅιδου δημαγωγῶν, ὡς ὁ Περικλῆς ὠνομάσθη τελευταῖος· ὅ τί περ κεφάλαιον τῶν κάτωθεν ἤγαγες, *Per.* 3.7 = Eupolis fr. 155 KA). The verse was of course spoken by a character; its content does not offer a reason for why Plutarch should ascribe it to Eupolis. It is not a gnome and does not link up to a position the author may have held. For our understanding, it is odd that Pericles has Eupolis 'make inquiries' that were in fact made by a character.

Even more striking is a reference in Athenaeus (12.551 = Hermippus fr. 36 KA). Noting that it is better to be poor and thin 'than to be much too rich and resemble the sea monster in Tanagra' (ὑπερπλουτοῦντας τῷ Ταναγραίῳ κήτει ἐοικέναι), he adds a quotation from a comedy by Hermippus: 'Hermippus says the following, addressing the speech to Dionysus: "Because now, since they're poor,/ they sacrifice little crippled cows to you/ who are thinner than Leotrophides and Thumantis"' (φησὶ δ' οὕτως ὁ Ἕρμιππος πρὸς τὸν Διόνυσον τὸν λόγον ποιούμενος· οἱ γὰρ πενόμενοι/ ἀνάπηρά σοι θύουσιν ἤδη βούδια,/ Λεωτροφίδου λεπτότερα καὶ Θουμάντιδος). Again, there seems to be no reason why the verses should reveal the author's viewpoint. What is more, Athenaeus not only attributes the words of a character to the author, he also mentions the character to whom the words were addressed. This reference to the charac-ter addressed highlights the conflation of author and character.

A parallel for this conflation can be found in Pollux's *Onomasticon* (9.102). Pollux discusses a game called εἰς ὤμιλλαν, in which the partici-pants throw dice into a ring so that they stay within it, and compares it with another game, in which a quail is placed in a ring and tapped on the head; when it leaves the circle, its owner loses. A quotation of three verses from Eupolis' *Taxiarchoi* closes the discussion: 'When in *Taxiarchoi* Phormion says: "Will you draw a circle around so we can take breakfast in it?", Eupolis responds: "What is this? Will we eat 'in the circle'?/ Or will we beat the cake just as a quail?"' (ἐν γοῦν Ταξιάρχοις Εὔπολις τοῦ Φορμίωνος εἰπόντος οὐκοῦν περιγράψεις ὅσον ἐναριστᾶν κύκλον; ἀποκρίνεται, τί δ' ἔστιν; εἰς ὤμιλλαν ἀριστήσομεν;/ ἢ κόψομεν τὴν μᾶζαν ὥσπερ ὄρτυγα; fr. 269 KA). It has been shown that Phormion converses with Dionysus, but Pollux ascribes the rejoinder made by Dionysus to the author, who thus directly interacts with one of his characters.

The ascription of one part to a character and the other to the author also indicates that the conflation of author and character stems not necessarily from the source from which such writers as Athenaeus and Pollux are quoting. They may not have been reading full scripts of the plays but rather quoting from excerpts and anthologies. The references to characters, however, indicate that they knew the names of the speakers. At least in these cases, it is not the absence of the speakers from anthologies that was the reason for the assignment of the verses to the author (it is also unlikely that the quotations by Plutarch and Athenaeus quoted above stem from anthologies). The examples, which could be easily multiplied, thus force upon us the following question: did ancient readers fail to distinguish between authorial and character speech? Were they insensitive to something that we consider a basic tenet of literary interpretation?

There is, on the other hand, strong evidence that ancient readers had a clear sense of the difference between authors and characters. One of the interpretative principles on which the scholiasts relied when facing contradictions within a text is 'the solution from the character' (λύσις ἐκ τοῦ προσώπου).[20] The Neoplatonic scholar Porphyry aptly explains the principle (on *Il.* 6.265, vol. 1, p. 100.4–9):

οὐδὲν δὲ θαυμαστὸν εἰ παρὰ τῷ ποιητῇ ἐναντία λέγεται ὑπὸ διαφόρων φωνῶν. ὅσα μὲν γὰρ ἔφη αὐτὸς ἀφ' ἑαυτοῦ ἐξ ἰδίου προσώπου, ταῦτα δεῖ ἀκόλουθα εἶναι καὶ μὴ ἐναντία ἀλλήλοις· ὅσα δὲ προσώποις περιτίθησιν, οὐκ αὐτοῦ εἰσιν ἀλλὰ τῶν λεγόντων νοεῖται.

No wonder when in Homer different things are said by different voices. Whatever is said by the poet in propria persona should be consistent and not contradictory. All the views he attributes to the characters are not his, but are understood as being said by the speakers.

Porphyry wrote in the 3rd century CE, but other scholia reveal that Aristarchus already noticed that Homer used different words and referred to things differently from his characters. Aristarchus was chiefly concerned with the gap between Homer's world and the world of his characters in order to avoid anachronisms:[21] whereas Homer says 'Corinth', his heroes speak of 'Ephyra' (on *Il.* 2.570a), since the city was not yet called 'Corinth' in ancient times. At the same time, such comments also bespeak an awareness of the difference between authorial and character speech. Most importantly, Plato and Aristotle gave much weight to the distinction between representation through simple diegesis and representation through mimesis in discussions that I will scrutinize in the subsequent section.

There can thus be no doubt as to the ability of ancient readers to draw a line between author and characters. This said, the passages quoted above

---

[20] Compare Dachs 1913; Nünlist 2009: 116–19.   [21] Nünlist 2009: 117–19.

demonstrate that ancient readers not only identified the poetic 'I' with the author but were also inclined to ascribe character speech to the author. The tension with which we are thus confronted is encapsulated in a treatise already referred to in Chapter 2, *de audiendis poetis* – Plutarch's attempt to show in what ways young readers may benefit from reading poems. Writing in the Platonic tradition, Plutarch sets out strategies that can save poetry from Plato's harsh verdict in the *Republic*. For example, young readers need to be instructed that, instead of taking questionable actions as models, they should appreciate the quality of their representation. Likewise, utterances of malign characters such as Thersites do not reflect the opinion of the poet (17f–18f). Here, character speech and authorial narrative are carefully kept apart.

When, however, Plutarch suggests another strategy, namely to disarm and to correct questionable utterances with other utterances from the same or other texts (20d–22a), he unhesitatingly ascribes quotations from tragic characters to the authors. He writes for example: 'Again, when Euripides speaks at this rate "The Gods deceive us through many kinds of tricks, although they are stronger", we may do well to quote him elsewhere "If Gods do wrong, surely no Gods there are". This has been said better by him' (πάλιν Εὐριπίδου λέγοντος "πολλαῖσι μορφαῖς οἱ θεοὶ σοφισμάτων/ σφάλλουσιν ἡμᾶς κρείττονες πεφυκότες" οὐ χεῖρόν ἐστιν ὑπενεγκεῖν τὸ "εἰ θεοί τι δρῶσι φαῦλον, οὔκ εἰσιν θεοί", βέλτιον εἰρημένον ὑπ' αὐτοῦ, 20f–21a). On the one hand, Plutarch sharply distinguishes between author and characters; on the other, he unflinchingly assigns character speech to the author. It may be a convenient brachylogy to say 'Homer says X' instead of 'Homer has A say X'. And yet, as Nünlist points out, 'the frequency of comments such as "Homer says X" gives rise to the suspicion that some critics did not always pay sufficient attention to a distinction that is, after all, crucial'.[22]

3   Authorial Impersonation

Is it, however, true that ancient critics were negligent and 'did not always pay sufficient attention' when they ascribed utterances of characters to their authors? I think the case is more intricate. When ancient readers identify the poetic 'I' with the author or when they hear the author in utterances of characters, they are not simply conflating distinct narrative levels, but following a different logic of viewing the relationship between

---

[22] Nünlist 2009: 133.

an author and their characters. Before tracing this logic, I will adduce another aspect of ancient narrative that in some cases facilitated references to the author where character speech was involved, namely the moral expectations of ancient readers.

One of the points that has emerged from the investigation in Chapter 2 is an emphasis on the moral dimension of literature in antiquity. There were also critics who stressed the entertaining function of poetry or concentrated on its euphonic quality, and yet, on the whole, there was a broad expectation that poets and other authors instructed their audiences, notably on morality. This concentration on the moral dimension of literature, I suggest, may have had an impact on how speeches of characters were read. The content of a moral message does not depend on whether it is put forward by the author or a character. Since it is the author from whom the reader expects instruction, it is unsurprising that ethical insights, even if characters voice them, are ascribed to the author.

Plutarch, for example, addresses Sophocles directly and states that 'we have also heard from you that "lies do not yield fruit"' (καὶ μὴν σοῦ γ᾽ ἀκηκόαμεν ὡς οὐκ ἐξάγουσι καρπὸν οἱ ψευδεῖς λόγοι, *de audiendis poetis* 21a), and because the play from which this gnome stems has been lost and Plutarch does not mention it, we do not know the speaker of the verse. In light of the gnomic character of the verse, it appears possible that Plutarch here quoted from an anthology and did not know the speaker himself. That said, in the examples adduced above, the critic knew the speakers and nonetheless ascribed the quote to the author. What is crucial is that for a reading that is primarily invested in moral insights the speaker does not matter. The moral focus of ancient literature made it easy to ignore the difference between author and characters and to envisage the former as the source of what the latter say.

This explanation, however, pertains only to moral references and does not grasp the essential point, namely, a different way of envisaging character speech, which is part of a distinct model of narrative. For us, character speech is located at the level of the story-world, which is strictly separated from the world in which the author communicates with their readers. The idea of the fabula reinforces this separation of levels, as it suggests that the story exists independently of the narration. According to this understanding, the narrator, when they present direct speech, does not mediate but reproduces verbatim what the characters have said in the story-world. In the words of Genette, 'a perfect imitation is not an imitation, it is the thing itself'.[23]

---

[23] Genette 1966: 156.

If we look at how ancient critics talk about narrative, we encounter a very different model. Not only is there no narrator in addition to the author, but the author does not seem to be strictly separated from the narrated world and its characters. A central passage of ancient literary criticism, praised as a proto-narratology by modern scholars, is instructive. When in Plato's *Republic* Socrates discusses with Adeimantus whether or not the ideal city should admit poets, he first tackles the content and then the form of poetry. He distinguishes three different modes of presentation (392c6–398b8). Diegesis, signifying narrative in a broad sense, is divided into: (1) *haplē diēgēsis*, plain diegesis – narrative in the poet's voice, to be found in dithyramb; (2) *mimēsis* – direct speech of characters, as in drama; (3) *diēgēsis di' amphoterōn* – compound narrative such as Homeric epic, which combines both modes.

Many aspects of this passage have been discussed. Genette, for one, has closely analysed Socrates' illustrative example, a recasting of a passage with much direct speech in the *Iliad*, as plain diegesis.[24] Classicists such as Halliwell have sounded a note of caution, alerting theoreticians to the fact that 'this Platonic text is driven by normative, not purely descriptive, concerns'.[25] Socrates' typology of diegesis is ultimately a means of determining what kind of poetry is suited to edify the guardians of the ideal city. One aspect that has not received much attention from narratologists as well as scholars of Plato is the peculiar logic of mimesis. In order to characterize plain diegesis, Socrates observes that the poet 'does not try to turn our attention elsewhere as if someone else is speaking rather than he himself' (οὐδὲ ἐπιχειρεῖ ἡμῶν τὴν διάνοιαν ἄλλοσε τρέπειν ὡς ἄλλος τις ὁ λέγων ἢ αὐτός, 393a6–7). As to the speeches of characters, he says: 'What follows upon this, he [i.e. the poet] speaks as if he were himself Chryses and tries to sway us as far as possible so that the speaking subject seems to be not Homer but the priest, being old' (τὰ δὲ μετὰ ταῦτα ὥσπερ αὐτὸς ὢν ὁ Χρύσης λέγει καὶ πειρᾶται ἡμᾶς ὅτι μάλιστα ποιῆσαι μὴ Ὅμηρον δοκεῖν εἶναι τὸν λέγοντα ἀλλὰ τὸν ἱερέα, πρεσβύτην ὄντα, 393a7–b2). When characters say something, it is, on Socrates' and presumably Plato's view,[26] still the poet who is speaking and pretending to be the character. The best translation for *mimēsis* in this context is therefore 'impersonation'.[27]

---

[24] Genette 1972: 186–91.   [25] Halliwell 2014.
[26] I am aware of reproducing the ancient identification of the author's view with that of the character – however, this does not mean that Socrates always gives us direct access to Plato's position. For ancient readers identifying Plato's position with that of Socrates, see, for example, Aristot. *eth. Nic.* 1172b28 on Philebus and Quintilian, *Inst.* 2.15.26 on Gorgias.
[27] Compare Else 1972: 23; de Jong 1987: 3.

The difference from narratological concepts of direct speech is easy to ignore but crucial: whereas narratologists picture the narrator as reproducing the words that the character has uttered in the story-world, Socrates assumes that the author slides into the role of the character and speaks 'as if he were' the character. This is more than a clumsy expression for speaking in the voice of the character; it signifies a deep entanglement of the speaker with the character, which comes to the fore in the serious effects it can have on the speaker. Impersonation shapes the character and even the nature of the speaker (395d1–3). This power is one of the reasons why Plato is so concerned with mimesis: impersonating a flawed character corrupts the character of the speaker and, by extension, of the listeners, who engage in the same process as the speaker. What may appear to us as merely an odd and pre-technical way of talking about direct speech encapsulates an understanding of the author's position in relation to his characters that deviates significantly from the narratological view. Instead of rendering words spoken in the distinct world of the story, the narrator himself metamorphoses into the character.

The difference comes to the fore in Genette's interpretation of the passage. Genette claims that in Socrates' transformation of the Iliadic passage 'the scene in direct dialogue then becomes a narrative mediated by a narrator ... In the terms provisionally adopted, "pure narrative" will be considered more distant than "the imitation": it says less of it and in a form that is more strongly mediated.'[28] However, as Irene de Jong astutely observes, 'Plato would never think of *diēgēsis haplē* as "mediated": on the contrary, in the *diēgēsis haplē* the poet speaks as himself, in propria persona and if there is "mediation" at all, it is in the mimesis, where the poet impersonates a character.'[29] This discrepancy highlights where the ancient idea of the author and his or her relation to the characters differs from the narratological conception. Genette and his followers see distinct levels and a narrator who either speaks from his own superior level or reproduces what characters said in their own world. As a straight reproduction of words from the story-world, character speech is unmediated; in fact, it is not even an imitation. Differently from this, Socrates and with him Plato conceive of an author who can not only speak as himself but can also modulate his voice to fit that of a character. Character speech is thus just another mode of presentation that the author can adopt; like authorial speech and the

---

[28] Genette 1972: 184: 'La scène dialoguée directe devient alors un récit médiatisé par le narrateur ... Dans ces termes provisoirement adoptés, le "récit pur" sera tenu pour plus distant que "l'imitation": il en dit moins, et de façon plus médiate.'
[29] De Jong 1987: 4.

mixed mode, it is called diegesis by Plato. Instead of inhabiting an onto-logical level that is separate both from that of the narrator and from that of the characters, the author is viewed as the narrator who creates the story through plain narration and/or impersonation (Figure 3.1).

Plato's distinction of three modes of representation seems to have served as the model of mimetic modes that Aristotle outlines in *Poetics*, chapter 3. This is not the place to discuss Aristotle's terminological deviation from Plato's or the knotty problem of whether Aristotle introduces, like Plato, a tripartite or a bipartite system, which juxtaposes a dramatic with a diegetic mode and subdivides the latter into a pure form and one that also contains dramatic elements.[30] Crucial for my argument is the way in which Aristotle speaks of the dramatic mode: he says that here the poet 'is becoming another' (ἕτερόν τι γιγνόμενον, *poet.* 1448a21–2).[31] Aristotle's approach to mimesis differs starkly from Plato's; for him, poetic represen-tation is an anthropological need whose articulations he wishes to dissect, not something that needs to be censured. And yet, the phrasing shows that Aristotle shares Plato's understanding of the relationship between author and text. Instead of separating the author ontologically from the characters, he assumes that in character speech the author has turned into the character.

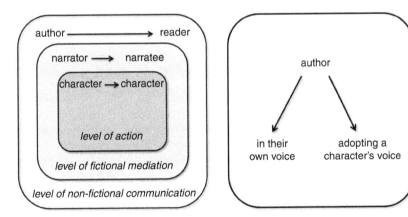

Figure 3.1 The modern and ancient models of narrative

---

[30] For bibliography, see Lattmann 2005: 30–1.
[31] On the curious neuter of ἕτερόν τι, see Lucas 1968 on 1448a21.

Together, Plato's and Aristotle's models of narrative modes have exerted a massive influence on literary criticism in antiquity and beyond. Terminology varies wildly, but the distinction of narrative in the voice of the author, narrative through the voices of characters and a mixed mode pervades ancient commentaries on various authors ranging from Homer to the tragedians, from Hesiod to Theocritus and even on Plato himself.[32] The idea that the author morphs into the characters reverberates, for example, in comments on shifts from authorial speech to character speech without a proper speech introduction in Homer. Commenting on *Il.* 15.346–9, Pseudo-Longinus notes: 'Sometimes a writer, while speaking about a person, suddenly turns and changes into the person himself, a sort of outbreak of emotion' (Ἔτι γε μὴν ἔσθ' ὅτε περὶ προσώπου διηγούμενος ὁ συγγραφεὺς ἐξαίφνης παρενεχθεὶς εἰς τὸ αὐτὸ πρόσωπον ἀντιμεθίσταται, καὶ ἔστι τὸ τοιοῦτον εἶδος ἐκβολή τις πάθους, 27.1).[33] Pseudo-Plutarch singles out the same verses: 'For he switches from the diegematic mode to the mimetic mode' (ἀπὸ γὰρ τοῦ διηγηματικοῦ μετέβαλεν εἰς τὸ μιμητικόν, *On Homer* 57.2). Both authors are interested in the strong emotional effect of the device. For our purposes, the phrasing is crucial, as it reveals the same understanding of direct speech that we have found in Plato and Aristotle.

That this understanding was widespread is evident from the Homeric scholia and their recurring phrase: 'He [i.e. the poet] goes from the diegematic mode to the mimetic mode of representation' (ἀπὸ τοῦ διηγηματικοῦ δὲ ἐπὶ τὸ μιμητικὸν μέτεισιν).[34] In other passages, the ancient commentators write that the poet 'turns over' (ἀποστρέφει) from the diegematic mode to the mimetic mode.[35] In an intriguing comment, the late antique rhetor Choricius compares Homer with a pantomime – after elaborating on all the roles a pantomime can adopt, he adds (21.2):

οὕτω καὶ Ὅμηρος ὀρχεῖται τοῖς ἔπεσιν. ἢ οὐχ ὁρᾶτε τὸν ποιητὴν ὅ τι ἂν ἐθέλῃ τοῦτο εἶναι δοκοῦντα; ἐμοὶ μέν, εὖ ἴστε, παρασύρει τὴν φαντασίαν, καὶ εἴ που νεανίσκον ἐξ Αἰτωλίας ἢ γέροντα Πύλιον ὑποκρίνοιτο ἤ τινα ὅλως τῶν Ἀχαιῶν καὶ οἷς ἐπολέμουν οἱ Ἕλληνες, αὐτὸν ὁρᾶν μοι δοκῶ, ὃν ἂν ἐκεῖνος ὑποκρινόμενος τύχοι.

[32] For the categorization of Platonic dialogues, see Diog. Laert. 3.50; Plut. *Quaest. Conv.* 7.8.1 (711B–C); Procl. *In Rep.* 1.14–15.
[33] The following quote is: "Ἕκτωρ δὲ Τρώεσσιν ἐκέκλετο μακρὸν ἀΰσας/ νηυσὶν ἐπισσεύεσθαι, ἐᾶν δ' ἔναρα βροτόεντα./ ὃν δ' ἂν ἐγὼν ἀπάνευθε νεῶν ἐθέλοντα νοήσω,/ αὐτοῦ οἱ θάνατον μητίσομαι."
[34] Compare scholion on *Il.* 1.17b bT; 4.303b bT; 6.45–6 bT; 23.855b bT.
[35] Compare scholion on *Il.* 16.203 a, and also on 4.127 T.

> In this way Homer dances with his verses. Or do you not see that the poet seems to be whatever he wishes? For you have to know he carries away my phantasy, and when he speaks the part of a young man from Aitolia or that of the Pylian old man or that of the men with whom the Greeks fought, I seem to see the one whose part he happens to speak.

Author and character are not imagined as residing at different ontological levels, with the level of the narrator couched in between, but the author rather appears as speaking either in his own voice or in that of the characters.

It is this view of the author, I contend, that inclined ancient critics to ascribe to authors utterances that were spoken by their characters. As the salience of the distinction between mimetic, diegetic and mixed representation in ancient commentaries illustrates, ancient critics followed Plato and Aristotle in the assumption that in direct speech authors impersonate their characters. Instead of ontologically separating the author from the characters in the way that modern scholars do, ancient critics saw the author as metamorphosing into his or her characters. If the author is not envisaged as reproducing what characters said in their own world, but as producing their speeches through a modulation of his or her voice, it is easy to ascribe to the author their utterances, not only in cases where the content suggests such an identification, but also without such pointers.

Note that the ancient view does not erase the distinction between authorial and character speech – this distinction is well documented in ancient criticism. Yet the ancient model aligns the author closely with his or her characters, much more closely than the modern model. Just as Plato is concerned about the impact that reciting, or even listening to, the speeches of depraved characters has, the morally flawed utterance of a character can be held against the author, as in the antidosis trial against Euripides reported in the *Rhetoric*. Even if the author transforms his or her voice into that of the characters, it is still the author who is deemed to be speaking.

Augustine's comment on Apuleius, with which I began my discussion, ought to be envisaged against this backdrop. His reference to Apuleius as the 'I' of *The Golden Ass* not only bespeaks the specifically ancient understanding of first-person narrative but is also indebted to the view of the author cemented by Plato and Aristotle. It is the idea that the author is speaking, albeit in a modulated way, when characters of the story speak or narrate that lets Augustine claim that Apuleius is reporting, or rather feigning to report, his experience as an ass. Apuleius himself gestures playfully to his presence in Lucius' narrative when he has Lucius call himself 'a man from Madaurus' – Apuleius' hometown

(11.27.9).[36] What is disturbing to our distinction between different narratological levels emerges naturally from an understanding of character speech and narration as impersonation.

4   Oral Performance and Literary Composition

It is now time to ask why the ancient take on the author is so different from the narratological model. An important background for the ancient understanding of narrative is, I surmise, the salience of oral performance in antiquity.[37] Not only were plays – tragedy, comedy and satire play – written to be put on stage in Classical Greece, but until the fifth, and even into the fourth centuries BCE, poetry in general was received mostly in oral recitals. While bards recited the Homeric epics at such festivals as the Panathenaea, symposiasts entertained themselves by quoting verses from Archilochus, Simonides and Sappho. The performance culture of Archaic and Classical Greece forms the backdrop against which Plato advanced his critical views, which remained influential throughout antiquity.

Even after the emergence of a literary culture and its refinement in the Hellenistic period, public performances remained prominent.[38] The culture of rhetorical *epideixis*, for example, flourished especially in the Imperial era; the declamations of such orators as Dio and Philostratus attracted large crowds. Much of Latin literature was produced for the individual reader, but prose as well as poetry was read in small circles in the Roman Republic and then also in public in the Imperial age.[39] Pliny reports in one of his letters that in April there was barely a day without a recitation (1.13.1). Importantly, even the individual perusal of literature seems to have been at least partly different from ours: besides the practice of individual reading, the use of slaves to read out texts is attested.[40] And while ancient readers were able to read in silence, the reading aloud of literary texts seems to have been widespread.[41]

There is evidence that ancient readers were trained specifically to modulate their voices to render character speech. When Quintilian comments on exercises in reading aloud as part of the *grammaticus'* elementary

---

[36] See Tilg 2014: 107–31 for an interpretation of the *Metamorphoses'* epilogue that emphasizes further elements that refer to Apuleius' presence behind Lucius.

[37] Whitmarsh 2013: 240 adduces the 'world of performance' 'to offer some psychological contextualization' for the idea that fictional autobiography involves the idea of impersonation.

[38] On ancient literacy in general, see Harris 1989; Johnson and Parker 2009.

[39] Compare Binder 1995: 265–332; Valette-Cagnac 1997; Johnson 2010: 42–56.

[40] Compare Starr 1991; Horsfall 1995.

[41] For a survey of the debate on reading silently and aloud, see Johnson 2010: 4–9.

education, he notes that poetry should not be read like prose but sung just as poets sing their work; nonetheless, he takes issue with 'the effeminate modulations now in vogue' (*plasmate, ut nunc a plerisque fit, effeminata*, 1.8.2). Quintilian objects to the teachers who 'wish character as revealed by speeches to be indicated as it is by the comic actor' (*nec prosopopoeias, ut quibusdam placet, ad comicum morem pronuntiari velim*, 1.8.3), and yet even he thinks 'that there should be some modulation of the voice to distinguish such passages from those where the poet is speaking in person' (*esse tamen flexum quendam quo distinguantur ab iis in quibus poeta persona sua utetur*, 1.8.3). Diskin Clay observes the parallel to public performances: 'By a psychology well known to Plato, the reader of the book impersonated the poet as he became for a moment the "I" of the poem he was reciting or, in the case of a dramatic poet, he took the parts of his characters.'[42]

When somebody recites or reads out a text, they either slip into the role of the author or into the role of a character.[43] They may speak as Homer or as Achilles, as Vergil or as Aeneas, as Tacitus or as Tiberius. In a culture which predominantly listens to texts, it is thus more natural to see two different modes of presentation than to distinguish between different ontological planes on which author and characters operate. While the modern reader of a novel encounters direct speech as something that is embedded in the narrator's account and gives direct access to the narrated world, an ancient audience or individual listening to a slave attends to a voice which has been modulated either into that of the author or that of a character. As Augustine's comment on Apuleius demonstrates, this understanding of narrative, which has its root in an oral culture, persisted even in a highly literate culture. *The Golden Ass* is a text to be read – nonetheless, when Augustine hears Apuleius' voice in Lucius' narration, the idea of an author impersonating the narrator and main character is still preeminent.

It seems that oral performances were also a factor weighing in on medieval concepts of narration, which, as mentioned above (p. 55-6), did not envision a separate instance of the narrator. The 'I' of many romances, saints' legends and other texts, far from being an independent narrator with a clear psychological profile, offered a position to be taken up by the speaker, and even texts that were no longer written to be performed continued this use of the 'I' as a quasi-oral feature.[44] The medieval understanding of narrative voice was

---

[42] Clay 1998: 32.

[43] In this context, Jajdelska's (2007) thesis that the narrator as a fictive persona emerges together with the practice of silent reading in the late seventeenth and early eighteenth centuries CE in England is thought-provoking.

[44] See Schaefer 2004; Glauch 2009; 2010.

also shaped by other factors, some of them generating notable differences from that of antiquity. While, for example, parchment strips (*sillyboi/ tituli*) contained the names of author and work of ancient scrolls, there were no comparable paratexts in medieval manuscripts. The names of authors could be mentioned in prologues and epilogues, but these parts were not always copied. As Plotke argues, this practice reflects a very weak notion of authorship, markedly different from antiquity, which put a premium on authors.[45] This said, in both the Middle Ages and antiquity, the tradition of oral performances and the continuation of oral features even through later stages of literacy had a considerable influence on views of narrative that deviate from the narratological model.

Another point that aligns ancient and medieval authors and readers and may have an impact on how narrative is viewed is the meagre presence of the idea of fictionality. Walsh's studies suggest that the prominence of the narrator as a distinct and inherent instance of narrative in modern theory is linked to the idea of fiction: 'Indeed, the narrator's promotion from representational accidence to structural essence has occurred specifically to the qualities of fiction, not narrative per se.'[46] The instance of the narrator establishes 'a representational frame within which the narrative discourse may be read as report rather than invention'. If Walsh is correct, the modern focus on the referential status has fostered the identification of an independent narratorial instance that allows critics to consider the narrated action and world without regarding them as invented. In cultures that paid less attention to fictionality, on the other hand, there was less pressure to forge the notion of an independent narrator.

In antiquity, the idea of impersonation, so crucial for the understanding of character speech, is also prominent in rhetoric. In forensic oratory, the rhetor played roles when he put himself into the position of protagonists and adopted their voices in order to reinforce the appeal of his presentation. *Ethopoiia*, sometimes also called *prosopopoiia*, was an essential exercise in elementary education: the pupils embodied mythological or historical characters and voiced their views and positions. This type of play was also used by professional rhetoricians to display their skills – in *meletai*, they gave speeches embedded in past or fictive situations, often sliding into different roles. Given the central role of rhetoric in ancient education and society, it is a compelling suggestion that rhetoric helped cement the notion of impersonation as a key model for understanding the representation of speech in other contexts as well.

---

[45] Plotke 2017: 63–84.   [46] Walsh 1997: 496.

The conception of character speech as a modulation of the author's voice is also embedded in a larger view of the process of literary composition. Chapter 15 of *de sublimitate* commences with a definition of *phantasia* as 'every idea of the mind, in whatever form it presents itself, which gives birth to speech. But at the present day the word is predominantly used in cases where, carried away by enthusiasm and passion, you think you see what you describe, and you place it before the eyes of your hearers' (πᾶν τὸ ὁπωσοῦν ἐννόημα γεννητικὸν λόγου παριστάμενον· ἤδη δ᾽ ἐπὶ τούτων κεκράτηκε τοὔνομα ὅταν ἃ λέγεις ὑπ᾽ ἐνθουσιασμοῦ καὶ πάθους βλέπειν δοκῇς καὶ ὑπ᾽ ὄψιν τιθῇς τοῖς ἀκούουσιν, 1). The first two examples adduced demonstrate the extreme images a poet can evoke: Orestes' words illustrating his frenzy in Euripides' *Orestes* and *Iphigenia in Tauris* and the description of Phaethon's celestial ride in Euripides' *Medea*. Pseudo-Longinus' discussion in chapter 15 foregrounds the effects on the audience and raises many questions, for example about the juxtaposition of poetic *ekplêxis* with rhetorical *enargeia*.[47] Crucial for my argument here, however, is the underlying idea of *phantasia*: that in order to place the narrated scene and action before an audience's eyes, a poet has to transport themselves to the scene in their imagination and to enact whatever the characters are doing. In the preceding chapter, I made a case that the experiential quality of narrative was a central concern of ancient criticism – now we see that in Pseudo-Longinus the immersion of the recipients is prefigured by the immersion of the author.

The meaning that Pseudo-Longinus ascribes to *phantasia* is a recent development.[48] In Plato and Aristotle, *phantasia* still signifies chiefly the appearance of things as perceived by the senses. While the meaning that Pseudo-Longinus adduces as traditional bears Stoic hallmarks, the rhetorical and poetological use is explicitly introduced as being of recent date.[49] That being said, *phantasia* understood as imagination and the object imagined and vividly presented crystallizes ideas that can be traced back to at least the Classical age.[50] We have already encountered Socrates' question as to what state Ion is in when he performs the epics – it is worth quoting in full here (*Ion* 535b–c):

ὅταν εὖ εἴπῃς ἔπη καὶ ἐκπλήξῃς μάλιστα τοὺς θεωμένους, ἢ τὸν Ὀδυσσέα ὅταν ἐπὶ τὸν οὐδὸν ἐφαλλόμενον ᾄδῃς, ἐκφανῆ γιγνόμενον τοῖς μνηστῆρσι καὶ ἐκχέοντα τοὺς ὀιστοὺς πρὸ τῶν ποδῶν, ἢ Ἀχιλλέα ἐπὶ τὸν Ἕκτορα

---

[47] See Halliwell 2011: 347–50; 2021: 299.
[48] Besides Manieri 1998: 27-94, see also Sheppard 2014 and Otto 2009: 91–101.
[49] See, however, Otto 2009: 94 for the observation that the view of *phantasia* as a faculty of the mind is indebted to Aristotelian ideas.
[50] Compare Sheppard 2014: 2–10. See however n. 51 for where I part company with Sheppard.

ὁρμῶντα, ἢ καὶ τῶν περὶ Ἀνδρομάχην ἐλεινῶν τι ἢ περὶ Ἑκάβην ἢ περὶ
Πρίαμον, τότε πότερον ἔμφρων εἶ ἢ ἔξω σαυτοῦ γίγνῃ καὶ παρὰ τοῖς
πράγμασιν οἴεταί σου εἶναι ἡ ψυχὴ οἷς λέγεις ἐνθουσιάζουσα, ἢ ἐν Ἰθάκῃ
οὖσιν ἢ ἐν Τροίᾳ ἢ ὅπως ἂν καὶ τὰ ἔπη ἔχῃ;

When you give a good recitation and specially thrill your audience, either
with the lay of Odysseus leaping forth on to the threshold, revealing himself
to the suitors and pouring out the arrows before his feet, or of Achilles
dashing at Hector, or some part of the sad story of Andromache or of
Hecuba, or of Priam, are you then in your senses, or are you carried out of
yourself, and does your soul in an ecstasy suppose itself to be among the
scenes you are describing, whether they be in Ithaca, or in Troy, or as the
poems may chance to place them?

Socrates' piercing questions make clear that Ion's self-understanding
needs to be faced with a healthy dose of reservation; it quickly emerges
that Ion also needs to stay in control somehow if he wants his performance to
succeed: 'If I make them weep, I shall be laughing myself as I take my money,
but if I make them laugh, I shall myself be weeping because I will lose
money' (ὡς ἐὰν μὲν κλάοντας αὐτοὺς καθίσω, αὐτὸς γελάσομαι ἀργύριον
λαμβάνων, ἐὰν δὲ γελῶντας, αὐτὸς κλαύσομαι ἀργύριον ἀπολλύς, 535e).
While Ion's description of his emotional involvement provides early evidence for the idea that a performer, who comes to embody the author, needs
to experience what he is describing in his imagination, the reflexive distance
to which he also lays claim is premised on a separation of the reciter from his
characters and their experiences. Viewed thus, the performer encapsulates in
one person the ambiguity that we have noted in the corpus of scholia: some
scholia separate authors and characters, while others conflate them.

When Aristotle in the *Poetics* discusses how dramatists should work out
their plots, he mentions the importance of visualization (17.1455a22–32):

Δεῖ δὲ τοὺς μύθους συνιστάναι καὶ τῇ λέξει συναπεργάζεσθαι ὅτι μάλιστα
πρὸ ὀμμάτων τιθέμενον· οὕτω γὰρ ἂν ἐναργέστατα ὁρῶν ὥσπερ παρ'
αὐτοῖς γιγνόμενος τοῖς πραττομένοις εὑρίσκοι τὸ πρέπον καὶ ἥκιστα ἂν
λανθάνοι τὰ ὑπεναντία ... ὅσα δὲ δυνατὸν καὶ τοῖς σχήμασιν
συναπεργαζόμενον· πιθανώτατοι γὰρ ἀπὸ τῆς αὐτῆς φύσεως οἱ ἐν τοῖς
πάθεσίν εἰσιν, καὶ χειμαίνει ὁ χειμαζόμενος καὶ χαλεπαίνει ὁ ὀργιζόμενος
ἀληθινώτατα.

A poet ought to imagine his material to the fullest possible extent while
composing his plot-structures and elaborating them in language. By seeing
them as vividly as possible in this way – as if present at the very occurrence of
the events – he is likely to discover what is appropriate, and least likely to
miss contradictions ... So far as possible, the poet should even include

gestures in the process of composition: for, assuming the same natural talent, the most convincing effect comes from those who actually put themselves in the emotions; and the truest impression of distress or anger is given by the person who experiences these feelings.

A comic parody of this idea of the authorial imagination indicates that it was widely disseminated in the Classical era. In *Thesmophoriazusae*, the in-law bumps into the poet Agathon, who has to explain why he is dressed as a woman: 'I change my clothing accordingly as I change my mentality. A man who is a poet must adopt habits that match the play he is committed to composing. For example, if one is writing plays about women, one's body must participate in their habits' (ἐγὼ δὲ τὴν ἐσθῆθ' ἅμα γνώμῃ φορῶ./ χρὴ γὰρ ποιητὴν ἄνδρα πρὸς τὰ δράματα/ ἃ δεῖ ποιεῖν, πρὸς ταῦτα τοὺς τρόπους ἔχειν./ αὐτίκα γυναικεῖ' ἢν ποιῇ τις δράματα,/ μετουσίαν δεῖ τῶν τρόπων τὸ σῶμ' ἔχειν, 148–52). Aristophanes has his rival not only imaginatively enact what he is writing, but, with due comic exaggeration, even adjust his own appearance to match that of his characters.

Phantasia may not have become the standard term for visualization in art and literature until the Imperial era, but, as Ion's reflections in Plato, Aristotle's comment on visualization and the cross-dressing of Agathon in *Thesmophoriazusae* prove, the idea that a poet needs to visualize and to go through the action was a familiar one.[51] The concept of character speech as an author's impersonation of a character thus seems to be a special case of the broader idea that an author has to transport himself to the scene of his narrative and to imagine doing what he is describing. Just as Euripides imaginatively has to embark on Helius' chariot in order to present a vivid account of Phaethon's ride, Homer has to step into the shoes of Achilles when he makes him speak.

This link between the understanding of direct speech gleaned from Plato, Aristotle and the scholia, on the one hand, and the concept of poetic imagination tangible in *de sublimitate* 15, on the other hand, is corroborated by the fact that ancient readers not only ascribe character speech to the author but also have the author actually do what their characters do. At the

[51] The passages from the *Ion*, *Poetics* and *Thesmophoriazusae* are often quoted together with such passages as Eur. *Supp.* 180–3: a songwriter needs to be happy while composing happy songs; Ar. *Ach.* 410–13: Euripides is fond of ragged and ill heroes on account of his own sleazy habits (e.g., Muecke 1982: 52–3; Sommerstein on Ar. *Thesm.* 149–50; Collard ad Eur. *Supp.* 180–3; Sheppard 2014: 21). They may not be unrelated, but there is one crucial difference: whereas Plato, Aristotle and, in comic exaggeration, Aristophanes anticipate the role of the imagination in the later notion of *phantasia*, these passages are premised on the idea that poetry and its characters reflect the nature or feeling of the poet but do not involve the idea of imagination.

beginning of the *Frogs*, Xanthias complains that he is not permitted 'to do any of the things that Phrynichus is always doing. Lycis and Ameipsias, too, they carry luggage every time in their comedies' (εἴπερ ποιήσω μηδὲν ὧνπερ Φρύνιχος/ εἴωθε ποιεῖν; καὶ Λύκις κἀμειψίας/ σκεύη φέρουσ᾽ ἑκάστοτ᾽ ἐν κωμῳδίᾳ, 13–15). There is irony in that Aristophanes has a character in a comedy refer the action of other comic characters back to their authors,[52] but the idea of an author doing what his characters do is not a comic one. While Pseudo-Moschus has Bion produce syringes and milk a young cow (3.82), the *Iliad* scholia note such things as that Homer 'has taken down the wall' (καθελὼν τὸ τεῖχος, bT on *Il.* 14.0) and that he 'has wounded the majority of the best with the exception of Ajax son of Telamon' (τοὺς πλείους τῶν ἀρίστων τρώσας πλὴν Αἴαντος τοῦ Τελαμωνίου, bT on *Il.* 11.598).[53] Illustrating what the 'great nature' in an author means, Pseudo-Longinus describes that Homer 'in these cases fully shares in the combat [lit. with fair wind breathes together with the combat] and he has suffered nothing less than that "he raged, as when destructive fire or spear-shaking Ares/ rages among the mountains and dense places of the deep forest. Slaver came out of his mouth"' (ἀλλὰ γὰρ Ὅμηρος μὲν ἐνθάδε οὔριος συνεμπνεῖ τοῖς ἀγῶσι, καὶ οὐκ ἄλλο τι αὐτὸς πέπονθεν ἢ 'μαίνεται, ὡς ὅτ᾽ Ἄρης ἐγχέσπαλος ἢ ὀλοὸν πῦρ/ οὔρεσι μαίνεται, βαθέης ἐν τάρφεσιν ὕλης,/ ἀφλοισμὸς δὲ περὶ στόμα γίγνεται', 9.11). Pseudo-Longinus not only ascribes to Homer the activity of a character, in this case Hector, but makes him its grammatical subject through the quotation.

Like the 'author says x' statements, these references to an author's activity within the narrated world are more than a simple *façon de parler*; they reflect a specific understanding of literary composition. The tendency to identify the poetic 'I' with the author is part of a far broader difference that encompasses the representation of character speech and action in general. In modern narratology, the narrator is ontologically separated from the characters and their actions. The distinction between fabula and sujet suggests that he moulds into a form what exists independently of his narration. Ancient critics, however, instead of erecting a boundary, have the author imaginatively step into the narrated world. In order to endow their accounts with force, they have to transform themselves into their characters, speaking their words and doing their deeds. The presence of the narrated action is not only, as argued in Chapter 2, an important

---

[52] On the different comic layers in the scene, see Halliwell 2014: 191–3.
[53] For further examples, see Lieberg 1982; Kassel 1991: 366–8.

element of ancient meditations on reception, it is also the background for the understanding of the author's relation to the characters.

5   From Metalepsis to Immersion

In an article that explores what narratologists label 'first-person narratives' and what he prefers to call 'fictional autobiography' in ancient literature, Whitmarsh argues that the illusion of the author's identity with the fictional 'I' constitutes a case of metalepsis: in order to turn into the fictional 'I', the author has to break the wall between their world and the fictional worlds.[54] However, as I now wish to show, the ancient understanding of the relationship between author and narrated world undermines the very framework of metalepsis. This does not mean that we ought not to speak of metalepsis in ancient literature, but it alerts us to the fact that the ancient view of author and narrated world was decisively unmetaleptic. Instead, I will finally suggest, the ancient view rather ties in nicely with recent insights of cognitive studies.

Whitmarsh quotes Genette's classical definition of metalepsis and calls metalepsis 'the elision of two different narrative levels, the traversal of a "shifting but sacred frontier between two worlds"'.[55] When, for example, Homer addresses Patroclus in the second person, he transgresses the boundary between the narrator or author and the characters in the narrated world. Normally, an author cannot converse with their characters, just as the characters are not able to address directly the reader. However, in the case of fictional autobiography, Whitmarsh argues, this boundary is erased: there is a metalepsis in that the author steps into the narrated world and plays the role of the character.

Whitmarsh's argument about 'fictional autobiography' is compelling; however, as the preceding sections have shown, the phenomenon on which Whitmarsh touches is significantly wider – it is not limited to first-person narrative and concerns more broadly an understanding of the relationship between the author and the characters of their narrative that can be traced across ancient criticism. What is more, it ultimately explodes the conceptual frame with which Whitmarsh tries to capture it. The modern concept of metalepsis is predicated on a 'frontier between two worlds' that keeps the author and the characters strictly apart. If my argument so far is correct, then the ancient understanding of narrative does not assume this frontier. Ancient readers distinguished between author and character speech, but

[54] Whitmarsh 2013.   [55] Whitmarsh 2013: 241.

they did not envisage the author on a different plane from the characters; instead, with the help of their imagination, they saw them as transporting them to the scene, themselves enacting the action and metamorphosing into their characters. This conception denies the very premises on which the idea of metalepsis is based, namely the ontological gap between author and characters.

I am far from claiming that Augustine's identification of Apuleius with Lucius and the other cases that Whitmarsh discusses ought not to be analysed as metalepsis. Here, and in general, it is possible and often fruitful, if not inevitable, to rely on concepts that are alien to the culture under analysis.[56] In fact, metalepsis has proven a highly stimulating concept for Classicists over the course of the last years.[57] As fruitful as such explorations of metalepsis are, however, they ought not to be mistaken for the attempt to elucidate the internal logic of ancient narrative. We can certainly describe as metaleptic the ancient tendency to detect the author's view in character speech; this, however, fails to capture the ancient sense of how authors relate to their characters. If direct speech is as a rule understood as a modulation of the author's voice and if, more broadly, the author is envisaged as themselves enacting the action in their imagination, then the strict ontological boundary on which the notion of metalepsis is based does not exist. The author does not violate a boundary in a paradoxical act; the very act of composing is predicated on their immersion in the narrated world.

This bestows a fine irony on Whitmarsh's argument about ancient fictional biography. Whitmarsh expresses the dissatisfaction that he and other scholars have come to feel about narratology in Classics. The narratological toolkit can analyse any kind of narrative, but it does not necessarily help to appreciate the specificities of the ancient understanding of narrative. Whitmarsh's test case is the narrator, a category that is key to modern narratology but absent from ancient criticism. However, in criticizing the application of the category of the narrator to ancient narrative as anachronistic, Whitmarsh is invoking another category, namely metalepsis, that is equally at odds with the logic of ancient narrative.

While incompatible with the narratological concept of metalepsis, the ancient idea of the author's use of *phantasia* chimes with so-called second-generation models of cognition. We have already seen in Chapter 2 that ancient authors and readers, in their focus on immersion, zeroed in on the

---

[56] See the distinction between emic and etic approaches in anthropology.
[57] Compare de Jong 2009; Eisen and Möllendorff 2013; Matzner and Trimble 2020. I return to the topic of metalepsis in Chapter 6, see p. 155–61.

dynamics of the reception process in ways that, despite obvious differences, parallel cognitive inquiries. The ancient view of the relation between authors and characters permits me to expand on this – at first sight certainly surprising – affinity of ancient criticism with current cognitive approaches.

What is now labelled the first generation of cognitive studies was based on computational models of the mind, which, it was assumed, formed internal representations of the world on the basis of the agent's perceptions. Against this view, a new generation of scientists and philosophers such as Noë and Gallagher have made a case for the embodied and enactive nature of perception.[58] Instead of forming an internal picture of our environment, we attend to it in terms of potential interactions that involve our bodies. Perception proceeds through the sensorimotor response to what it would be like to interact with our environment. For example, when we see a hammer, we do not form an internal representation of it but attend to the aspects of it that pertain to how we could use it. Perception is thus closely related to action; in fact, it has been demonstrated that seeing an action activates partly the same areas in the brain as those which are activated when engaging in this action.

What is more, experiments reveal that these regions of the brain are also put to work when we merely imagine these objects. When we imagine a hammer, our response is similar to when we actually see a hammer: the areas in the brain responsible for gripping an object and swinging it become active. In this case, not the immediate environment but our memory triggers the sensorimotor resonances. Literary scholars have just started to use this embodied and enactive view of cognition and imagination for a better understanding of reader response.[59] Against the intuition of most scholars, it is not detail in itself that renders literature vivid.[60] On the contrary, stories highly invested in descriptive details are not cognitively realist, for they do not conform to how we perceive the world around us. Our perception does not provide us with photographic images of our environment; instead, it is highly selective and focuses on things in terms of actual and possible interaction. Narratives that adopt this focus and do not try to deliver picture-like descriptions are cognitively realist and therefore feel experiential.

---

[58] Noë 2004; Gallagher 2005.
[59] Bolens 2008; Kuzmičová 2012; Kuzmičová 2013; Troscianko 2014; Cave 2016. In Classics, see, for example, Grethlein and Huitink 2017; Gaifman and Platt 2018; Lather 2021.
[60] See Grethlein and Huitink 2017 for a fuller explanation with references to scholarship.

The exploration of the style that renders narrative enactive is still in its infancy, but some important features have already been identified. For example, a focus on things only when they matter to the action, the so-called principle of 'just-in-time', corresponds to our perception, which assesses the environment in terms of actual and possible interaction. Likewise, a concentration on 'affordances', that is on qualities of things relevant to potential and actual ways of interacting with them, is cognitively realist. As to the action itself, the description of simple bodily movements triggers the reader's sensorimotor system and thus helps to bind the reader in. Finally, the assimilation of narrative time to narrated time, however difficult it is to define, generates 'dynamic veracity'. Together with an emphasis on bodily movement and a focus on things as and when they are relevant to the action, dynamic veracity helps to induce in the reader the feeling of directly witnessing the action of the narrative, without, however, forgetting that they are attending to a representation.

Now, cognitive literary studies elaborate on the response of readers, whereas the argument of this chapter has focused on the author. This being said, if we follow up on the ancient idea that the imagination of the writer parallels the imagination of the reader, that, in fact, only the author's immersion can bring about the immersion of the recipient, then the description of the author's *phantasia* in *de sublimitate* and other ancient texts anticipates, with due qualification, the embodied and enactive account of imagination. The description of how the author steps onto Helius' chariot and embarks on the ride with Phaethon illustrates the thesis that when we imagine something, whether as reader or as writer, the very areas in the brain are turned on that we use when we actually witness or even ourselves do what we imagine.

Take, for instance, the approach of the cognitive psychologist Rolf Zwaan, who argues that language comprehension involves an embodied, if vicarious experience: 'Language is a set of cues to the comprehender to construct an experiential (perception plus action) simulation of the described situation. In this conceptualization, the comprehender is an immersed experiencer of the described situation, and comprehension is the vicarious experience of the described situation.'[61] According to Zwaan's 'Immersed Experiencer Framework' (IEF), processing a narrative triggers the same sensorimotor and emotional responses as the actual experience. There is obviously a difference in that, whereas Pseudo-Longinus seems to consider the author's imaginative transferral to the depicted scene a special case of poetic and rhetorical ingenuity and its reception, Zwaan speaks about

---

[61] Zwaan 2004: 36.

language comprehension in general.[62] This difference notwithstanding, it is striking that recent cognitive models of cognition and imagination yield a more productive framework for thinking about ancient views of authors and their texts than the category of metalepsis. The embodied and enactive account of imagination is closer to the dynamic sense of composition and reception held by ancient critics than a concept that erects a 'shifting but sacred frontier between two worlds'. Without questioning the merits of narratology, one could say that ancient models of the author are cognitively more realist than the ontological model of structuralist narratology.

The resonance between current cognitive theory and ancient models of the author highlight that it is worthwhile considering more recent approaches in narrative theory, notably those that are inspired by cognitive research.[63] The taxonomies of structuralist narratology will remain useful, but their heuristic limits become clearer and clearer. Whilst providing useful tools for the analysis of individual texts, they are inadequate as a means for capturing the specifically ancient understanding of narrative. The parallel between cognitive theory and ancient concepts is illuminating in several regards. Cognitive studies have an experimental basis and are therefore per se 'presentist'. We do not have a chance to question ancient readers or to produce MRI scans of their brains in order to explore their responses to literature. That said, as the ancient notion of *phantasia* illustrates, cognitive studies may provide us with models that permit us to understand better the claims of ancient criticism. Pseudo-Longinus' assertions about the transportation of readers suddenly appear less outlandish when they are seen in light of cognitive research in immersion.

Another case in point is Gorgias' comments on the strong effects of poetry in *Helen* referred to in Chapter 2. Unlike Aristotle, Gorgias has not received much attention from modern theoreticians – under the auspices of critique, it has been easy to ignore his claims as inflated rhetoric.[64] Seen in the light of cognitive approaches, however, his description of the response elicited by poetry is worth reconsidering: 'Those who hear it are penetrated by a terribly

---

[62] Interestingly, in a more recent article Zwaan qualifies his IEF and juxtaposes immersive language comprehension with another mode of language comprehension that focuses more strongly on abstract, amodal symbols (2014).

[63] It is disappointing that de Jong, who did much to introduce narratology to Classics with her dissertation (1987), in her recent monograph (2014) ignores further developments in narrative theory after the structuralist theories of the 1960s and 1970s. First attempts to make second-generation cognitive theory fruitful for the study of ancient literature can be found in Grethlein and Huitink 2017 and Anderson, Cairns and Sprevak 2019. See now also the webpage https://cognitiveclassics .blogs.sas.ac.uk/.

[64] Cassin 1995 is a noteworthy exception that takes Gorgias' reflection on language seriously.

fearful shuddering, a much-weeping pity and a yearning that desires grief, and on the basis of the fortunes and misfortunes of other people's actions and bodies, their soul is affected, by an affection of its own, by the medium of words' (ἧς τοὺς ἀκούοντας εἰσῆλθε καὶ φρίκη περίφοβος καὶ ἔλεος πολύδακρυς καὶ πόθος φιλοπενθής, ἐπ᾽ ἀλλοτρίων τε πραγμάτων καὶ σωμάτων εὐτυχίαις καὶ δυσπραγίαις ἴδιόν τι πάθημα διὰ τῶν λόγων ἔπαθεν ἡ ψυχή, fr. B 11.9 DK). Gorgias captures not the experiential quality of the response, he also highlights its emotional and physiological dimensions. The reference to 'the fortunes and misfortunes of other people's actions and bodies' can even be read to gesture to an embodied and enactive account of the reception.[65]

The parallels to cognitive theory also reveal the value that ancient criticism may have not only for our understanding of ancient models of narrative but also for our own interpretive practice. Needless to say, ancient criticism does not provide a compulsory framework for our own readings. The assumption that we understand ancient texts better if we read them through the lens of an ancient reader is wrong on many counts.[66] At the same time, comments of ancient critics may stimulate our own interpretations. As we have seen, they alert us to the limits of structuralist narratology and may also enrich reader-response approaches. Many of the studies inspired by Wolfgang Iser and Stanley Fish tilt towards the intellectual and focus on the conjectures that readers make about the further course of the plot. Ancient critics, however, highlight that our response is significantly richer, that it also has an affective dimension and even a physiological dimension. They may therefore direct us to a fuller understanding of how texts captivate their readers.

Besides letting us see ancient criticism and literature with new eyes, cognitive studies stand to benefit inversely from this dialogue. Cognitive studies mostly focus on the present world; as I have just mentioned, this is natural given their experimental background. At the same time, it is highly desirable that the essentialism of cognitive studies be somehow mediated with the historicism of cultural studies. It seems to take very long periods for the human apparatus of cognition to change, and yet it would be naive to assume that cognition is not also shaped by cultural factors. The concepts and categories of a culture undoubtedly have an impact on our perception. So far, however, this impact has been widely ignored in cognitive studies. The rich tradition of ancient criticism affords a unique opportunity for providing cognitive approaches with a historical perspective and for mediating their essentialist claims with the insights given by cultural studies.

---

[65] Compare Grethlein 2021: 17–18.   [66] See, for example, the compelling criticism by Feeney 1995.

CHAPTER 4

Minds

1 Cognitivism: The New Holy Grail?

In the two preceding chapters, we saw that the focus on fictionality and the taxonomies of structuralist narratology, helpful as they may be in some regards, also occlude essential aspects of ancient narrative. Surprisingly, cognitive approaches turned out to provide a better framework for capturing the ancient understanding of narrative. The emphasis of ancient critics on the strong effects of narrative resonates with the concept of immersion, just as the idea of the author's impersonation of characters corresponds with cognitive models such as Zwaan's 'Immersed Experiencer Framework'. Unfortunately, this does not mean that cognitivism is the new holy grail for studies of ancient narrative. In this chapter, I will argue that perhaps the most prominent reception of a cognitive concept in recent narratology fails to do justice to ancient texts.

In the past two decades, scholars of narrative have enthusiastically declared that the Theory of Mind is key to our reading process, that, in other words, 'narrative is the description of fictional mental functioning'.[1] Some Classicists have latched onto this approach. Felix Budelmann and Pat Easterling, for example, identified 'mind reading' as a helpful concept for the analysis of tragedy and its reception – it permits us to tackle some of the issues previously discussed under the label of 'character' without having its baggage.[2] The scholar who has arguably done the most to establish the Theory of Mind as a concept in Classical Studies is Ruth Scodel. In *Epic Facework. Self-Presentation and Social Interaction in Homer* and related articles, she argues that the Homeric heroes are constantly engaged in processes of mind reading, which we have to reconstruct in order to fully understand their interactions.[3] The psychology of Homer's characters, she contends, is far more intricate than had been assumed in previous scholarship.

---

[1] Palmer 2004: 12.   [2] Budelmann and Easterling 2010.   [3] Scodel 2008; 2012; 2014b.

There can be no doubt that characters in ancient epic, drama and other genres such as historiography read each others' minds and that we as readers are prompted to engage with the interior lives of characters.[4] And yet I wish to argue in this chapter that the Theory of Mind is less central to the engagement with ancient narratives in general than previously asserted. In fact, ancient literature challenges the thesis that 'narrative is the description of fictional mental functioning'. The problem with this claim is ultimately similar to that of structuralist narratology – it is related to the tendency of theoreticians to deduce transhistorical claims about narrative mostly from modern novels. The pioneers of the Theory of Mind in narrative studies are eager to distance themselves from the structuralist founding fathers of narratology, who had little interest in psychologizing interpretations, and yet they focus on the same small canon of texts. As we will see in this chapter, their claims are not only inadequate for ancient texts, but an inquiry into premodern material has the capacity to enrich theories of narrative at large. Besides continuing the project of getting a better sense of the specificities of ancient narrative as in the two preceding chapters, this chapter will also exploit the ancient material as a provocation for theoretical reflection.

I will first introduce two of the most prominent cognitive scholars, who, in their studies, have put a premium on the Theory of Mind, while ignoring that this concept is problematic and heavily disputed in cognitive science (§2 The Theory of Mind in Psychology and Narratology). I will then turn to my test case – Heliodorus' *Ethiopica*. Although recent work shows that character portrayal in the ancient novel is more intricate than has been widely assumed, the reader of the *Ethiopica* does not get much mileage out of the Theory of Mind. Instead, Heliodorus' novel draws our attention to the temporal dynamics of narrative – the plot is crucial to the experiential dimension that, as argued in Chapter 2, is so important for ancient views of narrative (§3 Heliodorus' *Ethiopica*: From Fictional Minds to Narrative Time). What is more, the reflections on narrative and response encapsulated in the *Ethiopica* highlight that the reader is enticed primarily by plot features such as suspense and curiosity (§4 Reflections on Narrative and Time in the *Ethiopica*). The prominence of plot that can be detected in the *Ethiopica* and its meta-narrative reflections is a central point of Aristotle's *Poetics* that merits reconsideration in this context. Other works of criticism also corroborate the thesis that the Theory of Mind is not key to the responses elicited

---

[4] Further applications of the Theory of Mind in Classics can be found in Lauwers, Schwall and Opsomer 2018; Meineck, Short and Devereaux 2019; Budelmann and Sluiter forthcoming.

by ancient narratives (§5 Plot and Character in Aristotle's *Poetics* and Ancient Criticism). By no means, however, should plot be played off against character. Their entwinement in narrative can be grasped, I finally suggest, by the concept of experience, which is also capable of capturing the cognitive processes of readers as well as characters (§6 The Entwinement of Narrative Time with Character: Experience).

2   The Theory of Mind in Psychology and Narratology

Considering various concepts recruited to elucidate the interface between mind and narrative, Marie-Laure Ryan notes that 'the most popular of these imports is the ... notion of theory of mind'.[5] This concept, sometimes also circulating under the label of folk psychology, was first developed by comparative psychologists who investigated the ability in primates to impute mental states to others.[6] It was then applied to the human mind in developmental psychology and triggered a wave of clinical research. Broadly defined as the human capacity to explain the behaviour of others in terms of their beliefs, feelings and desires, the Theory of Mind has been identified by literary scholars as a key to the reader's engagement with narrative across media.

Let me single out the approaches of two particularly influential scholars from the bulk of works that claim the notion of Theory of Mind for literary scholarship.[7] In two monographs, Alan Palmer advances the thesis that 'narrative is the description of fictional mental functioning'.[8] Some aspects of 'fictional mental functioning' are covered by investigations of speech categories, focalization, characterization and plot structures, others come to the fore in possible-worlds theory; and yet Palmer reckoned that we need the new label of 'fictional minds' to fully grasp what hitherto had been called the presentation of consciousness. Following characters' 'fictional mental functioning' is 'the fundamental and principal way by which we understand narrative'.[9] For Palmer, the Theory of Mind, which helps us navigate our social world, is at the core of our response to narrative.

---

[5] Ryan 2010: 485.   [6] Premack and Woodruff 1978.

[7] For further recent literary scholarship indebted to the Theory of Mind, see, for example, Mar, Djikic and Oatley 2008; Oatley 2009; Leverage, Mancing, Schweickert and William 2011; Herman 2011a; Pagan 2014.

[8] Palmer 2004: 12. Compare Palmer 2010: 9: 'Fictional narrative is, in essence, the presentation of mental functioning.' While advancing close readings of new texts, the theoretical agenda of Palmer 2010 is more or less the same as that of Palmer 2004, parts of which are simply rephrased or repeated verbatim.

[9] Palmer 2010: 17.

In order to describe the reading process thus envisaged, Palmer coins the term 'continuing-consciousness frame', that is, 'the ability to take a reference to a character in the text and attach it to a presumed consciousness that exists continuously within the storyworld between the various, more or less intermittent references to that character'.[10] The readers' activity produces what Palmer calls 'embedded narratives' in his first book and 'cognitive narratives' in his second book:[11] 'the total perceptual and cognitive viewpoint, ideological worldview, memories of the past, and the set of beliefs, desires, intentions, motives, and plans for the future of each character in the story as presented in the discourse'.[12] It is through such 'embedded/cognitive narratives' that readers access story-worlds.

Palmer offsets his investigation against traditional approaches to the presentation of consciousness by focusing on 'the social nature of thought'.[13] Besides intramental thought, there is intermental thought. While the former is located within the individual mind, the latter is shared by a group, be it a couple, a nation or a random crowd. Believing that socially distributed cognition is important in real life, Palmer argues that it is also pervasive in the novel. One of his test cases is Eliot's *Middlemarch*. There is a Middlemarch mind formed by the inhabitants of the town, embracing various subgroups. Palmer goes out of his way to assert that his use of mind in this case is not metaphorical: 'The town actually and literally does have a mind of its own.'[14]

Like Palmer, albeit from a different angle, Lisa Zunshine considers the Theory of Mind pivotal to the reading process. In her book *Why We Read Fiction*, she draws on the work of cognitive evolutionary psychologists such as Robin Dunbar and Simon Baron-Cohen, who understand the Theory of Mind as an evolutionary adaptation: 'The emergence of a Theory of Mind "module" was evolution's answer to the "staggeringly complex" challenge faced by our ancestors, who needed to make sense of the behavior of other people in their group, which could include up to 200 individuals.'[15] Works of fiction, she argues, 'provide grist for the mills of our mind-reading adaptations that have evolved to deal with real people'.[16] Besides subscribing to an evolutionary approach, *Why We Read Fiction* puts much stock in psychological investigations that explain autism as a drastically reduced ability of mind reading: 'Fiction presents a challenge to people with autism because in many ways it calls for the same kind of mind-reading – that is,

---

[10] Palmer 2010: 10.   [11] Palmer 2010: 11–12.   [12] Palmer 2010: 11.
[13] Palmer 2004: 11. On Palmer's concept of social minds, see the special issue of *Narrative* 23.2 (2015).
[14] Palmer 2010: 74.   [15] Zunshine 2006: 7.   [16] Zunshine 2006: 16–17.

the inference of the mental state from the behavior – that is necessary in regular human communication.'[17]

Zunshine argues that fiction confronts us with multiple embedded levels of intentionality that often exceed the complexity of real-life encounters. Here, her take is nuanced in a different way to that of Palmer. While Palmer is inclined to stress the transparency of the minds of others in real life, Zunshine gives more space to the possibility of misunderstanding and highlights that 'the joys of reading fictional minds are subject to some of the same instabilities that render our real-life mindreading both exciting and exasperating'.[18] Nonetheless, novels and other narratives 'test the functioning of our cognitive adaptations for mind-reading while keeping us pleasantly aware that the "test" is proceeding quite smoothly'.[19]

As central as the notion of the Theory of Mind is in the works of Palmer, Zunshine and other literary scholars, it has been forcefully challenged in recent psychology.[20] To start with, the usage of the term Theory of Mind varies significantly. Some limit the Theory of Mind to so-called theory theory, that is, approaches which presume that our inferences about other people hinge on a theory or quasi-Theory of Minds. Then the Theory of Mind is opposed to simulation theories which identify empathy as the key to our social interactions.[21] Other scholars, however, are happy to subsume both theory theory and simulation theory under the heading of Theory of Mind.[22]

More disconcerting than such terminological issues are the methodological flaws of the experiments on which the Theory of Mind is premised, especially the 'false-belief' task. The experiments that test the ability to meta-represent, that is to distinguish somebody's thought about an object from its reality, not only require no theory or quasi-theory about minds, they also prove nothing about how our interaction with other humans proceeds: 'The experiments themselves were *stipulative*, defining the very phenomenon they claim to investigate'.[23] There are alternative modes of conducting social interactions: often social rules permit us to make sense of the behaviour of others, and instead of inferring the desires and beliefs of others we can ask

---

[17] Zunshine 2006: 11. More recently, Zunshine has recanted her position on narrative and autism. In an interview with the neuroscientist Savarese, she advocates a dialogue between literary studies and the approach of neurodiversity in the sciences (Savarese and Zunshine 2014).

[18] Zunshine 2006: 20.   [19] Zunshine 2006: 18.

[20] See, for example, Hutto 2007; 2008; and the contributions to Leudar and Costall 2009a.

[21] Cf. Goldman 2006. For a juxtaposition of theory theory and simulation theory, see the double issue of *Mind and Language* 7 (1–2) 1992.

[22] For example, Gallagher 2001. See also Palmer 2010: 24 who uses the term 'in a more general sense, as a kind of umbrella or generic label for our ability to understand others'.

[23] Leudar and Costall 2009b: 6–7.

them directly.[24] The experimental focus of the Theory of Mind has also led to a neglect of the social circumstances in which communication takes place. While the experiments concentrate on third-person contexts, many of our interactions are second-person.[25] The Theory of Mind, it appears, is far less salient in our social lives than its advocates take for granted.

It has also been criticized that the Theory of Mind is predicated on a dualism: the juxtaposition of behaviour and mind underlying the idea of mind reading is superseded by more recent approaches which aim at integrated and embodied concepts of mind.[26] Psychologists and philosophers have further marshalled the concept of intersubjectivity to identify a primordial connection with other individuals and to question the idea of a primary separation between self and other on which the Theory of Mind is premised.[27] The arguments of *Why We Read Fiction* in particular are challenged by the discovery that many people diagnosed with autism are actually able to meta-present.[28] To cut a long story short, a glance at recent literature on the mind shows that, by invoking the Theory of Mind, literary scholars are building their theories on a cognitive approach that has lost much of its lustre since the 1990s.[29]

It is also worth wondering if some of the examples discussed by Zunshine actually put the Theory of Mind to good use. Many novels, she contends, intrigue us because of the complexity of the mind reading they prompt us to do. Her case in point is a passage from Virginia Woolf's *Mrs Dalloway*.[30] While in everyday life our mind is used to computing three, sometimes four levels of embedded information, this passage, Zunshine claims, features seven levels of intentionality: A believes that B assumes that C wishes that D hopes . . . However, not only does a closer inspection reveal that, instead of being stacked on top of each other, the mental activities partly parallel one another, it is also doubtful that such accounts actually require our Theory of Mind.[31] In the passage under discussion, Woolf gives us full insight into the interior processes of the characters; the Theory of Mind, on the other hand, however we define it exactly, is the attempt to conjecture about interior processes to which we have no access. Woolf's novels and other modernist works intrigue us

---

[24] Hutto 2007: 44–6.   [25] Gallagher 2005: 213.   [26] Leudar and Costall 2009b: 10.
[27] Zlatev 2008.   [28] Boucher 1996: 223–41.
[29] It is odd that Herman 2011b adduces some recent critics of the Theory of Mind to destabilize the assumption that we have no access to other minds in the everyday world but fails to draw the appropriate conclusions for its applications to narrative. How can a theory that is insufficient to account for social interaction furnish a model for our response to narrative that claims to be based on everyday cognitive processes?
[30] Zunshine 2006: 31–6.   [31] Compare Ryan 2015: 297.

through their use of introspection, but their extensive portrayals of consciousness processes do not necessarily and primarily activate our Theory of Mind.

In this chapter, I wish to show that the general claims about the Theory of Mind and narrative, so popular in current scholarship, do not work for ancient texts.[32] Palmer, Zunshine and other disciples of the Theory of Mind tend to focus on modern narrative, particularly realist novels.[33] This genre lends itself to them on account of its prominent consciousness presentation, but once we start to look outside this narrow canon, it is hard to sustain the assertion that the anthropological significance of narrative is predicated on the Theory of Mind. Ancient narrative highlights an aspect that is in danger of being downplayed in cognitive narratology, although it is not confined to premodern texts.

3   Heliodorus' *Ethiopica*: From Fictional Minds to Narrative Time

Recent scholarship has been eager to correct the traditional view that the characters in the ancient novel are 'soulless … figures' ('seelenlose … Gestalten'), merely 'jointed dolls' ('Gliederpuppen')[34]. Gender studies in particular have inspired a more refined analysis of the novel's protagonists.[35] Most recently, Koen de Temmerman presented a monograph on characterization in the novel from a literary point of view.[36] Mustering the five ancient Greek novels that have been fully preserved, he argues that their heroes are by no means only typified, idealistic and static characters, but dynamic, realistically sketched and well individuated. De Temmerman challenges in particular Christopher Gill's take on characterization in ancient literature. In a series of monographs and articles, Gill has explored the ancient notion of selfhood in a wide range of literary genres and philosophical works. A summary will not be able to reproduce the nuances of his readings nor to account for the

---

[32] For a critical assessment of Zunshine's approach, see Boyd 2006. A special issue of *Style* on social minds also features essays that are critical of Palmer's work (see especially Bortolussi 2011; Hogan 2011; Jahn 2011), but while most of these articles disagree with the notion of intermental thought, I will try to challenge the application of Theory of Mind.

[33] The contributions to Herman 2011a are a noteworthy exception. While not going so far as to question the Theory of Mind, some of the chapters reveal that in premodern narrative fictional minds work differently.

[34] Rohde 1914: 476.   [35] Egger 1994; Konstan 1994; Goldhill 1995; Haynes 2003; Jones 2012.

[36] De Temmerman 2014. See also the volume of the *Studies in Ancient Greek Narrative* on characterization, De Temmerman and van Emde Boas 2018a.

conceptual changes made over the course of decades, and yet on the whole it can be said that Gill juxtaposes the ancient emphasis on moral judgement which constitutes in his terms *character* with what he labels *personality*, shaped essentially by introspection and the Cartesian idea of selfhood.[37] Combining a psychological dimension which can be subjective or objective with an ethical dimension which can be premised on an individualist or a participant conception of the person, Gill contrasts the objective-participant stance dominating in antiquity with the subjective-individualist stance defined by Cartesian and Kantian philosophy.[38] Note that the objective-participant concept of personhood is consonant with the strong moral dimension of ancient literature for which I argued in Chapter 2.

De Temmerman takes pains to trace the subjective and individualist aspects of *personality* in the ancient novel. The reader, he contends, is invited not only to evaluate, but also to understand the protagonists. As illuminating as de Temmerman's interpretations and qualifications are, they cannot detract from the overall plausibility of Gill's argument. While it is possible to challenge some of Gill's interpretations and to identify texts in which aspects of personality come to the fore (as Gill himself did), the tendency to consider characters along ethical lines distinguishes ancient authors from the modern obsession with the uniqueness of characters' interior processes.[39] Most importantly for my argument, the heroes in the Greek novels are not portrayed in a way that puts the Theory of Mind in the centre of the reader's response. It is not the consciousness of the characters but the temporal dynamics of narrative that pulls the reader into the story – the workings of plot are crucial for the experiential quality on which ancient readers put a premium; this was one of the major points of Chapter 2.

I wish to illustrate this claim through arguably the most complex of the five preserved Greek novels, the *Ethiopica*. Heliodorus' novel follows the

---

[37] See Gill 1983; 1986; 1990; 1996; 2006: 338–42. Note that, in the course of his interventions, Gill modified parameters of the character–personality dichotomy (see esp. 1990: 3–9) and was happy to identify ancient texts that privilege personality over character (1986). Sorabji 2006 argues that subjectivist and individualist notions of selfhood were more prominent than Gill allows for. See Sorabji 2008 and Gill 2008 for a critical discussion of the differences between their reconstructions.

[38] In Gill 1990, there is a third dimension, namely the explanation of action, notably if actions are explained with reference to beliefs and desires or psychological causes distinct from conscious motives (see also Gill 1984). I leave this aspect aside as it is less pertinent to my focus.

[39] On differences of characterization in ancient and modern literature, see also Goldhill 1986: 179; 1990: 100–5 and, last not least, the contributions to Pelling 1990. For a more recent assessment, see De Temmerman and van Emde Boas 2018b.

pattern that we know from the other ancient and also early modern romances.[40] A couple, in this case Theagenes and Charicleia, has to brave various ordeals before they are united in marriage. After the first scene of the *Ethiopica* shows us Theagenes and Charicleia on a beach at the mouth of the Nile, most of the novel's first half is taken up by an embedded narrative in which the Egyptian priest Calasiris reveals its prehistory: in Delphi, Theagenes meets Charicleia, an Ethiopian princess raised by a priest of Apollo. They fall in love and escape with his help. After a first series of adventures, notably a sea storm, pirates and several men who lust after Charicleia, the hero couple arrive in Egypt. The second half of the *Ethiopica* is more straightforward: undergoing further trials, including separation, captivity and a lecherous woman, Charicleia and Theagenes come to Ethiopia and are finally married.

Written probably in the third or fourth century CE, the *Ethiopica* has been called 'the ancient world's narratological summa'[41]. Heliodorus had a huge impact on the emergence of the modern novel and was extolled by such critics as Scaliger;[42] nowadays, however, his novel is studied mostly by a small, if devoted group of experts.[43] As I hope to show though, its formal complexity and high degree of reflexivity make it a text worthy of the attention of students of narrative. I will begin with the portrayal of the heroine, taking de Temmerman's reading as my starting point; I will then consider the use of internal focalization in the opening scene and finally discuss Charicleia's *Scheintod* at the beginning of book 2.

According to de Temmerman, two features in particular define Charicleia: mental strength (φρόνημα) and chastity (σωφροσύνη).[44] De Temmerman argues that while both traits may seem to be static at the beginning, their dynamic and shapeable nature comes to the fore as the narrative proceeds. Calasiris narrates how Charicleia's mental strength is challenged by her passion for Theagenes and reinforced when she learns about her royal descent: *noblesse oblige*. Charicleia first sees her chastity threatened by Theagenes; she is then, however, instructed by Calasiris that only sex, not marriage, is incompatible with chastity. This reassessment allows her to keep her vows while eloping with Theagenes. De Temmerman stresses Charicleia's

---

[40] On the plot dynamics of the *Ethiopica*, see, for example, Lowe 2000: 249–58; Whitmarsh 2011: 139–252, for a discussion of the narrative dynamics of all five preserved Greek novels.

[41] Lowe 2000: 258.   [42] For a survey, see Sandy 1982: 95–124.

[43] Pavel 2003 is a noteworthy exception in granting Heliodorus a prominent place in his genealogy of the novel, but I doubt that his emphasis on the tension between individual and world works well for the ancient novel.

[44] De Temmerman 2014: 246–58.

clever use of rhetoric to defend her chastity.[45] In book 1, she successfully fends off the brigand Thyamis, who is eager to marry her. Pretending to be a priestess of Artemis and the sister of Theagenes, she makes Thyamis postpone his marriage plans until they reach Memphis. As we later learn in Calasiris' narrative, he taught her the art of speaking 'as a basis for choosing the best way of life'.[46] Further on, in the second half of the *Ethiopica*, Charicleia tries to pass on her skills to Theagenes, who has now become the victim of illicit desire.

De Temmerman brilliantly teases out the nuances of the portrayal of Charicleia. And yet, even his overly subtle analysis yields a strictly confined character sketch that throws into relief the limits of characterization in the ancient novel. The development for which de Temmerman argues is minimal. Neither the reassessment of chastity nor the confirmation of mental strength furnishes a serious change of character. Charicleia's character is tested rather than transformed in the manner of a modern *Bildungsroman*. Note also that the traits by which Charicleia is defined have a strong moral bearing. Both chastity and mental strength firmly belong to Gill's realm of *character* and do not impinge on the inner features that are part of what Gill labels *personality*. There is far more to evaluate than to understand in Charicleia.

Most importantly, it is clearly not the character of Charicleia and other protagonists that drives the narrative and entices the reader. Take for instance Charicleia's dealings with the head of the brigands, Thyamis, in book 1.[47] Beguiled by her beauty, Thyamis falls for Charicleia. Although she is in his hands, he avoids the use of force and instead proposes marriage. Charicleia senses that she is not in a position to reject this proposal; hence she slyly asks him to wait until she has had a chance to lay down her priesthood at the temple of Apollo in Memphis. In their exchange, Thyamis reveals himself to be a righteous brigand, while Charicleia showcases her savviness and shrewdness. This is fair enough, but the reader's attention is directed less at the nuances of the characters than at the plot. On the one hand, the reader is bound to wonder about the identity and prehistory of Charicleia and Theagenes.[48] We have followed the beautiful couple from the mouth of the Nile to the village of the brigands and still do not know who they are and what brought them to the shores of Egypt. Charicleia's self-identification as the sister of Theagenes is obviously a ruse,

---

[45] De Temmerman 2014: 258–77.   [46] De Temmerman 2014: 264.

[47] De Temmerman 2014: 258–69.

[48] On the delayed revelation of essential information in the *Ethiopica*, see Winkler 1999: 296–307; Morgan 1999: 265–9.

and yet the reader wonders whether her speech to Thyamis could also feature true elements. Her claim that they suffered shipwreck chimes with the tableau of the initial scene; but did they actually come from Ephesus, and were they really on a religious mission? On the other hand, the reader will feel suspense as to whether or not Charicleia's strategy will work out. Thyamis accepts her story, but for how long will she be able to postpone the wedding? Once in Memphis, will she have to marry him? It is not so much the interior lives of Charicleia and Thyamis as the action that engages the reader.[49]

Priority of plot over character can also be noted in other passages. Take for example the final book: Theagenes and Charicleia have been caught by the Ethiopian army and are due to be sacrificed. Before that, however, they need to undergo a chastity test, as only virgin victims are legitimate. An intriguing tension proliferates: an oracle reported at the end of book 2 suggests that Charicleia and Theagenes will eventually be married on account of their chastity. Now, however, Charicleia is liable to be sacrificed if she turns out to be a virgin. De Temmerman notes that the scene deconstructs both the 'Artemisian' and 'Apollonian' sides of Charicleia, the former concerning her chastity, the latter her rhetorical skills.[50] When Charicleia's sexual abstinence almost leads to her sacrifice, then 'the novelistic *topos* of chastity is fundamentally perverted'.[51] At the same time, Charicleia's rhetorical shrewdness fails to reach its goal this time. She does not manage to convince the Ethiopian king and queen that 'as their daughter, she is not a suitable victim for sacrifice in a ritual that traditionally requires foreign prisoners of war'.[52] It is only through the intervention of the crowd that she will be spared.

De Temmerman nicely teases out how the virginity test undercuts central traits of Charicleia's earlier presentation, and yet his own analysis ultimately drives home that character portrayal is not at the core of the scene: 'At this point, then, the "Artemisian" side of her character, high-lighted since the first pages of the novel, turns out to be the main *obstacle* to a happy ending.'[53] It is not the presentation of Charicleia's character in itself, but its role as an '*obstacle* to a happy ending' that arrests the reader's attention. The virginity test is one of many events that create suspense by

---

[49] Fludernik 2015: 290 ignores these hermeneutic challenges related to the plot when she asks: 'Why indeed should we care for those two lovers and their trials unless it were for the cognitive and emotional transposition (i.e., immersion) into their situation, which crucially includes their hopes, desires, fears, and disappointments?'

[50] De Temmerman 2014: 293–4.   [51] De Temmerman 2014: 293.

[52] De Temmerman 2014: 294.   [53] De Temmerman 2014: 293.

veering off into a direction which conflicts with the anticipated ending. As John Morgan notes in his fine analysis of the narrative dynamics of the *Ethiopica*'s final book, 'the narrative is full of signs that point wrong trails'.[54] Seen in this light, Charicleia's response to Theagenes' query as to why she does not simply reveal her identity to her parents has a meta-narrative quality to it: 'Great ends can only be achieved by means of equal greatness. A story whose beginnings heaven has made convoluted cannot be quickly resolved' (τὰ μεγάλα τῶν πραγμάτων μεγάλων δεῖται κατασκευῶν. Ὧν γὰρ πολυπλόκους τὰς ἀρχὰς ὁ δαίμων καταβέβληται, τούτων ἀνάγκη καὶ τὰ τέλη διὰ μακροτέρων συμπεραίνεσθαι, 9.24.3–4).[55]

Furthermore, the initial scene of the *Ethiopica* hammers home that Heliodorus is more invested in the dynamics of plot than the intricacies of character (1.1.1–8):

> The smile of daybreak was just beginning to brighten the sky, the sunlight to catch the hilltops, when a group of men in brigand gear peered over the mountain that overlooks the place where the Nile flows into the sea at the mouth that men call the Heracleotic. They stood there for a moment, scanning the expanse of sea beneath them: first they gazed out over the ocean, but as there was nothing sailing there that held out hope of spoil and plunder, their eyes were drawn to the beach nearby. This is what they saw: a merchant ship was riding there, moored by her stern, empty of crew but laden with freight. This much could be surmised even from a distance, for the weight of her cargo forced the water up to the third line of boards on the ship's side. But the beach! – a mass of newly slain bodies, some of them quite dead, others half-alive and still twitching, testimony that the fighting had only just ended. To judge by the signs this had been no proper battle. Amongst the carnage were the miserable remnants of festivities that had come to this unhappy end. There were tables still set with food, and others upset on the ground, held in dead men's hands; in the fray they had served some as weapons, for this had been an impromptu conflict; beneath other tables men had crawled in the vain hope of hiding there. There were wine bowls upturned, and some slipping from the hands that held them; some had been drinking from them, others using them like stones, for the suddenness of the catastrophe had caused objects to be put to strange, new uses and taught men to use drinking vessels as missiles. There they lay, here a man felled by an axe, there another struck down by a stone picked up then and there from the shingly beach; here a man battered to death with a club, there another burned to death with a brand from the fire. Various were the forms of their deaths, but most were the victims of arrows and archery. In that small space the deity had contrived an infinitely varied

---

[54] Morgan 1989: 318.
[55] Cf. Morgan 1989: 308–9; Elmer 2008: 429–30; Whitmarsh 2011: 230–1.

spectacle, defiling wine with blood and unleashing war at the party, combining wining and dining, pouring of drink and spilling of blood, and staging this tragic show for the Egyptian bandits. They stood on the mountainside like the audience in a theater, unable to comprehend the scene: the vanquished were there, but the victors were nowhere to be seem; the victory was unequivocal, but the spoils had not been taken, and the ship lay there by herself, crewless but otherwise intact, riding peacefully at anchor as if protected by a great force of men. But although they were at a loss to know what it all meant, they still had an eye for plunder and a quick profit. So they cast themselves in the role of victors and set off down the hillside.

A camera-like movement gives the description a cinematographic quality:[56] the narrator starts with a pan shot of the scenery – the reference to 'men in thievish attire' is restricted to what can be seen – and, in a type of reverse shot, turns around to adopt the viewpoint of these men. Following the movement of their gaze, the narrator describes first the sea and then the beach. His report adheres to the perspective of the internal beholders, reporting only what they see and reckon without imparting any additional information: 'this much could be surmised even from a distance . . . to judge by the signs this had been no proper battle' (καὶ τοῦτο παρῆν συμβάλλειν καὶ τοῖς πόρρωθεν . . . Ἦν δὲ οὐ πολέμου καθαροῦ τὰ φαινόμενα σύμβολα). The beginning of the *Ethiopica* is an impressive instance of internal focalization in ancient narrative.[57]

Internal focalization is an important means of giving the reader access to the minds of characters. It thus figures prominently in studies of 'fictional minds'. At the beginning of the *Ethiopica*, however, internal focalization is not used to interest the reader in the characters whose perspective the narrative adopts. The brigands through whose eyes the reader sees the beach play no further role; they simply leave when another group of brigands arrives. The limitation of sensual and intellectual perception to the perspective of an internal audience serves to put the reader right on the spot of the action. It makes the account mimetic and bestows on it the graphic vividness which ancient critics label *enargeia*.[58] More specifically, the *enargeia* at the beginning of the *Ethiopica* reinforces the reader's curiosity which the scene is bound to arouse. What has happened on the beach? How can the mysterious blending of party with war and wine with blood be explained? Who is the couple that the narrator describes in the subsequent paragraphs, a gorgeous girl, statue-like with a bow in her hand,

---

[56] Compare Bühler 1976 on the cinematographic character of the *Ethiopica*'s opening. See also Winkler 1999: 289–3; Morgan 1991: 86–90; Tagliabue 2015. I am unconvinced by the argument Telò 2011 makes for far-reaching allusions to the *Odyssey* in the *Ethiopica* that imply a predatory poetics.

[57] Compare Effe 1975: 152–7.   [58] See n. 58 in Chapter 2.

and at her feet a young man, heavily injured, but nonetheless of astounding beauty? Instead of engaging the reader in the process of mind reading and involving her with the characters, the internal focalization on the first pages of the *Ethiopica* inserts the reader into the plot.[59] In an artful play with different story lines and embedded narratives, the *Ethiopica* will continue to tickle the reader's curiosity – the prehistory which lets them understand the starting scene will not be revealed fully until the end of book 5,

By now it should be clear that the *Ethiopica* fails Palmer's formula for narrative as a 'description of fictional mental functioning'. It is not the Theory of Mind, however understood, that grabs the reader's attention and immerses them into the world of the *Ethiopica*. We do not access the story through 'embedded/cognitive narratives' but are gripped by the forceful plot. Of course, the narrator reports on the feelings, motives and goals of the characters. However, what entices the reader is not the rather schematic consciousness processes, but the drive of the action.[60] At the same time, what modern readers may be inclined to shrug off as tedious moralizing will have appealed to ancient readers, who, as we have seen in Chapter 2, by and large expected moral instruction. While falling short of our psychological standards, Heliodorus' emphasis on Charicleia's mental strength and chastity corresponds to the strong moral dimension of ancient narrative.

It is not incidental that ancient grammarians define *enargeia* as the ability to 'bring something before the eye' (Anon. Segu. 96) or 'to turn readers into spectators' (Nicolaus, *prog.* 68.12). Instead of leading readers and audiences into the consciousness of characters, the absorption effected by *enargeia* makes them witnesses of actions. Take, for example, the first definition of *enargeia* found in ancient literature, by Dionysius, who commends Lysias for his vividness (Lys. 7):

> ἔχει δὲ καὶ τὴν ἐνάργειαν πολλὴν ἡ Λυσίου λέξις. αὕτη δ᾽ ἐστὶ δύναμίς τις ὑπὸ τὰς αἰσθήσεις ἄγουσα τὰ λεγόμενα, γίγνεται δ᾽ ἐκ τῆς τῶν παρακολουθούντων λήψεως. ὁ δὴ προσέχων τὴν διάνοιαν τοῖς Λυσίου λόγοις οὐχ οὕτως ἔσται σκαιὸς ἢ δυσάρεστος ἢ βραδὺς τὸν νοῦν, ὃς οὐχ ὑπολήψεται γινόμενα τὰ δηλούμενα ὁρᾶν καὶ ὥσπερ παροῦσιν οἷς ἂν ὁ ῥήτωρ εἰσάγῃ προσώποις ὁμιλεῖν.

---

[59] This point is ignored by Fludernik 2015: 232 when she adduces the scene as 'a wonderful example of collective mind well before the Renaissance' that provides evidence against my argument. I am however far from denying the existence of fictional minds, whether individual or collective, as Fludernik's response insinuates – what I contend is that it is not the engagement with minds but the dynamics of plot that chiefly captures the reader.

[60] See also Morgan 2018: 649, who concludes his analysis of minor characters in books 7 and 8 by noting that 'Heliodorus' characterization has more to do with character types, both of persons and of ethnicities, than with individuated psychologies'.

Vividness is a quality which the style of Lysias has in abundance. It is a certain power of conveying what he describes to the senses. It arises out of his grasp of circumstantial detail. Nobody who applies his mind to the speeches of Lysias will be so obtuse, insensitive or slow-witted that he will not feel he can see the action described going on and meet the characters, introduced by the orator, as if they were present.

After mentioning the action on which Lysias knows to bestow presence, Dionysius also refers to characters – but as people we are made to meet in our imagination, not as people whose mind we are allowed to enter. To give another example, Plutarch praises Xenophon for his account of the battle of Cunaxa in the Anabasis (*Art.* 8.1):

Ξενοφῶντος δὲ μονονουχὶ δεικνύοντος ὄψει καὶ τοῖς πράγμασιν ὡς οὐ γεγενημένοις, ἀλλὰ γινομένοις ἐφιστάντος ἀεὶ τὸν ἀκροατὴν ἐμπαθῆ καὶ συγκινδυνεύοντα διὰ τὴν ἐνάργειαν.

Xenophon brings it all but before the eyes and through his vividness all the time places the reader, much affected and sharing in the dangers, near to the action, as if it had not been concluded, but is going on.

Here and in many other references in ancient authors, *enargeia* signifies the presence of an action, not access to the minds of characters. The experiential dimension of narrative, which was of great concern to ancient authors and readers, is a matter not so much of introspection as of action.

A small but pertinent formal observation reinforces my point – the use of free indirect discourse: 'He would return home, marry his beloved and show them what he had achieved.' On the one hand, person and tense conform to the template of indirect speech: 'He said that he would return home, marry his beloved and show them what he had achieved.' On the other hand, the verb of saying or thinking to which the statement is subordinated in indirect speech is missing – therefore the indirect discourse is free. Free indirect discourse is a powerful means of consciousness presentation in the modern novel; we find it in the works of modern authors such as Gustave Flaubert, Jane Austen and Henry James, but also in the novels of Jonathan Franzen, Ulrich Peltzer and other contemporary writers: 'It is actually difficult to find novelists, past or present, respected or otherwise, who do *not* write sentences in this mode, and who do not seem to be writing them most of the time. It is a technique that has been seen to constitute the essence not only of the novel but of literariness itself.'[61]

---

[61] Laird 2008: 202.

In the *Ethiopica*, however, there is no free indirect discourse. What is more, free indirect discourse is nearly completely missing in the ancient novel and rare in ancient narrative in general.[62] There are of course other means of rendering internal reflection, notably direct thought representation and thought report, and yet the absence of free indirect discourse which blends the character's subjectivity and language with the narrator's voice is emblematic of the minor role that the presentation of consciousness plays in the *Ethiopica* and other ancient narratives.

While challenging the claims of Palmer, Zunshine and others, the examples just discussed suggest another model for narrative, a model that has not consciousness but time at its core. Suspense and curiosity have emerged to be more prominent than character portrayal. They form two of the three master tropes that constitute narrative according to Meir Sternberg: 'I define *narrativity* as the play of suspense/curiosity/surprise between represented and communicative time (in whatever combination, whatever medium, whatever manifest or latent form).'[63] As this definition indicates, the relation between represented or narrated time and communicative or narrative time is the crux of Sternberg's model. The narrative itself is a temporal sequence that represents the unfolding of events in the narrated time. However, narrative time need not, and in fact often does not, simply mimic narrated time. As Sternberg shows, the reconfiguration of narrated time in narrative time engenders suspense, curiosity and surprise, thereby shaping our response.

Elsewhere, I linked Sternberg's definition of narrativity to Ricoeur's understanding of narrative as a mode of coming to grips with time.[64] Against Ricoeur's idea of a triple mimesis and the interweaving of factual and fictional elements, I suggested that it is the interplay of narrated time with narrative time which reconfigures time and allows the recipient to engage with time. The reader is subjected to the same temporal structure as in the everyday world, albeit without pragmatic constraints. The orchestration of time which Sternberg views as the hallmark of narrative encapsulates a reflection on time, of course not an explicit meditation, but, more profoundly, a playful enactment of our temporality in the frame of 'as-if'. Given the *Ethiopica*'s virtuoso play with suspense and curiosity, such an approach captures their dynamics

---

[62] Compare Laird 2008: 201–3 on the absence of free indirect discourse from the ancient novel. See also Bakker 2009: 121–2; Beck 2012: 9–10; 57–78 argues that there is free indirect discourse in Homer, but she considers free indirect speech any clause that is not directly subordinated to a verb of speaking – consequently, free indirect speech does not stand between direct and indirect speech, but between narrator text and indirect speech. Beck 2009: 139–40 acknowledges that what she considers free indirect speech in Homer differs from free indirect speech in the novel in that it mainly represents speech, not thought. On free indirect discourse in Latin epic, see Auhagen 1998.

[63] Sternberg 1992b: 529.   [64] Grethlein 2010; 2017b: 53–9.

much better than theories homing in on consciousness presentation. While the first half of the novel has the reader try to grasp the prehistory, the second half sends them on a roller coaster of suspense. Both make them experience the force of time in the safe framework of 'as-if'.

Surprise, Sternberg's third master trope, also comes into play in the *Ethiopica* as the following example illustrates. In the village of Thyamis and his brigands, Theagenes and Charicleia meet a young Athenian, Cnemon, who tells them of his adventures. Roughly summarized, Cnemon is the victim of his stepmother Demainete, whose love he rejected. Out of revenge and with the aid of a servant named Thisbe, Demainete schemed against Cnemon, who was then driven into exile and, once in Egypt, fell into the hands of the brigands. When the village of the brigands is attacked, Thyamis hides Charicleia in a cave. Sensing that the battle is lost, he rushes back to the cave to kill her so she will not fall into the hands of his enemies. After the raid, Theagenes and Cnemon enter the cave in order to fetch Charicleia. Finding a corpse, Theagenes breaks out in an excessive lament. It turns out, however, that Charicleia is alive – the corpse is Thisbe's!

Heliodorus gives a detailed description of Theagenes' mourning that is partly rendered in direct speech. And yet the report does not aim at rousing the reader's empathy through the piercing description of an individual's feelings. Brimming with rhetorical commonplaces, the lament rather prepares the surprise which Heliodorus springs on both characters and readers when they learn that the corpse is Thisbe's. Charicleia wonders: 'How can someone ... suddenly be spirited away by a sort of theatrical special effect, out of the heart of Greece to the remotest parts of Egypt?' (πῶς ἦν εἰκός ... τὴν ἐκ μέσης τῆς Ἑλλάδος ἐπ᾽ ἐσχάτοις γῆς Αἰγύπτου καθάπερ ἐκ μηχανῆς ἀναπεμφθῆναι, 2.8.3). In the words of a modern critic: 'As if by magic, Thisbe emerges from the pre-history and unexpectedly turns out to be directly involved in the main action.'[65] Familiar with the conventions of the novel, the reader may expect that the corpse is not Charicleia, but nothing steers them to suspect that it is Thisbe. Only now are they informed how Thisbe also had to leave Athens and finally came to Egypt. Note that the reader's response does not hinge on an engagement with the minds of the characters but is triggered by the action itself. Their surprise does not require that they access the story through Theagenes' 'embedded/ cognitive narrative' – it is caused by the appearance of Thisbe herself.

In addition to drawing on Ricoeur in order to grasp the existential dimension of narrative time, I think Sternberg's theory needs to be modified in one

---

[65] Pinheiro 1998: 3157.

important respect. Surprise, it seems, is not really equivalent to curiosity and suspense. While the latter two describe a durative expectation, surprise is a momentary feeling.[66] Strangely, the master strategy which Sternberg treats first and to which he devotes most attention is less important for the reading process than the others. It is easy though to see why surprise has this prominent place in his system. Sternberg starts from Aristotle and finds in surprise the only element in the *Poetics* that works well for his approach focusing on the tension between narrative and narrated time. It is the Aristotelian heritage that prompts Sternberg to overrate the significance of surprise.

Sternberg's definition of curiosity as retrospection and of suspense as prospection also needs qualification. It makes good sense to distinguish the desire to learn something about the past from expectations about the future, but it is important to note that these temporal directions only operate on the level of narrated time. Narrated time, however, is mediated by narrative time, which only moves forward. Thus, not only in suspense, but also in curiosity, which is levelled at the past of narrated time, is attention directed at the future of narrative time. While in suspense the prospection towards the futures of narrative and narrated time converges, curiosity embeds the retrospective turn to the past of narrated time in the prospective movement of reading. As important as the refraction of narrated time in narrative time is, it is based on the simple sequence of signs.

To avoid misunderstanding, I am far from claiming that the *Ethiopica* lacks the presentation of consciousness. There are 'fictional minds' in Heliodorus, and yet it is clearly not the engagement with them that drives the reading process. Heliodorus speaks loudly against the view that the Theory of Mind is 'the fundamental and principal way by which we understand narrative'[67] and the anthropological reason for our infatuation with narrative. He alerts us to the significance of time for narrative, an aspect that has been given ample attention in the Neo-Aristotelian and phenomenological traditions[68] but gets short thrift from cognitive scholars obsessed with the Theory of Mind.[69] Not mind reading but the temporal dynamics of the plot entice the reader of the *Ethiopica*. Suspense, curiosity and, to a lesser degree, surprise let them engage with time.

---

[66] Compare Baroni 2007: 297. Baroni also doubts that surprise ought to be analysed as a gap in the plot (299 with n. 1).

[67] Palmer 2010: 17.

[68] Besides the work of Sternberg, esp. 1978; 1992, see also Baroni 2007; 2009.

[69] Palmer 2004: 212–14 has some interesting remarks on the 'thought–action continuum', but the few pages he devotes to it highlight that his interest lies with fictional minds.

4   Reflections on Narrative and Time in the *Ethiopica*

The *Ethiopica* itself reflects the significance of the narrative reconfiguration of time for captivating readers. Winkler's seminal paper on 'The mendacity of Kalasiris and the narrative strategy of Heliodorus' "Aithiopika"' has drawn our attention to the novel's strong self-referential dimension.[70] The long embedded narrative in which Calasiris reveals the prehistory to Cnemon in particular can be read as a nuanced reflection on narrative and its reception. Winkler argued that the *Ethiopica*'s self-referentiality throws into relief its narrative complexity and the need for a sophisticated reader. In this section, I wish to show that the temporal dimension of narrative looms large in the *Ethiopica*'s implicit reflections, corroborating my argument for their orientation towards plot.

In his extended narration, Calasiris reproduces the report of the priest of Apollo Charicles at Delphi on how he received Charicleia. An Ethiopian ambassador asked him to take care of the child. The ambassador had to leave before he could inform him about the origin and identity of the child but promised to do so the next day. However, he did not show up for this meeting (2.32.3):

"Υπέστρεφον ἀνιαρῶς ἄγαν διατεθεὶς καὶ ὥσπερ οἱ βαρεῖάν τινα πληγὴν εἰληφότες ὅτι δή μοι γνῶναι μὴ ἐξεγένετο τὰ κατὰ τὴν κόρην τίς ἢ πόθεν ἢ τίνων." "Μὴ θαυμάσῃς" εἶπεν ὁ Κνήμων· "ἀσχάλλω γὰρ καὶ αὐτὸς οὐκ ἀκούσας, ἀλλ᾿ ἴσως ἀκούσομαι." "Ἀκούσῃ" ἔφη ὁ Καλάσιρις.

'I trudged home with heavy heart, stunned and like those who have received a heavy blow, because I had not had the chance to hear all about the girl – who she was, where she came from, who her parents were.' 'It is not surprising,' said Cnemon. 'I am dismayed myself not to have heard. But perhaps I shall.' 'Indeed you will,' said Calasiris.

Cnemon's response resembles the disappointment Charicles himself felt and simultaneously prefigures that of Heliodorus' reader. The embedded audience, namely Cnemon, signals the alignment of reader with character: our curiosity is piqued like that of Charicles. Charicles, Cnemon and we alike puzzle over Charicleia. Cnemon's response thus reflects the dynamic of curiosity that draws the attention of the reader to the prehistory of the plot.[71]

---

[70] Winkler 1999.

[71] In emphasizing the curiosity about who Charicleia is, the embedded reflection on our response is a powerful warning against Fludernik's claim that readers simply immerse themselves in Charicleia and Theagenes (2015: 290). See n. 49 above.

At the same time, the brief dialogue intimates the rift between real life and reading experiences. While Charicles cannot know whether or not he will learn of Charicleia's origin at some point, Calasiris assures Cnemon and us that our curiosity will be satisfied. Calasiris' reply 'indeed you will' (ἀκούσῃ) highlights the fundamental gap that separates characters from readers. In real life, the future is open and contingent. The universe of narratives, on the other hand, is closed. Narrative economy tends to avoid information that is unnecessary. Calasiris' assurance makes explicit the reader's expectation that questions raised will be answered.

Like curiosity, suspense and its spell on the reader of the *Ethiopica* are reflected in the response of internal audiences, for example in Calasiris' account of a foot race at Delphi in which Theagenes challenges a prize-winning athlete (4.3.2–4):

> "Ἐκεκίνητο μὲν δὴ καὶ πᾶσα πρὸς τὸ παράδοξον ἡ Ἑλλὰς καὶ Θεαγένει νίκην
> ηὔχετο καθάπερ αὐτός τις ἕκαστος ἀγωνιζόμενος, ἐπακτικὸν γάρ τι καὶ
> πρῶτον ὁρώντων εἰς εὔνοιαν τὸ κάλλος· ἐκεκίνητο δὲ ἡ Χαρίκλεια πρὸς
> πᾶσαν ὑπερβολὴν καὶ εἶδον ἐκ πολλοῦ παρατηρῶν παντοίας μεταβαλλομένην
> ἰδέας. Ὡς γὰρ εἰς ἀκοὴν πάντων ὁ κῆρυξ τοὺς δραμουμένους κατήγγειλεν
> ἀνεῖπέ τε "Ὅρμενος Ἀρκὰς καὶ Θεαγένης Θετταλός', ἔσχαστο μὲν ἡ
> ὕσπληξ τέτατο δὲ ὁ δρόμος μικροῦ καὶ τὴν τῶν ὀφθαλμῶν κατάληψιν
> ὑποτέμνων· ἐνταῦθα οὔτε ἀτρεμεῖν ἔτι κατεῖχεν ἡ κόρη ἀλλ' ἐσφάδαζεν ἡ
> βάσις καὶ οἱ πόδες ἔσκαιρον ὥσπερ, οἶμαι, τῆς ψυχῆς τῷ Θεαγένει
> συνεξαιρομένης καὶ τὸν δρόμον συμπροθυμουμένης. Οἱ μὲν δὴ θεαταὶ
> μετέωρος ἅπας ἐπὶ τὸ μέλλον καὶ ἀγωνίας ἀνάμεστος, ἐγὼ δὲ καὶ πλέον ἅτε
> μοι λοιπὸν ὡς παιδὸς ὑπερφροντίζειν προῃρημένον." "Οὐδὲν θαυμαστὸν" ἔφη
> ὁ Κνήμων "ὁρῶντας καὶ παρόντας ἀγωνιᾶν, ὅτε κἀγὼ νυνὶ περὶ τῷ Θεαγένει
> δέδια καί σου δέομαι θᾶττον εἰ νικῶν ἀνηγορεύθη διελθεῖν."

'The whole of Greece thrilled with emotion at this dramatic turn of events and prayed for Theagenes to win as fervently as if each man were himself competing; for nothing wins the sympathy of beholders like beauty. Charicleia's emotion passed all bounds; I had been observing her carefully for some while and I saw every conceivable expression pass in succession over her face. The herald proclaimed the names of those entered for the race for all to hear, "Ormenos of Arcadia and Theagenes of Thessaly". The starting gate opened, and they were off, running at such a speed that the eye could barely keep pace. Now the maiden could not stay still; her feet began to skip and dance, as if, in my estimation, her soul were flying together with Theagenes and sharing his passion for the race. The viewers were all buoyed up, anticipating the outcome, and full of anxiety; I myself even more so, now that I had decided to care for Theagenes in the future as for a son.' 'It is not surprising,' said Cnemon, 'that those who were there watching were anxious. Even now I fear for Theagenes and beg you to make haste and tell me whether he was proclaimed victor.'

The passage nests multiple audiences into each other: we read about Cnemon listening to an account of the crowd witnessing the scene. The concentric circles of reception bridge the gap between reader and action, drawing them close to the foot race. Cnemon prefigures the reader in the framing narrative. Through his ears, the reader follows Calasiris' account that puts internal and external audience into the shoes of the spectators present. The immersion of the spectators is explicitly stressed and subtly underlined by the repeated use of the stem *agōn-* (ἀγωνιζόμενος, ἀγωνίας, ἀγωνιᾶν) which is poetologically charged. Ancient critics refer to the involvement of the reader as *agōnia*.[72] Demetrius' *de elocutione*, a treatise on the four styles from the Imperial era, for example, elaborates on suspense as constituting *enargeia*: 'One should not say right away what has happened, but unfold it gradually, thus keeping the reader in suspense (lit. "hanging up") and forcing him to share the anxiety' (δεῖ τὰ γενόμενα οὐκ εὐθὺς λέγειν, ὅτι ἐγένετο, ἀλλὰ κατὰ μικρόν, κρεμῶντα τὸν ἀκροατὴν καὶ ἀναγκάζοντα συναγωνιᾶν, 216). Heliodorus adopts this critical usage and grafts it onto a literal *agōn*. Using words of the same stem for the race and the beholders' response highlights their absorption in the scene. Cnemon's comment drives home that the listener is as affected as the viewers and makes explicit the workings of suspense which immerse the reader in the story.

The detailed account of the audience in the stadium illustrates the possibility of a variety of responses. All cheer for Theagenes, but for distinct reasons and with different intensity. The crowd is allured by his beauty; Calasiris' feelings are even stronger due to his care for the runner; the involvement of Charicleia, who is in love with Theagenes, is the most intense. The double use of compound verbs with the prefix *sun-* linguistically expresses her bond with Theagenes (συνεξαιρομένης, συμπροθυμουμένης). Charicleia's immersion in his current situation goes so far that she starts moving her feet and thereby mimics his running. The graded response of the internal audience underscores the impact of identification on suspense. And yet the different intensities notwithstanding, the entire audience is kept on their toes. Suspense is intensified by identification but does not hinge on it.[73]

The interaction of external and internal responses again merits our attention. When Cnemon begs Calasiris to hurry with his recital, he is fully absorbed by the story. The reader, however, who is equally eager to

---

[72] In addition to Dem. *de eloc.* 216 quoted above, see for example Ps.-Plut. *Hom.* 6 and scholion bT *Il.* 7.479: 'The poet rouses the reader beforehand and makes him feel anxious (ἀγωνιᾶν) in view of the future events' (προκινεῖ καὶ ἀγωνιᾶν ποιεῖ τὸν ἀκροατὴν ἐπὶ τοῖς ἐσομένοις ὁ ποιητής). Cf. Nannini 1986: 41–9.

[73] Compare Baroni 2007: 271–8.

learn the outcome of the race, is forcefully reminded of the narratorial mediation: they are not witnessing the foot race but attending to an account embedded in a narrative. Thus, instead of prefiguring the reader's response, Cnemon's absorption makes the reader reflect on the mediation. In another way, though, Cnemon's interruption may contribute to the spell the text casts on the reader. The retardation heightens suspense and thereby helps to bind the reader into the story. Here as in other cases, the responses of internal and external audiences do not fully map onto one another but chafe against each other in multiple ways.

Reflections on narrative suspense are by no means confined to Calasiris' report. They can also be found for instance in Cnemon's narration of how he came to Egypt (1.14.1–2):

> "Κἀγὼ μὲν οὕτως ἐξηλαυνόμην ἑστίας τε πατρῴας καὶ τῆς ἐνεγκούσης· οὐ μὴν ἀτιμώρητός γε ἡ θεοῖς ἐχθρὰ Δημαινέτη περιελείφθη. Τὸν δὲ τρόπον εἰσαῦθις ἀκούσεσθε, τὸ δὲ νῦν καὶ ὕπνου μεταληπτέον, τό τε γὰρ πολὺ προέβη τῆς νυκτὸς καὶ ὑμῖν πολλῆς δεῖτῆς ἀναπαύσεως." "Καὶ μὴν προσεπιτρίψεις γε ἡμᾶς" ἔφη ὁ Θεαγένης "εἰ τὴν κακίστην ἀτιμώρητον ἐάσεις ἐν τῷ λόγῳ Δημαινέτην."

'Thus I was banished from my family home and the land of my birth; but Demainete, enemy to the gods, was not left unpunished. The mode of her punishment you will hear, but now it is time for sleep, for we are far into the night and you badly need rest.' 'But you only afflict us further,' said Theagenes, 'if you will leave the wicked Demainete unpunished in your story.'

The force of narrative suspense is so strong that Theagenes presses Cnemon to go on despite the hour and unflinchingly sacrifices his sleep. The phrase 'if you will leave the wicked Demainete unpunished in your story' (εἰ τὴν κακίστην ἀτιμώρητον ἐάσεις ἐν τῷ λόγῳ Δημαινέτην) is metaleptic in that it suggests a direct interaction between narrator and character.[74] The erasure of the boundary between the act of narrating and the world of the narrative underscores the immersive capacity of the story.

This passage is of special interest as it foregrounds the kind of suspense that is most prominent in the *Ethiopica*. Theagenes and Charicleia are informed that Demainete will be punished and have to wait to learn about the 'mode of her punishment' (τρόπον). Theagenes' feeling of suspense as to how Demainete will find her deserved end not only prefigures the reader's response at this particular juncture but also mirrors the narrative

---

[74] On metalepsis, see 75–80; 156–61.

dynamics of the *Ethiopica* at large. The strong generic conventions of the novel minimize room for suspense as to what will happen. Instead, the suspense triggered by Heliodorus concentrates rather on how the known end will be realized. What Baroni calls 'suspense moyen' is dominant in the *Ethiopica*.[75]

Theagenes' desire to see Demainete punished also draws our attention to another point: the character of an expected *telos* can help heighten suspense. Here, the end of Demainete is phrased in moral terms. Being ethically charged, the *telos* gains in momentum and enriches the suspense the audience is feeling. This applies to the *Ethiopica* at large: the purity of Charicleia and Theagenes and the depravity of their opponents endow the plot with a strong ethical dimension and heighten the reader's investment. The expectation of the *telos* is reinforced by its moral desirability. The two foci of ancient views of narrative spotlighted in Chapter 2 are combined – it is a morally laden plot that enthrals the reader.

As these passages illustrate, the reflexivity of the *Ethiopica* supports the salience of the interplay between narrative time and narrated time for which I have argued. While not directly prefiguring the response of the *Ethiopica*'s readers, the reactions of Cnemon and other internal audiences illustrate the process of reception. Not mind reading but the temporal dynamics of plot emerge as its foundation. Suspense and curiosity are pivotal to the characters' experience of being immersed in the embedded stories and to the reader's absorption into the plot of the *Ethiopica*.

5 Plot and Character in Aristotle's *Poetics* and Ancient Criticism

By no means can Aristotle's *Poetics* lay claim to special authority as a framework for the analysis of Greek tragedy or ancient narrative more generally. Had we only the *Poetics* and no tragedies, we would for example have no idea of the role of the gods in the plays of Aeschylus, Sophocles and Euripides. That said, the *Poetics*, despite its textual form of what could be a lecture script, is an inquiry not only driven by a strong systematic agenda but also premised on many astute observations. For the argument of this chapter, it is noteworthy what Aristotle has to say about plot and character.[76] He lists them as two of six elements of tragedy, the others

---

[75] Baroni 2007: 269–78.
[76] Jones 1962 remains an important study that duly criticizes Romantic interpretations of the *Poetics* which focus on the idea of a tragic hero and instead rightly emphasizes that for Aristotle, tragedy is

being style (λέξις), thought (διάνοια), spectacle (ὄψις) and lyric poetry (μελοποιία). There is a clear hierarchy of these elements headed by plot (1450a15–23):

μέγιστον δὲ τούτων ἐστὶν ἡ τῶν πραγμάτων σύστασις. ἡ γὰρ τραγῳδία μίμησίς ἐστιν οὐκ ἀνθρώπων ἀλλὰ πράξεων καὶ βίου ... οὔκουν ὅπως τὰ ἤθη μιμήσωνται πράττουσιν, ἀλλὰ τὰ ἤθη συμπεριλαμβάνουσιν διὰ τὰς πράξεις· ὥστε τὰ πράγματα καὶ ὁ μῦθος τέλος τῆς τραγῳδίας, τὸ δὲ τέλος μέγιστον ἁπάντων.

The most important of these elements is the structure of events, because tragedy is a representation not of people as such but of actions and life ... It is not, therefore, the function of the agents' actions to allow the portrayal of their characters; it is, rather, for the sake of their actions that characterization is included. So, the events and the plot-structure are the goal of tragedy, and the goal is what matters most of all.

Aristotle adds a string of arguments as evidence for the priority of plot over character (1450a23–38): whereas tragedy without character is feasible, it needs to have action. Tragedies' greatest means of emotional power are elements of *mythos*, namely, reversals and recognitions. Style and character are easier to master than plot construction (1450a38–1450b4):

ἀρχὴ μὲν οὖν καὶ οἷον ψυχὴ ὁ μῦθος τῆς τραγῳδίας, δεύτερον δὲ τὰ ἤθη (παραπλήσιον γάρ ἐστιν καὶ ἐπὶ τῆς γραφικῆς· εἰ γάρ τις ἐναλείψειε τοῖς καλλίστοι φαρμάκοις χύδην, οὐκ ἂν ὁμοίως εὐφράνειεν καὶ λευκογραφήσας εἰκόνα)· ἔστιν τε μίμησις πράξεως καὶ διὰ ταύτην μάλιστα τῶν πραττόντων.

And so, the plot-structure is the first principle and, so to speak, the soul of tragedy, while characterization is the element of second importance (an analogous point holds for painting: a random distribution of the most attractive colours would never yield as much pleasure as a definite image without colour). Tragedy is a mimesis of action, and only for the sake of this is it mimesis of the agents themselves.

Now Aristotle discusses primarily tragedy and, to a lesser extent, epic in the *Poetics*, as we have it – a choice that itself reflects his predilection for the mimesis of action, which is less prominent in lyric poetry. Nonetheless, his emphasis on plot as the primary element of tragedy also works well for other ancient narrative genres including the novel. As I have argued above (§4), what enthrals the reader of the *Ethiopica* is not the rich interior lives of

a mimesis not of characters but of actions. See also Lloyd-Jones 1982: 111–15; Halliwell 1986: 164–5; Heath 1987: 115–23.

the characters, but the dynamics of the plot. Instead of being arrested by extensive accounts of their thoughts, hopes and desires or instead of investing most of our energy in deducing these consciousness processes from sparse hints in the text, we are enticed by curiosity and suspense, trying to grasp the prehistory and to fathom how the action will arrive at the expected *telos*.

The *Poetics* not only makes explicit the view of narrative that the *Ethiopica* implicitly reflects; it can also help us identify the reasons for this privileging of plot over character. After devoting chapters 7 to 14 to the analysis of plot, Aristotle comes to *ethos*. In chapter 15, he elaborates on the definition of character in primarily ethical terms from chapter 6: the most important goal of characterization is 'that the characters be good. Characterization will arise, as earlier explained, where speech or action exhibits the nature of an ethical choice; and the character will be good when the choice is good.' (ὅπως χρηστὰ ᾖ. ἕξει δὲ ἦθος μὲν ἐὰν ὥσπερ ἐλέχθη ποιῇ φανερὸν ὁ λόγος ἢ ἡ πρᾶξις προαίρεσίν τινα <ἥ τις ἂν> ᾖ, χρηστὸν δὲ ἐὰν χρηστήν, 1454a16–19). Appropriateness, likeness and consistency are added as further criteria of characterization (1454a22–6).

For Aristotle, *ethos* is not about the uniqueness of a person that comes to our mind when we think about intriguing characters in modern novels; instead, it focuses on ethical qualities, being fully in tune with Gill's notion of character and an objectivist-participant conception of person: characters are seen from a third-person standpoint chiefly in their social relations. As Aristotle puts it, the ethical quality of characters is defined by their choices – ethics is thus closely tied to action.[77] If character reveals itself chiefly through ethically meaningful action, then plot has particular significance. It is through plot design that an author can show the quality of his characters. Far from revealing a disinterest in character, Aristotle's emphasis on plot is premised on an understanding of character that, instead of homing in on their distinct interior qualities, is formed through how they choose to act.[78]

Both the importance of plot and the ethical focus on character are also tangible in a treatise that, like the *Ethiopica*, belongs to the world of Imperial *pepaideumenoi*. In Chapters 2 and 3, I have already had recourse to Plutarch's *de audiendis poetis*, the attempt of a Platonist, who shares

---

[77] In modern theory, Aristotle's focus on characters as doers is taken up by Propp 1968: 25–65; Lotman 1977: 352–4. See, however, also Forster 1993 (1927), who, right before giving his famous definition of plot, notes that Aristotle's approach to the character falls short of the modern novel (58): 'We have already decided that Aristotle is wrong.'

[78] Halliwell 1987: 94 notes that Aristotle's ethical concept of character jars with modern approaches.

Plato's anxiety about the effects of poetry, to show that it should neverthe-less have a place in the educational curriculum. One of the things that renders *de audiendis poetis* still thought-provoking is its focus on the reader and their activity.[79] In an intriguing comparison, Plutarch distinguishes three different kinds of reader: 'Now just as in pasturage the bee seeks the flower, the goat the tender shoot, the swine the root, and other animals the seed and the fruit, so in the reading of poetry one person culls the flowers of the story, another rivets his attention upon the beauty of the diction and the arrangement of the words' (Ἐπεὶ δ' ὥσπερ ἐν ταῖς νομαῖς ἡ μὲν μέλιττα διώκει τὸ ἄνθος, ἡ δ' αἲξ τὸν θαλλόν, ἡ δ' ὗς τὴν ῥίζαν, ἄλλα δὲ ζῷα τὸ σπέρμα καὶ τὸν καρπόν, οὕτως ἐν ταῖς ἀναγνώσεσι τῶν ποιημάτων ὁ μὲν ἀπανθίζεται τὴν ἱστορίαν, ὁ δ' ἐμφύεται τῷ κάλλει καὶ τῇ κατασκευῇ τῶν ὀνομάτων, 30 c–d).

Plutarch is most interested in a third kind of reader (30d–e):

> οἳ δὲ τῶν πρὸς τὸ ἦθος εἰρημένων ὠφελίμως ἔχονται, πρὸς οὓς δὴ νῦν ἡμῖν ὁ λόγος ἐστίν, ὑπομιμνήσκωμεν αὐτοὺς ὅτι δεινόν ἐστι τὸν μὲν φιλόμυθον μὴ λανθάνειν τὰ καινῶς ἱστορούμενα καὶ περιττῶς, μηδὲ τὸν φιλόλογον ἐκφεύγειν τὰ καθαρῶς πεφρασμένα καὶ ῥητορικῶς, τὸν δὲ φιλότιμον καὶ φιλόκαλον καὶ μὴ παιγνίας ἀλλὰ παιδείας ἕνεκα ποιημάτων ἁπτόμενον ἀργῶς καὶ ἀμελῶς ἀκούειν τῶν πρὸς ἀνδρείαν ἢ σωφροσύνην ἢ δικαιοσύνην ἀναπεφωνημένων.

> but as for those who are concerned with what is said as being useful for character (and it is to these that our present discourse is directed), let us remind them how strange it is if the lover of fables does not fail to observe the novel and unusual points in the story, and the lover of language does not allow faultless and elegant forms of expression to escape him, whereas the lover of the honourable and good, who takes up poetry not for amusement but for education, should give but a slack and careless hearing to utterances that look toward manliness or sobriety or uprightness.

A quotation from the *Iliad*, Agamemnon's appeal to Diomedes to fight bravely, illustrates the kind of utterances that Plutarch has in mind.

Unlike Aristotle in the *Poetics*, Plutarch places a premium on character, and yet his focus on character is, despite the different intellectual back-grounds and poetological agendas, in line with Aristotle's concept of character. Both concentrate on the moral dimension of character, not on individuality; both view choice and action as the chief modalities by which it can be apprehended, not introspection. Plot is crucial for the kind of character presentation of which Plutarch thinks, as an exemplary character

---

[79] Compare Konstan 2004; Grethlein 2021: 137–65.

is defined by their actions. When Plutarch juxtaposes his 'lover of the honourable and good' (φιλόκαλος καὶ φιλότιμος) with a 'lover of fables' (φιλόμυθος), he does not go against plot, only against a focus on formal features that fails to consider the content and its ethical dimension.

In fact, at the beginning of *de audiendis poetis*, Plutarch acknowledges the salience of plot (16b–c):

> οὔτε γὰρ μέτρον οὔτε τρόπος οὔτε λέξεως ὄγκος οὔτ' εὐκαιρία μεταφορᾶς οὔθ' ἁρμονία καὶ σύνθεσις ἔχει τοσοῦτον αἱμυλίας καὶ χάριτος ὅσον εὖ πεπλεγμένη διάθεσις μυθολογίας· ἀλλ' ὥσπερ ἐν γραφαῖς κινητικώτερόν ἐστι χρῶμα γραμμῆς διὰ τὸ ἀνδρείκελον καὶ ἀπατηλόν, οὕτως ἐν ποιήμασι μεμιγμένον πιθανότητι ψεῦδος ἐκπλήττει καὶ ἀγαπᾶται μᾶλλον τῆς ἀμύθου καὶ ἀπλάστου περὶ μέτρον καὶ λέξιν κατασκευῆς.

> For not metre nor figure of speech nor loftiness of diction nor aptness of metaphor nor harmonious composition has so much allurement and charm, as a clever interweaving of fabulous narrative. But, just as in pictures, colour is more stimulating than line-drawing because it is life-like, and creates an illusion, so in poetry falsehood combined with plausibility is more striking, and gives more satisfaction, than the work which is elaborate in metre and diction, but devoid of myth and fiction.

Here Plutarch is chiefly concerned with the 'falsehood' (ψεῦδος) of poetry – it is the first lesson young readers have to learn that the poets freely fabricate their stories – but the 'clever interweaving of fabulous narrative' (εὖ πεπλεγμένη διάθεσις μυθολογίας) also refers to the construction of plot, which is key to the effect of poetry. Plutarch uses the juxtaposition of outline and colour differently from Aristotle.[80] In the *Poetics*, the outline stands for the plot, colour for character; here, it is colour that illustrates the importance of fictional plots. And yet, Plutarch is in line with Aristotle when he emphasizes the strong effect of plot on readers.

The elements with which Plutarch compares the 'clever interweaving of fabulous narrative' (εὖ πεπλεγμένη διάθεσις μυθολογίας) indicate other approaches to poetry in ancient criticism. The euphonists, for example, put a premium on sound; one of them, Pausimachus, even seems to have gone so far as to sever sound from content. Pseudo-Longinus extolled the sublime as poetry's ultimate goal, which could be reached by various means. There was thus no consensus about the salience of plot among ancient critics. But Plutarch's view of plot and character in *de audiendis poetis* highlights the astuteness of Aristotle's observations about the key element of tragedy and, in extension, of ancient Greek narrative: plot is

---

[80] On the juxtaposition of colour and shade, see Hunter and Russell 2011 on 16b: 83–4.

crucial for a view of narrative that envisages characters less as distinct individuals than as moral agents. The salience of the moral dimension in narrative, which we encountered in Chapter 2, is an important reason for the prominence of plot discussed in this chapter. It is therefore not surprising that aspects of plot loom large in the questions discussed in the scholia.[81]

The exegetic scholia furnish the opportunity to compare ancient responses to specific passages with the interpretations advanced by modern scholars. Let me give an example which illustrates that ancient readers viewed narrative differently from modern scholars foregrounding the Theory of Mind – the arrival of Phoenix, Odysseus and Ajax at Achilles' tent from the embassy scene in *Iliad* 9 (9.185–91):

Μυρμιδόνων δ' ἐπί τε κλισίας καὶ νῆας ἱκέσθην,
τὸν δ' εὖρον φρένα τερπόμενον φόρμιγγι λιγείη
καλῆ δαιδαλέη, ἐπὶ δ' ἀργύρεον ζυγὸν ἦεν,
τὴν ἄρετ' ἐξ ἐνάρων πόλιν Ἠετίωνος ὀλέσσας·
τῆ ὅ γε θυμὸν ἔτερπεν, ἄειδε δ' ἄρα κλέα ἀνδρῶν.
Πάτροκλος δέ οἱ οἶος ἐναντίος ἦστο σιωπῆ,
δέγμενος Αἰακίδην ὁπότε λήξειεν ἀείδων.

Now they came beside the shelters and ships of the Myrmidons
And they found Achilleus delighting his heart in a lyre, clear-sounding,
Splendid and carefully wrought, with a bridge of silver upon it,
Which he won out of the spoils when he ruined Eetion's city.
With this he was pleasuring his heart, and singing of men's fame,
As Patroclus was sitting over against him, alone in silence,
Watching Aiacides and the time he would leave off singing.

In her interpretation, Ruth Scodel, one of the most prominent advocates of Theory of Mind in Classics, starts from the ambassadors' wish to persuade Achilles: 'Persuasion is an attempt to change another person's mental state, so the audience is primed to believe that the ambassadors will be trying to understand what Achilles is thinking and feeling and themselves to consider what Achilles may be thinking and feeling.'[82] She admits that it is hard to determine who perceives the details of the scene, the ambassadors or the narrator, but continues:

the ambassadors are the emotional centre . . . Since we have been led to care about his [i.e., Achilles'] state of mind at this point primarily as it affects the Achaeans, although we do not watch these actions *through* the ambassadors,

---

[81] Compare Nünlist 2009: 23–68.   [82] Scodel 2014b: 65.

we still watch *with* them, hoping that the warm reception Achilles gives them indicates that he will also be open to their mission.[83]

It is of course possible to read the scene like this and to adopt the perspective of the ambassadors. In the preceding lines not quoted by Scodel, Homer explicitly mentions their goal of persuading Achilles. However, the scholia reveal that the scene was read very differently in antiquity. The ancient commentators were interested chiefly in Achilles' musical activity, the origin of his lyre and his solitary companionship with Patroclus. Their strongest concern is the question of why Achilles the hero is singing. Different answers are given (T and bT 9.186): It is 'not inappropriate' (οὐκ ἀνοίκειος), because song offers encouragement; Achilles is young and 'a lover of the Muses' (φιλόμουσος); in the absence of his beloved, he spends his time well in singing; while not fighting, he still prepares his soul for the coming deeds; the topic of the great deeds of men is highly appropriate for the hero (for this see also AbT 9.189b). It is also deemed fitting that he did not bring the instrument from home but captured it during a siege (A 9.188a; b; c). Finally, Patroclus is explicitly mentioned because Automedon was there too or because 'the recital is sweet among friends' (ἡδεῖα γὰρ ἐπίδειξις ἡ ἐπὶ τῶν φίλων, A and bT 9.190a; b).

Some of these points are taken up and developed further by other ancient authors: Pseudo-Plutarch in *de musica* notes that the topic of *klea andrōn* is highly appropriate for Achilles and quotes the passage as an example of the right use of music – it shows that music has the power to appease anger (1145d–f), a point also made by Sextus (*math.* 6.10).[84] Dio refers to the passage as a proof that the gentle and kingly man is always concerned with virtue (2.30–1). There is no evidence in either scholia or other ancient texts for the framework of Scodel's reading, a reading of the scene through the lens of the ambassadors. Ancient readers were familiar with mind reading – the scholia also suggest that Achilles sings in order to signal his disregard for the Greeks (T and bT 9.186), but this is not the main focus of how they approached this scene. Instead of adopting the perspective of the ambassadors and wondering if Achilles, alone with Patroclus and absorbed in his singing, will accept their gifts, the ancient commentators concentrated on Achilles' character. Their concern is fully in line with what we find in the *Poetics*: what kind of behaviour is

---

[83] Scodel 2014b: 66.

[84] On Achilles' musical engagement in Pseudo-Plutarch's *de musica*, especially on its sources, see Raffa 2011.

appropriate for what kind of character? The assessment of *ethos* is far more prominent than mind reading.

It would not be difficult to list other passages that are alleged to engage readers through the Theory of Mind while being discussed along rather different lines in the scholia,[85] but this example may suffice to make my point: by no means are fictional minds absent from ancient narratives, and yet they played a far smaller role in enticing readers than modern novels lead scholars to expect today. The view of characters as moral agents rather than individual personalities privileged action over introspection.

I am far from claiming that the presentation of consciousness plays no role in the ancient novel. Investigating the presentation of interior processes in ancient narrative is a rewarding exercise. Much work indeed remains to be done from a diachronic perspective in order to explore the different presentations and articulations of fictional minds in the history of narrative.[86] It is a pity that the high-flying agenda proposed by Palmer in *Fictional Minds* for a second book on the topic has not materialized.[87] The monograph on fictional minds discussing both 'the Bible (books from both the Old and New Testament)' and 'classical narratives' as well as a wide array of modern narratives, as eloquently announced and advertised by Palmer over the course of five pages, would have been most welcome. And yet it is easily understandable why Palmer instead wrote another book which concentrates on such texts as *Middlemarch* and *Little Dorrit*. A serious engagement with premodern texts, but also with modern literature beyond his canon, makes it difficult to sustain the conviction that 'following characters' fictional mental functioning' is 'the fundamental and principal way by which we understand narrative'.[88]

In his response to my original intervention, Palmer, after generously subsuming classical literature under the label of *paralittérature*, admits that his theory of fictional minds is in fact based on a narrow canon of texts but invokes the broad reach of Zunshine, who is 'a distinguished specialist on the *eighteenth* century novel' and whose 'seminal book, *Why We Read Fiction*, contains discussions of *Beowulf*, *Don Quixote*, and *Clarissa*.[89] At the risk of appearing stubborn, I continue to assume that the eighteenth century does not qualify as premodern. As for references to texts that would

---

[85] See, for example, my criticism of the conclusion of Scodel 2008, an interpretation of Achilles' proposal to award Agamemnon a prize in *Il.* 23.889–97 with the help of Theory of Mind (2011: 484–5). Even before working on the theory of fictional minds, its excessive application to Homeric epic struck me as misguided.

[86] For first investigations, see the contributions to Herman 2011a.   [87] Palmer 2004: 240–4.

[88] Palmer 2010: 17.   [89] Palmer 2015: 286.

be traditionally considered premodern, I wish to add that Zunshine even brings up the *Ethiopica*, naming it as her example for a premodern text that features, among other narrative devices, 'stream of consciousness'.[90]

6   The Entwinement of Narrative Time with Character: Experience

The *Ethiopica* and other ancient narratives revolt against the concept of narrative as a 'description of fictional mental functioning'. The reconfiguration of time is more salient than the presentation of consciousness in these and other narratives. By no means though do I wish to play off time against character. Both are important components of narrative; what is more, they are closely entwined with each other. In a final step, I will touch on this entwinement and suggest that experience is a more fruitful category for cognitive or phenomenological approaches to narrative than fictional minds.

To start with, modern consciousness novels go beyond a pure 'description of fictional mental functioning'[91]. They show the workings of narrative minds as part of a temporal sequence. Thoughts, feelings and conjectures figure in a plot, weak as it may be. While putting much emphasis on mind activities, modern novels embed the portrayal of the inner lives of characters in narrated time. Even experimental works that aspire to mimic spatial form are still bound to the sequential form of narrative.[92] On the other hand, action without introspection is in danger of being anaemic. Narratives that avoid revealing the inner lives of characters have the reader infer their feelings and motives. In reading such stories as Hemingway's *The Killers*, we constantly make conjectures about the minds of the characters.

The duplication of time which Sternberg's definition of narrativity zeroes in on comes in tandem with a duplication of consciousness. Just as the sequence of reading is grafted onto the sequence of the action, the consciousness of the reader parallels the consciousness of the characters. While the notion of mind is directed only at the duplication of consciousness, the concept of experience is able to conceptualize the twofold duplication – the doubling of time as well as that of consciousness. Let me first point out my understanding of experience and then show how it lends itself to describing the reading process as well as the unfolding of the plot. My concept of experience deviates significantly from the one Fludernik has

---

[90] Zunshine 2006: 41. She returns to the *Ethiopica* as an ancient example of what she considers a triangulation of minds in Zunshine 2011.

[91] Palmer 2004: 12.

[92] The classical treatment of spatial narrative is Frank 1945, republished with more material in 1991.

made popular in narrative studies.[93] For Fludernik, experience can be 'quite uneventful' and centre on 'mental situations'.[94] Opposing experientiality to the idea of plot, she states with refreshing frankness: 'In my view narrative thus properly comes into its own in the twentieth century when the rise of the consciousness novel starts to foreground fictional consciousness.'[95] The historical perspective makes Fludernik's 'natural narratology' superior to general claims about narrative and fictional minds, but her approach fails to exploit the conceptual capacity of experience.

A look at Continental philosophy can help refine our understanding of experience. The hermeneutic tradition provides a concept of experience that is apt to capture the sequential aspect of plot in addition to describing the interior lives of characters. Gadamer in particular has emphasized the temporal character of experiences.[96] Harking back to Hegel, he notes that experiences disappoint expectations. They are defined by a reversal undergone by our consciousness: 'If a new experience of an object occurs to us, this means that hitherto we have not seen the thing correctly and now know it better.'[97] As Gadamer stresses, experiences ought not to be reduced to the insight gained through the reversal; they can only be understood as processes. In addition to being essentially temporal, experiences also make us sense time: 'Experience is experience of human finitude'.[98] Thus understood, experience grasps not only the interior lives of characters, as the notion of mind, but also the sequential aspect of plot. It conveys the temporal dynamics that the notion of mind does not necessarily embrace.

Not only narrative characters but also readers have experiences.[99] We have, as we say, reading experiences. It is important though to heed the difference between real-life and reading experiences. While the heroes of a novel are tortured or killed, the reader sits comfortably in their favourite easy chair. Reading experiences are indirect. And yet, in attending to the plot, the reader's consciousness forms the same chain of protentions and retentions that define everyday experiences. The reader retains what has happened and conjectures the future course of the plot. Reading thus exposes one's consciousness to the same temporal dynamics as our everyday

---

[93] Fludernik 1996. For a fuller critical assessment of Fludernik's concept of experience, see Grethlein 2018.

[94] Fludernik 1996: 29.   [95] Fludernik 1996: 27.   [96] Gadamer 1990: 352–68.

[97] Gadamer 1990: 359 (English tr. 2004: 347): 'Wenn wir an einem Gegenstand eine Erfahrung machen, so heißt das, daß wir die Dinge bisher nicht richtig gesehen haben und nun besser wissen, wie es damit steht.'

[98] Gadamer 1990: 363 (English tr. 2004: 351): 'Erfahrung ist also Erfahrung der menschlichen Endlichkeit.'

[99] On this, see Grethlein 2017b: 41–73.

life, while bracketing it in the frame of 'as-if'. In the second chapter, we saw how sensitive ancient critics were to the intensity that reading experiences can acquire while not denying the vicarious character of these experiences.

Besides embracing the temporal dynamics of the plot as well as the presentation of consciousness, the concept of experience applies, with due qualifications, to both the world of the story and to its reception by the reader. The reading experience is shaped by its relation to the experiences of the narrative characters.[100] Depending on how the fabula is transformed into the sujet, the reader's experience can be aligned with or be distinct from the characters' experiences. While Homeric epic for example capitalizes on tragic irony by privileging the reader over its characters, stream of consciousness novels make the reader perceive the story-world through the lens of characters.

And yet it is important to note that the reading experience is not necessarily mediated through the experiences of the protagonists. In a thought-provoking attempt to make the model of the embodied reader more dynamic, Karin Kukkonen draws on recent work in cognitive research.[101] According to these investigations, our embodied engagement with our environment implies predictive inferences about the future that are constantly reassessed on the basis of new observations. This, Kukkonen argues, also applies to the reading process. The reader not only concentrates on the embodied experience of the characters but derives from it predictions of the further development of the plot. Kukkonen's model is much more sensitive to the temporal dimension of the reading process than other models of the embodied reader. And yet I part company with her when she assumes that the reader's inferences about the future develop from that of the characters, either adopting or reassessing them against the backdrop of further knowledge about the story-world. This may but need not be the case. The reading experience is not necessarily grafted onto the experience of the character; it hinges primarily on the sequential form of narrative.[102]

We have already encountered some examples in the course of the argument, for example the reader's surprise at the appearance of Thisbe in Egypt, which parallels Theagenes' surprise without hinging on it. Let me add a further illustration: when the pyre on which Chariclea stands is about to be kindled, the reader feels suspense. This suspense does not build

---

[100] Compare Grethlein 2010: 318–27.   [101] Kukkonen 2014.

[102] Ryan 2015 seems to miss this in her response to my original intervention when she, by and large, buys my argument but notes that Zunshine is a better target for it than Palmer and outlines his theory of fictional minds. My criticism is not directed against the theory of fictional minds, which, I agree, permits us to bring together aspects otherwise separated from each other, but against the claims with which it is framed, namely that we access stories only through the minds of characters.

on how she or other characters feel and assess her future; it is immediately directed towards the further course of the action. The reader wants to know what his going to happen next, how the situation can be reconciled with the anticipated ending. The sequential form of narrative – whatever the medium – prompts the recipient to conjecture about the further course of the plot independently of the content and presentation of fictional minds. That said, an analysis of the dynamics of plot needs to take into account the characters' consciousness, as the reading experience receives its special character from its relation to the experience of the characters. Time is the primary dimension of narrative, but it needs to be studied together with character.

All faults and problems notwithstanding, cognitive approaches have been very successful in opening up new horizons for the study of narrative. They can also help us appreciate important dimensions of ancient narrative and criticism, as I argued in Chapter 1. This said, the Theory of Mind, which has taken centre stage in many cognitive studies of narrative, is not able to provide a satisfying answer to the question as to how our response to narrative relates to our way of monitoring the everyday world. It is not only fiercely criticized in psychology but also fails to account for ancient narrative. Applied mostly to the study of the modern realist novels, the Theory of Mind does not provide a key for studying such plot-driven narratives as the *Ethiopica*. Ancient narrative seems not to be the only material that does not conform to the claims about the Theory of Mind – medievalists have also questioned the significance of the Theory of Mind for narratives from the Middle Ages, which had 'an action-oriented rather than a mind-oriented conception of self'.[103] And in Chapter 6, we will see that even the modern era produces a not-insignificant amount of narrative that does not appeal chiefly to the Theory of Mind.

That the focus on mind reading has led scholars to neglect the temporal dynamics of narrative is palpable in Palmer's definition of it as a '*description* of fictional mental functioning'. The lack of terminological precision unveils the lopsidedness of Palmer's concept of fictional minds. Experience, as conceptualized by Gadamer, is a better tool to grasp the relation of processing narrative to processing the everyday world: besides embracing the consciousness processes targeted by the concept of fictional minds, it captures also the crucial aspect of time and allows us to do justice to the salience of plot for narrative.

---

[103] Von Contzen 2015: 140.

CHAPTER 5

Motivation

I Motivation in Narrative Theory

Motivation is a central aspect of narrative. It is addressed not so much in the narratological tradition that analyses the 'discourse', namely, how the story is presented – for example in terms of time, voice and mood (Genette) – as in the strand of narratology that addresses the construction of the story, the course of the events.[1] An important founding father of story-centred narrative theory is Vladimir Propp – he segmented tales into functions, understood as actions of characters defined by their relevance to the course of the action. In his analysis of 100 Russian fairy tales, Propp identified a single action structure which, in its complete form encompassing thirty-one functions, is the backbone of all these tales.[2] Propp introduces motivation as 'the reasons and the aims of personages which cause them to commit various acts. Motivations often add to a tale a completely distinctive, vivid coloring, but nevertheless motivations belong to the most inconstant and unstable elements of the tale.'[3] Since the functions – the focus of Propp's analysis – can be motivated in many different ways, Propp does not examine motivation in detail. More about motivation can be found in Brémond's *Logique du récit*, which advances an actantial model that allows us to break down all narratives into the positions of subject, object, helper, opponent, sender and receiver. Brémond comments extensively on the motives that drive the protagonists and thereby make the plot unfold.[4]

However, motivation can be understood more broadly as concerned not only with the motives of characters but with how individual scenes, events and actions are integrated into a narrative. If we take up the metaphor of plot architecture, motivation is the glue that makes

---

[1] This strand of narratology has influenced Classics via the structuralist interpretations of the Paris school; see Zeitlin 1991: 6.
[2] Propp 1968.   [3] Propp 1968: 15.   [4] Brémond 1973.

a narrative stick together. The goals and intentions of characters are only one element that can establish links between the parts of a narrative. There are also other means of coherence: events can be linked to one another causally without being related to the plans of the characters.[5] Besides and often in addition to causal and psychological motivation, there is compositional motivation: the individual parts of a narrative serve a function in the plot, for example as elements necessary for the closure.[6] Scenes may also correspond to one another thematically and thereby add up to a greater whole or simply contribute to its mood. While it is a concept in need of further theorizing, motivation is not exclusively a category of modern scholarship; Aristotle's emphasis on the unity of plot indicates the salience of the idea of motivation in antiquity – what, however, justifies the existence of a scene depends on genre and changes over time.

As this chapter will show, the expectations of Classicists about motivation tend to be shaped by modern realist novels and are in danger of not doing justice to ancient narrative. Even where it seems prima facie unlikely, the sense of motivation in ancient texts may deviate from ours. In his magisterial sketch of the history of the classical Western plot, Nick Lowe identified the *Odyssey* as its central source.[7] Both the course of the action – the hero's departure, his travelling, his trials and his final return – and the economy with which Homer tells it engendered a narrative tradition that continues to be prominent today. Menander and other authors of New Comedy adopted both the *Odyssey*'s plot pattern and its presentation and themselves exerted a strong influence on the writers of the Imperial novel, who also deployed the same narrative devices to give an account of couples who are separated and, after undergoing various adventures, united in a grand finale. Translated into the vernacular European languages in the sixteenth century CE, *Daphnis and Chloe* and the *Ethiopica* in particular served as models for the early modern novel. There is of course no direct link between the *Odyssey* and, say, Flaubert's *Sentimental Education* and Kracht's *Faserland*, and yet romances, coming-of-age stories and adventure narratives ultimately all vary the plot pattern introduced by the *Odyssey* to the history of literature.

---

[5] On the construction of causality as a crucial element of the reading process, see Kafalenos 2006, who develops further Propp's morphology and Todorov's take on plot.

[6] For an attempt to systematize different forms of narrative motivation, see Martínez 1996: 13–36; Martínez and Scheffel 1999: 111–19, who distinguish between causal, final and compositional/ aesthetic motivation.

[7] Lowe 2000.

However, despite its huge impact on the art of storytelling in the Western world and its ongoing appeal to modern readers, there are aspects of the *Odyssey* that do not follow the logic that modern realist novels have made our default model. In this chapter, I will reconsider the motivation of the Penelope scenes in books 18 and 19. I will first review scholarship that has tried to make sense of Penelope and her comportment. These readings of Penelope's character are not necessarily wrong; in fact, many of them are thought-provoking, but, as I will try to make clear, even the most sophisticated interpretations bypass the peculiar narrative logic of the scenes (§2 Penelope: Analytical, Psychological and Feminist Readings). In the subsequent section, I will tease out this narrative logic, which, it will turn out, is closer to the conventions of medieval narratives than those of narratology's favourite case, modern realist novels (§3 Penelope and Narrative Logic). My exploration is expanded by the contemplation of whether this sense of motivation can be explained in terms of Homeric psychology or oral tradition. The answer will be a qualified no, corroborated by parallels from later Greek literature (§4 Compositional Motivation and Homeric Psychology and Oral Poetry). Finally, I consider how this narrative motivation, which is at odds with the conventions of modern realist novels, relates to the emphasis on causal links in Aristotle's *Poetics* and the scholia. I will suggest that, despite the differences, they all share a common ground, which sets off the ancient understanding of narrative against our approaches (§5 Motivation in Aristotle and Scholia).

2 Penelope: Analytical, Psychological and Feminist Readings

Homer's presentation of Penelope has posed challenges to modern readers. Both her appearance before the suitors in book 18 and the bow contest she initiates in book 19 have been felt to sit uncomfortably with other scenes in the plot.[8] In book 17, Telemachus reports to Penelope what he has learnt from Menelaus. As Proteus had revealed to Menelaus, Odysseus was being held captive by Calypso (17.108–49). Theoclymenus then prophesies that 'Odysseus is already here in the land of his fathers,/ sitting still or advancing, learning of all these evil/ actions, and devising evils for all of the suitors' (ὡς ἦ τοι Ὀδυσεὺς ἤδη ἐν πατρίδι γαίῃ,/ ἥμενος ἦ ἕρπων, τάδε πευθόμενος κακὰ ἔργα,/ ἔστιν, ἀτὰρ μνηστῆρσι κακὸν πάντεσσι φυτεύει, 17.157–9). Penelope feels encouraged: Telemachus' report 'aroused the heart in her [Penelope's] breast' (τῇ δ' ἄρα θυμὸν ἐνὶ στήθεσσιν ὄρινε, 17.150), and in response to

---

[8] For example, Büchner 1940: 139–55; Katz 1991: 104–20.

Theoclymenus' prophecy she utters the wish: 'If only this word, stranger and guest, were brought to fulfilment!' (αἲ γὰρ τοῦτο, ξεῖνε, ἔπος τετελεσμένον εἴη, 17.163). Later, conversing with Eumaeus, Penelope renews her wish, and when Telemachus sneezes, interprets this as a confirmation: 'Do you not see how my son sneezed for everything I have spoken?/ May it mean that death, accomplished in full, befall the suitors/ each and all, not one avoiding death and destruction' (οὐχ ὁράᾳς, ὅ μοι υἱὸς ἐπέπταρε πᾶσιν ἔπεσσι;/ τῷ κε καὶ οὐκ ἀτελὴς θάνατος μνηστῆρσι γένοιτο/ πᾶσι μάλ', οὐδέ κέ τις θάνατον καὶ κῆρας ἀλύξει, 17.545–7). The air is thick with signs of Odysseus' return, and Penelope is obviously full of hope. Modern scholars are thus bewildered when in book 18 Penelope shows herself to the suitors and announces that she will now remarry (18.251–80).

In book 19, a similar tension between Penelope's action and the situation emerges. Penelope meets the beggar, who claims with credibility that he has seen Odysseus. He also swears an oath that Odysseus is about to come home (19.269–72, 300–2). Penelope's dream of the geese and the eagle, as interpreted by Odysseus in the dream and by the beggar in their conversation, further suggests that Odysseus' return is imminent (19.535–58). Unlike in book 18, Penelope is sceptical (19.312–4, 571–2), but still her decision to set up the bow contest seems to sit jarringly with the situation. Why should Penelope, who longs for her husband and is given reason to expect his appearance, accelerate her marriage with one of the odious suitors?

Unsurprisingly, the tension between Penelope's feelings, her actions and the situation has prompted Analysts and Neo-Analysts to argue for the contamination of different versions.[9] The bow test in particular has been thought to stem from a folk tale in which Penelope already recognizes her husband and acts in support of him.[10] The tension in our transmitted text is thus explained genetically. Analytical scholarship, however, has declined in popularity, giving way to other forms of readings.[11] In the course of the twentieth century, pressure mounted to replace diachronic explanation with synchronic interpretation. In a paper from 1950, Harsh put forward

---

[9] See Schwartz 1924: 220; von Wilamowitz-Moellendorff 1927: 87; Woodhouse 1930: 80–91; Merkelbach 1951: 9–15; Page 1955: 119–29; Kirk 1962: 245–7. Following a Neo-analytical path, Currie 2016: 48–55 explains the inconsistencies as Homer's allusion to other epic traditions, in which Penelope recognizes Odysseus at an early stage.

[10] Amphimedon's account of the killing of the suitors in the second *nekyia* is an important element of this interpretation; see below, p. 134.

[11] For a critique of analytical approaches to Penelope, see, for example, Büchner 1940; Vester 1968.

the thesis that Penelope in fact recognizes Odysseus in book 19.[12] She keeps her knowledge secret in order not to jeopardize her husband and herself, but nonetheless actively, if clandestinely, supports his revenge plan. As ingenious as this idea is, it only found a few followers and was widely rejected. There are too many elements that fly in the face of Harsh's argument, not least Penelope's prayer that she die and see her husband in Hades (20.61–90) and her hesitation in recognizing him in book 23.[13]

At the same time, Harsh's idea has survived and become popular in a modified form. A wide range of scholars have subscribed to and developed further Amory's thesis that Penelope recognizes Odysseus, but only subconsciously.[14] The inconsistency of her acting can thus be ascribed to different levels of her personality. Penelope does not fully know that the beggar is Odysseus in disguise, and yet she somehow intuits that her husband has come back and acts in accordance with this feeling when she appears before the suitors and later announces the bow contest. It is Penelope's complex psychological make-up that explains why she, despite not knowing Odysseus' plotting, engages in actions that play into Odysseus' hands. This interpretation has been developed with different nuances. While Russo, for example, spells out the many ways in which the beggar conjures up Odysseus for Penelope until she takes a gamble, Austin emphasizes the miraculous consonance that emerges between Penelope and Odysseus. More recently, Struck has invoked the Homeric Penelope as evidence for his thesis that ancient divination can be understood as a form of intuition. Penelope's intuitive knowledge of Odysseus' presence is fostered by various signs and *omina*, and this, he contends, proves the link between divination and intuition.

The thesis of a subconscious recognition appeals to what Rita Felski has labeled the hermeneutics of suspicion, the scholarly predilection for points that do not immediately strike the reader. Critics prefer meaning that is somewhere hidden in the text, they 'read against the grain and between the lines; their self-appointed task is to draw out what a text fails – or willfully refuses – to see'.[15] The hermeneutics of suspicion have found particularly fruitful ground in Classics, a discipline under pressure to prove its mettle.

---

[12] Harsh 1950.   [13] For a careful recent reading of the recognition scene in book 23, see Kelly 2012.

[14] Besides Amory 1963, see also Mariani 1978: 141–2; Austin 1975; van Nortwick 1979; Russo 1982; Winkler 1990: 143–56; Steiner 2010: 27–8; Struck 2016: 251–62. When Christensen 2020: 198–9 argues that 'her reluctance to reveal this (i.e. the knowledge that the beggar is her husband) is connected to cultural demands of restraint and passivity', he even seems willing to entertain the thesis of a full recognition. See also Vlahos 2011, who argues that Penelope may recognize her husband even earlier than in book 19, and the responses to his article in *College Literature* 38/2, 2011.

[15] Felski 2015: 1.

The credit that Homer gets from readings of Penelope comes to the fore in Russo's concluding remarks: Odysseus and Penelope '"know" and express much more on sub-conscious levels than they can process consciously and state explicitly. It is because Homer has understood and described so much, that is subtle, so well, enhancing and refining an ancient and familiar story, that he is ranked as our first poet.'[16]

Despite its allure, this psychological reading is open to challenge.[17] A subconscious recognition is not mentioned by Homer; it is not even alluded to and needs to be concluded from Penelope's actions. Why, it must be asked, does Homer not make explicit such an important fact? He knows how to present complex inner processes and is not shy of spelling them out.[18] Nothing, however, indicates the kind of feeling in Penelope for which Amory, Russo and others have insistently argued. If Penelope has been dimly aware of the beggar's identity, why is she so reluctant to acknowledge it after the killing of the suitors? What is more, the idea that Penelope intuits Odysseus' presence is aligned with dubious assumptions about gender.[19] Penelope is described as 'passive and intuitive',[20] as 'a woman of strong intuitions'.[21] Her intuition bespeaks an idea of the female that uncannily resembles popular gender clichés (not only) at the time this interpretation was forged.

Feminist critics have not failed to pick on such gendered readings. Emphasizing Penelope's active stance, they have instead proposed elaborate readings that envisage her more strongly in conjunction with the plot.[22] Felson-Rubin, for one, approaches Penelope as 'multivalent', as a 'spinner of plots'. Penelope is 'far more prudent about her own security and attentive to her own pleasures than others (both characters and critics) have acknowledged'. Facing a situation with many variables, Penelope shrewdly prepares for different scenarios. More precisely, she creates four possible plots, namely 'Courtship and Marriage', 'Dalliance', 'Disdain and

---

[16] Russo 1982: 18.

[17] For example, Emlyn-Jones: 1984; Heitman 2005: 6–7, 48; Alden 2017: 145: 'The theory of early recognition infers unexpressed unconscious motivation and subconscious intuition, neither of which can be substantiated.'

[18] See below, p. 133.   [19] Cf. Murnaghan 1987: 138–9; Felson-Rubin 1987: 63 n. 13.

[20] Amory 1966: 55.

[21] Russo 1982: 10. Harsh's 1950: 4, 7 as well as analytical readings are also predicated on questionable assumptions about gender: compare, for example, Merkelbach 1951: 5.

[22] See also Winkler 1990, who stresses Penelope's *mētis* and capacity for intrigue, but, unlike Felson-Rubin and Katz, assumes that Penelope has somehow identified Odysseus. Foley 2001: 126–46 foregrounds the moral decision made by Penelope: 'In full recognition of the suffering it will bring her, she moves to subordinate her own desires to the needs of her son and the parting instructions of her husband.'

Bride of Death' and 'Patience'.[23] What may appear as inconsistency is Penelope's attempt to stay abreast of all four trajectories. Her multivalence, Felson-Rubin argues, is crucial for captivating the attention of the readers. All the way until book 23, Homer has us rack our brains about what Penelope actually desires.[24]

In a similar vein, Marylin Katz makes indeterminacy the cornerstone of her reading of Penelope's character. She argues 'that the narrative of Books 18–21 is governed by the paradigm of alternatives introduced by Telemachus at the beginning of Book 16, which Penelope acknowledges in Book 19.524ff. as her state of mind: either to remain in the halls by the side of Telemachus, or to marry whichever suitor brings the most gifts'.[25] Hence, it is pointless to look for consistency in Penelope's comportment. The two options of resisting or giving in to the suitors alternately come to the foreground; they not only shape Penelope's behaviour but are also refracted in the interventions and comments of other characters.

Whereas the readings of Amory, Russo and others detect the *Odyssey*'s complexity in its subtle psychological portrayal of characters, the feminist interpretations introduce us to a Homer who tackles the instability of meaning with a sophistication that would have made the post-structuralist theorists of the twentieth century proud. Despite the glaring differences, the feminist approach is aligned with the readings that assert a subconscious recognition in one important regard. Both interpretations focus on the psychology of Penelope. This comes to the fore in Felson-Rubin's argument:

> Building up Penelope's features as a spinner of plots requires that we know, at each plot moment, what she knows, what beliefs and convictions she holds, what she desires and fears, and what actions she thinks are possible and permissible for her to take. We must treat her as if she were a character in real life, with a world of her own.[26]

Katz may claim that 'the scene as a whole retains its plausibility and its narrative integrity only if it is read not from the point of view of psychological realism, but rather of narrative strategy'.[27] And yet her focus remains with Penelope's mind, as she understands the actions as an expression of Penelope's indeterminate psychological make-up: 'In this way, Penelope's state of mind is exteriorized, and the plot is enacted as the "drama of inmost being" that Telemachus attributes to Penelope in 16.73

---

[23] Felson-Rubin 1987: 77. See also Felson-Rubin 1994.   [24] Felson-Rubin 1987: 62.
[25] Katz 1991: 93.   [26] Felson-Rubin 1987: 64.   [27] Katz 1991: 93.

(θυμὸς ἐνὶ φρεσὶ μερμηρίζει) though without permitting us access to any truth of ultimate intention.'[28]

I would not claim that the interpretations concentrating on Penelope's mind are necessarily wrong. Some of them open up illuminating perspectives on Penelope and the final part of the *Odyssey*. And yet, in looking for motivation in the character's psychology, these readings follow expectations shaped by modern realist novels. Such narratives as *Pride and Prejudice, Mrs Dalloway* and *The Ambassadors* give ample space to consciousness processes and carefully motivate actions psychologically. In the preceding chapter, I argued that, while there is no lack of fictional minds in ancient texts, the ancient sense of characterization was different from ours. Ancient writers and readers were, by and large, more invested in the moral dimension of characters and its manifestation through action than in how their interior lives rendered them unique. By no means does this rule out the psychological motivation of scenes – there are, in fact, numerous examples of it – but it should make us hesitant to argue for consciousness processes without clear indicators in the text. I contend that, in trying to pinpoint the motivation of books 18 and 19 in Penelope's mind, modern interpreters miss the distinct logic of the scenes in the *Odyssey*. In the subsequent section, I will try to unravel this logic, which will ultimately help explain why Penelope has proven so thought-provoking for modern readers.

3   Penelope and Narrative Logic

It is, to start with, striking that the tension between plot and Penelope's psychology that has kept generations of modern scholars busy does not seem to have been a concern for ancient readers. The rich literary reception of Penelope attests the fascination this Homeric figure held for ancient readers. In addition to Penelope – the model of female chastity – we also find, for example in Duris and Lycophron, a deeply un-Homeric Penelope, a lecherous woman, who indulges in the suitors' embraces.[29] As Jacobson notes, this portrayal of Penelope forms part of the playful, often agonistic engagement with mythical traditions in antiquity: 'What could be more delightful and more of a challenge than to turn the obviously loyal Homeric heroine into a slut?'[30] This misogynistic view of Penelope is

---

[28] Katz 1991: 93.

[29] Duris *FGrHist* 76 F 21; Lycophr. *Alex.* 771–3; 792. A survey of the ancient tradition of Penelope can be found in Jacobson 1974: 245–9.

[30] Jacobson 1974: 248.

obviously diametrically opposed to her appraisal as the incarnation of chastity, and yet both traditions bespeak the moral focus on character which we encountered in Chapter 4.

A scholion on the first verse of book 21 illustrates that ancient readers even wondered about Penelope's thoughts in the *Odyssey*: Penelope sets up the contest 'so that, if several manage to string [the bow], they start to fight, if none, they are revealed to be unworthy' (τίθησι δὲ τὸ τόξον ἵνα, ἐὰν μὲν πλείους ἐντείνωσι, στασιάσωσιν, ἐὰν δὲ μηδεὶς, ἀνάξιοι τῆς μνηστείας φανῶσιν, scholion V on 21.1). In one of his letters, Seneca mentions the question of 'whether she [Penelope] suspected that the person she saw was Ulysses before she was told' as the kind of topic discussed in the study of liberal arts (*An Vlixem illum esse, quem videbat, antequam sciret, suspicata sit?* 88.8). And yet, there is no trace of discomfort with Penelope's motivation in ancient responses to the *Odyssey*.

The presentation of Penelope in *Odyssey* 18 and 19, I wish to show, relies on a sense of motivation that does not square with the expectations of modern readers. In order to tease out this narrative logic, I will build on the comments of a few Homerists and reassess them in the light of a remarkable analysis of medieval and early modern narrative from the 1930s. In *Die Heimkehr des Odysseus*, Wilamowitz, while defending the authenticity of Penelope's speech in 19.124–63, criticizes scholars who argued for various atheteses: 'And again the critics only think of what the figures should do or not do in order to behave reasonably in the sense of an average human being instead of heeding what the poet needs and wants.'[31] The poet's needs are further spelled out by Woodhouse, who notices that Penelope's appearance before the suitors and the bow test are psychologically unmotivated but necessary for the plot.[32] Along similar lines, Allen observes: 'Homer had some trouble in producing the immediate motivation for Odysseus to begin the slaying of the suitors, and it is at that point that he again sacrifices the credibility of the character of Penelope to his plot.'[33] Seen against the backdrop of Chapter 4, it is interesting that these authors observe a preponderance of plot over character, which apparently disagrees with their own preferences. The phrasing of the last sentence – Homer 'sacrifices the credibility of the character of Penelope to the plot' – illustrates that this concentration on plot is felt to be a flaw of the *Odyssey*.

In the second half of the twentieth century, psychological readings of Penelope were clearly dominant, but a few scholars continued to consider the exigencies of the plot and the design of individual scenes. Fenik, for

---

[31] Von Wilamowitz-Moellendorff 1927: 40.   [32] Woodhouse 1930: 88–91.   [33] Allen 1939: 106.

one, stressed Homer's heedfulness of powerful scenes at the expense of
other factors: 'Clear, logical cause and effect, airtight motivation or strict
verisimilitude are not his concern. His interest is in emotion, irony, and
pathos.'[34] Homer, he argues, 'loses sight of (or willingly ignores) strict
motivation in direct proportion to the extent to which he develops his
favorite situations with their special emotions and ironies.'[35] Sheila
Murnaghan sees a conflict between Penelope's inner life and the role she
plays in the plot. While the latter yields a perspective in which Penelope
appears as the master of her own destiny and her actions as 'anticipations or
preliminary versions of this destined recognition' in book 23,[36] the former
presents her as a victim of the circumstances, pinning the spotlight on the
'painful, disorienting rifts that can exist between character and social
role'.[37] Fenik and Murnaghan underline the significance of the plot without sharing the negative evaluation of earlier works, but both simultaneously have a firm eye on Penelope's psychology. While Murnaghan notes
a tension between 'the figures in an orderly artistic design and as representations of human beings acting their way through experiences whose
patterns they cannot perceive or predict',[38] Fenik is at pains to show that,
by and large, Penelope's comportment is fully in keeping with her
character.[39]

A seminal analysis of medieval and early modern narrative can help us
identify more precisely the distinct narrative logic undergirding Penelope's
portrayal in the *Odyssey*. Published in 1932, Clemens Lugowski's *Die Form
der Individualität im Roman* contends that premodern narrative is predicated
on a 'mythical analogon'. The authors and readers may not believe in
a mythical world anymore, but their narratives sustain 'a perspective that
perceives the world largely as an all-embracing, coherent entity'.[40] Narrative
is the residuum of a mindset that believes in a magic connection of things
across time. This logic manifests itself in various features that deviate
markedly from the conventions of modern realist novel. Perhaps most
importantly, 'retroactive motivation' ('Motivation von hinten') has causes
hinge on the result: 'It is therefore not the case that the outcome is determined by the premises of the plot, but the opposite: namely that the

---

[34] Fenik 1974: 47.   [35] Fenik 1974: 120.   [36] Murnaghan 1987: 128.   [37] Murnaghan 1987: 138.
[38] Murnaghan 1987: 128.
[39] Fenik's willingness to psychologize is manifest for example when he rejects the idea that Penelope
   must recognize Odysseus (1974: 45): 'This is a Penelope frozen in an attitude of grief and wasting
   distress, practically without hope und uncertain of the proper course to take.'
[40] Lugowski 1976 [1932]: 41 (English tr. 38). For the value of Lugowski's concepts for a theory of the
   spatial dimensions of narrative, see Grethlein 2017b: 69–73.

individual strands of plot are determined by the outcome, which demands no more than that it should be revealed in advance.'[41] Now individual elements usually have their firm place also in the plot trajectories of modern novels. As Chekhov notes: 'If in the first chapter you say that a gun hung on the wall, in the second or in the third chapter it must without fail be discharged.'[42] However, modern authors tend not only to assign to events and elements a place in the plot, but also to motivate them causally and psychologically. In the narratives explored by Lugowski, on the other hand, things are often justified *only* as part of the plot and do not emerge naturally within the world of the action. It is this absence of motivation in the story-world that strikes us as implausible in retroactive motivation.

Closely linked with retroactive motivation is a preference for linear narrative, a willingness to add events to each other without establishing links, a reduction of characters to their function within the plot and a repetition of patterns that undermines the agency of the characters.[43] All these features, Lugowski argues, are premised on the idea of a 'totality that is not structured chronologically'.[44] The plot is seen less as something that unfolds diachronically than as something that is fully present in any of its parts. Lugowski even goes so far as to distinguish this sense of timelessness from teleology, which, while envisaging the course of the action from the ending, is still temporal.[45]

The sequence of plot is sidelined in a different way by what Lugowski labels 'thematische Überfremdung', which may be translated as 'thematic isolation'. In the fourteenth chapter of the *Historie von den vier Heymons Kindern*, for instance, one of the main characters, Malegys, addresses the king repeatedly with his title. In a later conversation with him, however, he says that he did not know his identity – without provoking protest. While retroactive motivation challenges the sequence of the plot by motivating a cause through its result, here the focus on a single scene and its narrative requirements dissolves it from its narrative context and thereby ignores the sequence of the plot: 'As regards the plot, the isolation of specific situations from the rest corresponds to the isolation of these plot segments as they become the focal point of the narrative.'[46] The regal identity is felt so strongly that it is voiced by a character who does not know the king yet.

---

[41] Lugowski 1976 [1932]: 75 (English tr. 72).   [42] Chekhov 1974: 23.
[43] Lugowski 1976 [1932]: 52–80.   [44] Lugowski 1976 [1932]: 180 (English tr. 177).
[45] Lugowski 1976 [1932]: 79–80 (English tr. 77).
[46] Lugowski 1976 [1932]: 24 (English tr. 21): 'Im Hinblick auf die Handlungskette bedeutet diese Isolierung nackter Seinsverhalte eine Isolierung des jeweiligen, gerade im Blickfeld befindlichen "Kettengliedes".'

The detemporalization of the plot also comes to the fore in the replacement of suspense as to what is going to happen by suspense that is directed upon *how* it is going to happen. In Boccaccio's *Decamerone*, for instance, the headings at the beginning of nearly all days and summaries preceding the individual novellas anticipate the course of the plot.[47] Instead of wondering about what is going to happen, the reader attends to the fashion in which the anticipated outcome will be realized. As Lugowski notes, this narrative design smooths the tensions of the plot:

> The elimination of all result-orientated suspense serves to transfigure the brutality of the real world and smooth down the overall effect. It is this that lies at the root of that delightfully elegant lightness of touch that is always associated with these novellas. They have been relieved of that unremitting harshness that is always associated with a mysterious and impenetrable future.[48]

Lugowski focuses on Wickram, a German writer of the sixteenth century, and touches on other late medieval and early modern authors. It has however been noticed that his analysis provides a key to medieval narrative in general.[49] Many idiosyncrasies that scholars used to, and sometimes continue to, condemn are cases of retroactive motivation, thematic isolation and suspense as to how. They are not weaknesses but rather characteristics of medieval narrative. I suggest that Lugowski's approach can also help us better comprehend the case of Penelope in the *Odyssey*. There are of course glaring differences between Homer and Lugowski's authors, but the putative inconsistencies that continue to strike Homerists are due to a sense of motivation that is closer to medieval than modern narratives.

First, however, Lugowski's approach needs to be qualified. The concept of a mythical analogon is premised on a questionable evolutionary model tracing the ascent from mythos to logos.[50] The assumption of a primitive stage of mythical thinking, be it in the Middle Ages or in Archaic Greece, defies all evidence, just as the thesis of a disappearance of myth has been

---

[47] Lugowski 1976 [1932]: 39–46.

[48] Lugowski 1976 [1932]: 41 (English tr. 38): 'Die Ausschaltung der Spannung des "Ob überhaupt" bedeutet eine mildernde Glättung, Verklärung der brutalen Realität; hier ist die Wurzel der liebenswürdigen und grazilen Leichtigkeit, ohne die man sich jene Novellen nicht mehr denken kann. Die unerbittliche Härte, die in der finsteren Undurchdringlichkeit des Zukünftigen liegt, ist den Erzählungen genommen.'

[49] For example, Haferland 2014. For an instructive survey, see Schneider 2019. Martínez 1996, an exploration of motivation in narrative, is also indebted to Lugowski.

[50] See, however, Schlaffer 1990, who uses the notion of 'mythisches Analogon' to argue that even after the process of the scientific demystification the form of poetry still conveys the transcendent sense constituted by mythical thinking. Martínez 1996: 30–2 also subscribes to the link between 'final motivation' and mythical causality.

forcefully challenged.[51] This, however, ought not to detract from the value of Lugowski's textual analysis. Elsewhere, I suggest a different framework for his observations.[52] Many of the narrative features described by Lugowski, I argue, push to an extreme the synchronic dimension inherent in any narrative. Narrative, no matter the medium, doubles represented time with representing time, and yet its sequential nature is counterbalanced by synchronic elements. What has been labelled spatial form prompts readers to comprehend the plot or at least some of its aspects nonsequentially.[53] Retroactive motivation in particular, but also thematic isolation and suspense as to how, forgo the sequence of narrative and bring to the foreground its synchronic dimension. They express not so much an archaic worldview as a distinct narrative logic.

Homeric epic does certainly not harbour all the features discussed by Lugowski. For instance, neither *Odyssey* nor *Iliad* is straightforwardly linear. Numerous anachronies can be found in both poems. In fact, Odysseus' most spectacular adventures figure in the form of a review. The *Odyssey* also starts with two different strands of action, Telemachus on Ithaca and Odysseus' return to Ithaca, which are traced one after the other until they coalesce in book 16. At the same time, Homeric epic strikingly parallels other characteristics of medieval narrative. Not only will the ending have been familiar to most ancient audiences, but also frequent foreshadowing, partly embedded in the action, partly given by the narrator, adumbrates that Odysseus will finally succeed and enjoy a happy *nostos*. While this impedes suspense as to what will happen, Homer efficiently uses the devices of retardation and misdirection to create the kind of suspense described by Lugowski, suspense that concerns the how of the plot.[54]

What I now wish to specifically argue is that the treatment of Penelope in books 18 and 19 of the *Odyssey* reveals a narrative logic similar to the texts explored by Lugowski. First, it is important to note that Penelope's appearance before the suitors is by no means unmotivated. On the contrary, Homer has Athena intervene. The goddess puts into Penelope's mind the wish to show herself to the suitors, a wish that Penelope herself deems odd (18.164–5). It is Athena's intention that Penelope will spark the suitors' desire and increase the esteem in which her son and husband hold her.[55] As if this

---

[51] See, for example, Blumenberg 1979 and Horkheimer and Adorno 1969.

[52] Grethlein 2017b: 69–73   [53] Grethlein 2017b: 59–65.

[54] Morrison 1992; Grethlein 2006: 205–310.

[55] On the final clause in 18.160–2 as giving us Athena's, not Penelope's, motives, see, for example, Büchner 1940: 143; Bona 1966: 147–8; Emlyn-Jones 1984: 10–12. Whitman 1958: 303; Austin 1975: 208 and Winkler 1990: 146, on the other hand, read the final clause as expressing Penelope's motives.

were not enough motivation, Penelope herself announces to Eurynome that she needs to have a word with Telemachus, who ought 'not to always go among the insolent suitors' (μὴ πάντα μνηστῆρσιν ὑπερφιάλοισιν ὁμιλεῖν, 18.167).

This motivation of Penelope's entry notwithstanding, Penelope's announcement of a new wedding does sit uncomfortably with her desire for Odysseus and with the signs of his imminent return. A wide range of scholars including de Jong have tried to evade this tension by arguing that Penelope is just pulling another trick on the suitors.[56] Penelope, they claim, simply invents Odysseus' counsel that she should marry again once Telemachus has grown up. As clever as this suggestion is, it faces weighty objections. Deceptive speeches are not scarce in the *Odyssey*, but this would be the only one that is not unmistakably presented as untruthful. Odysseus' response – he 'was happy/ because she beguiled gifts out of them, and enchanted their spirits/ with blandishing words, while her mind was set on other things' (γήθησεν δὲ πολύτλας δῖος Ὀδυσσεύς,/ οὕνεκα τῶν μὲν δῶρα παρέλκετο, θέλγε δὲ θυμὸν/ μειλιχίοισ᾽ ἐπέεσσι, νόος δέ οἱ ἄλλα μενοίνα, 18.281–3) – does not prove that Penelope is tricking the suitors. As Uvo Hölscher has compellingly argued, Odysseus appreciates Penelope's mourning of her lost husband and the reluctance with which she, complying with his parting words, finally cedes to the suitors' wooing.[57] Most importantly, later in her conversation with the beggar, Penelope herself, after recounting the ruse of the shroud, says ruefully: 'Now I cannot escape from this marriage; I can no longer/ think of another plan' (νῦν δ᾽ οὔτ᾽ ἐκφυγέειν δύναμαι γάμον οὔτε τιν᾽ ἄλλην/ μῆτιν ἔθ᾽ εὑρίσκω, 19.157–8).

There is no clandestine scheming involved in Penelope's speech – Homer simply neglects the motivation of her decision to marry again. Modern critics have deemed it improbable that Penelope only now acquaints the suitors with Odysseus' orders: 'And why has Penelope not told the suitors before that Odysseus commanded her to marry again once Telemachus has come of age?'[58] Indeed, for our taste the sudden introduction of Odysseus' counsel is odd. Most modern authors would have made sure that it surfaced earlier in the narrative to avoid the impression that it is

---

[56] Stürmer 1921: 418–19; Büchner 1940: 137–46; Müller 1966: 121–2; Levine 1983; Winkler 1990: 146–7; De Jong 2001: 450.

[57] Hölscher 1967; Vester 1968: 430–2; Erbse 1972: 80–90; Emlyn-Jones 1984: 11; Rutherford 1992: 32 n. 26; and, with different nuances, Byre 1988: 165–73. See already Turolla 1930: 171–2.

[58] Büchner 1940: 140: 'Und warum hat Penelope den Freiern nicht schon längst erklärt, gemäß der Weisung ihres Gatten solle sie sich, sobald Telemach volljährig geworden sei, wieder verheiraten?'

only introduced to justify Penelope's initiative. As Lowe notes in his exploration of the classical plot: 'All moves must be seeded in the narrative before they are required . . . The gun must be on the wall, not stashed away in a drawer to be produced where needed.'[59] For the narrative logic described by Lugowski, however, this is not an issue – the reference to Odysseus' council is retroactively motivated. No attempt is made to conceal the fact that an element of the story, here Odysseus' parting words, owes its occurrence to the need to cause an effect, namely to explain Penelope's decision to remarry. Just as in Wickram's *Galmy* a messenger is simply there when he is needed,[60] a reason for Penelope's decision to remarry crops up when it is required by the plot.

The entire scene can be viewed as a case of retroactive motivation. As we have seen, Penelope's entry is motivated through Athena's intervention and Penelope's wish to have a word with Telemachus. This, however, does not make her change of mind psychologically plausible. Penelope's decision to remarry jars with our insights into her inner life. What fully justifies the scene is its crucial role for the further development of the plot. Penelope's announcement of the imminent wedding leads to the bow contest, which affords Odysseus the opportunity to start his revenge. It is therefore a crucial step in the *Odyssey*'s teleology. The function of the scene in the trajectory of the plot is more important than its psychological plausibility. Just as in medieval narrative, the dynamics of plot trump psychological motivation.[61] Homer thereby generates fine irony: the very steps that Penelope takes towards a new wedding ultimately help Odysseus to overpower the suitors and to reassert his role as Penelope's husband.[62]

Penelope's entry can also be viewed as an example of thematic isolation. A plausible emergence of the scene is sidelined by its significance. Penelope's change of mind is odd, but it leads to a powerful scene: in the very presence of Odysseus, Penelope declares that she has given up hope for his return and, following his parting words, will now take a new husband. Homer here construes a strong tension between Penelope's view and the real situation, to be savoured by his audience who knows that the beggar is Odysseus. He also gives his narrative an edge: Odysseus has returned in the nick of time. Had his return been delayed by a couple of days, he might have found Penelope married to Antinous or Eurymachus. As in medieval

---

[59] Lowe 2000: 77.   [60] Compare Lugowski 1976 [1932]: 60–1.
[61] See Lugowski 1976 [1932]: 76 on the Duke in Wickram: 'Mit einem Wort, es ist fraglich, ob im Verhalten des Herzogs überhaupt etwas Verstehbares im Sinne individueller Psychologie vorhanden ist.'
[62] Compare Murnaghan 1987: 129.

narrative, the mileage to be got from a scene proves more important than its plausible development in the world of the action.

Finally, the crisis delineated in book 18 generates suspense. As in many medieval narratives, this suspense does not consist in the uncertainty of the outcome. Foreshadowing as well as the familiarity of the myth allow no doubts to be raised about Odysseus' final triumph. However, Penelope's plan to marry quickly raises the question as to how this end will come about. Countering 108 young men eager to wed Penelope is a tall order by any standard; the temporal pressure now at work makes it even more challenging. There is no time left for drumming up support or any other sort of preparation – Odysseus has to act immediately. Entwined with the irony that Penelope's initiative ultimately works in Odysseus' favour, this suspense about the how gives the revenge narrative its texture.

To conclude, Penelope's behaviour in *Odyssey* 18 and 19 is not in fact reconciled with her thoughts and feelings, but this is not the product of poor composition. What we encounter is a narrative design that privileges the plot function of scenes and their significance above the full psychological motivation of the action. Penelope's decision to remarry is not the only case of this narrative logic in Homer. In order to corroborate my argument, let me select another instance that is thought-provoking also on a systematic level: the *teichoscopia* in *Iliad* 3.121–244. Iris commands Helen to watch the duel between Menelaus and her husband. Helen climbs up the wall of Troy, where she meets Priam and some Trojan elders. The king asks his daughter-in-law to identify the Greeks in front of the wall, and Helen starts to characterize the heroes they are looking at. Helen's conversation with Priam has struck modern readers as odd. Why should Priam now ask his daughter-in-law about the identity of the Greek heroes? After nearly ten years of battling, he must be thoroughly familiar with them: 'Notoriously, the scene is very peculiarly situated in the ninth year of the war, since such an episode would make sense only near the war's start.'[63]

One attempt to remedy the problem is emblematic of the interpretive strategies forged by our experiences of reading modern novels. Tsagarakis argues that Priam's question poses no problem, because it is not a real question. Priam, he claims, notices that Helen feels lost and engages her in a conversation so she feels better. In order to explain an odd action, Tsagarakis, as numerous scholars in other cases, has recourse to the interior lives of the characters. However, there is nothing in the text to

---

[63] Scodel 1997: 78; Krieter-Spiro 2009: 51 on 3.121–244.

justify Tsagarakis' assumption that Priam asks Helen about something he already knows in order to cheer her up – it is pure speculation. Even Ruth Scodel, one of the advocates of the Theory of Mind in Classics, cannot help but reject this interpretation: 'Although characters often do repeat information the hearers know, I do not see sufficient justification of that here.'[64]

Taking a different tack, some scholars argued that the scene is justified by its traditional character, but, as others observed, this is hard to prove.[65] Whether traditional or not, the *teichoscopia*, while unmotivated in the action, is motivated by reasons of composition. We are at the beginning of the battle narrative – Helen's identification gives Homer the opportunity to present the woman that caused the war in her relation to the Greeks and to give an extended introduction of some major Greek heroes. The *teichoscopia* provides the audience with a welcome line-up of the Greeks before the fighting starts. Together with the Catalogue of Ships, it also helps to embed the action of the *Iliad* into the larger panorama of the Trojan War.[66] Both passages give the audience the feeling of standing at the beginning of the war. The *teichoscopia* also contains references to the prehistory of the Trojan War. Like the fore-shadowing of Achilles' death and the fall of Troy in the final books, the *teichoscopia* and the Catalogue of Ships are instrumental for the integration of the fifty-one days to which the *Iliad*'s action is confined into the full story of the war. While unmotivated in the action, the *teichoscopia* has an important compositional function.

There is a broader systematic point in this interpretation. The term of 'retroactive motivation' suggests that the narrative logic described by Lugowski is bound to the ending, and the case of Penelope seems to bear this out. The bow contest initiated by her is a crucial step towards the endgame of the *Odyssey*. The *teichoscopia*, however, stands at the beginning, and its function is very much linked to the beginning. Helen's description of the Greeks introduces major players to the audience and conveys the sense of standing at the beginning. It is compositional reasons in general to which the motivation at the level of the action can cede. In the *teichoscopia*, the opportunity to introduce the audience to the heroes, who are about to

---

[64] Scodel 1997: 78 n. 2.
[65] Kirk 1985 on 3.161–246 and Edwards 1987: 189 claim that it is traditional; Wyatt 1989/90: 18 and Krieter-Spiro 2009 on 3.121–244: 51 are sceptical. On the *teichoscopia*, see also Fuhrer 2015.
[66] In Grethlein 2006: 272–80, I argue for a further temporal dynamic, as the conjuring up of the war's beginning coincides with the possibility of its ending through the duel. In the light of Helen's weaving in 3.125–8, it is easy to see here a reflection on the mythical tradition.

spring into action, proves more important than a full motivation of the
scene in the world of the action.

It is psychological plausibility in particular that receives short shrift in
such Homeric scenes, which are highly charged in themselves and
pivotal to the trajectory of the plot. Homer does not fail to motivate
the action, as Athena's intervention and Penelope's wish to talk to
Telemachus both highlight. In the *apologoi*, Homer even goes out of
his way to account for Odysseus' knowledge of a divine conversation.
When Odysseus reports that Helius asked Zeus to punish those who had
killed his cattle, he hastens to add his source, Circe, who herself had
learnt it from Hermes (12.389–90).[67] While concerned with motivation
in general, Homer does not always feel the need to make the actions of
his characters psychologically plausible. It is odd that Priam requests the
identification of familiar faces and that Penelope expects her husband's
return and nonetheless presses for a new wedding. But both scenes fulfil
important functions in the plot: the *teichoscopia* allows Homer to
describe some of the main Greek heroes individually before the battle
narrative begins, Penelope's intervention generates suspense and simultaneously creates a foothold for Odysseus' revenge. The alleged inconsistencies of Homeric narrative are part of a narrative logic that does not
conform with the conventions of modern realist novels but which is
closer to the peculiarities of medieval narrative as explored by
Lugowski.[68]

My approach ultimately explains why Penelope has proven such an
intriguing character for modern readers. Her actions are not fully motivated in psychological terms, but designed to fit the requirements of the plot
and the scene at hand. Used as they are to psychological motivation,
modern scholars feel the need to fill this gap by supplementing the working
of Penelope's mind with her actions and utterances. To many Homerists,
her behaviour has seemed understandable only if she consciously or subconsciously knows about Odysseus' presence. Other scholars have made
Penelope's indeterminacy the point of their interpretation. For them
Penelope's multifarious ambivalence forces the audience to reflect on her

---

[67] Ancient critics already took issue with the contradiction between Odysseus' assertion and book 5
(scholion on 5.79). For a survey of modern approaches and an attempt to mitigate the tension, see
Erbse 1972: 12–6.
[68] The unconcern with psychological motivation seems to be part of a broader tendency in Homer to
devote little attention to the inner lives of his characters, at least significantly less than we are used to
from modern realist novels. For this argument and a discussion of the case of Telemachus, see
Grethlein 2017a: 71–9.

motives. Neither interpretation is wrong. It is legitimate, even inevitable, to read texts in the light of one's own sensibilities, which, in our case, are decisively shaped by modern realist novels and their conventions of motivation. Nonetheless, it ought to be noted that the psychological motivation at the core of modern interpretations seems to have been of minor importance to Homer and his original audience. Ironically, it is the neglect of psychological plausibility that renders Penelope so fascinating for readers who expect characters to be round and coherent in psychological terms.

4   Compositional Motivation and Homeric Psychology and Oral Poetry

Can the compositional motivation found in the *teichoscopia* and the Penelope scenes of *Odyssey* 18 and 19 be explained in terms of Homeric psychology and/or oral poetry? Above all, it needs to be emphasized that my inquiry does not pander to the idea that Homer is too archaic to have a proper sense of human psychology.[69] Homer knows very well how to portray interior processes. Think for example of the beginning of book 20, when Odysseus becomes angry at the female servants but then reminds himself of far worse experiences and thereby appeases his anger (20.13–24). Homer first describes Odysseus' sentiment with a striking metaphor – 'the heart was growling within him' – follows this up with a dog simile and then has Odysseus express his feelings in direct speech. Odysseus' tossing back and forth, illustrated by another simile, a stomach turned at a fire (20.25–30), is a physical expression of his emotional turmoil. The scene showcases Homer's ability to use various forms of presentation for elaborating on consciousness processes.[70]

The epic does not confine itself to the depiction of interior processes, it also engages its characters in mind reading.[71] In *Iliad* 1, Agamemnon sends

---

[69] This idea was developed in the influential studies of Snell 1993 and Fränkel 1993. The *geistesgeschichtliche* approach to Homer has long been a favourite whipping boy, but its ideas have never entirely disappeared. Steiner 2010: 27, for instance, writes: 'Without presuming that the poet attributes to Penelope the complex inner life and psychology that belong to individuals in works that long postdate archaic epic . . .' More importantly, scholars have started to reassess Snell's thesis about Homer's idea of man in the light of post-human theory, see Holmes 2010: 1–40 and Purves 2015.

[70] Privitera 2018 offers a cognitivist reading of Homer's presentation of Odysseus at the beginning of book 20. For the various ways of presenting a character's interior life, see Palmer 2004.

[71] This is a different point from the one discussed in Chapter 4 – it refers to the mind reading of the characters within the narrative, not the question of whether mind reading is key to our response to the narrative.

two heralds to fetch Briseis from Achilles' tent. The heralds go reluctantly
on their mission (1.329–36):

> τὸν δ' εὗρον παρά τε κλισίῃ καὶ νηΐ μελαίνῃ
> ἥμενον· οὐδ' ἄρα τώ γε ἰδὼν γήθησεν Ἀχιλλεύς.
> τὼ μὲν ταρβήσαντε καὶ αἰδομένω βασιλῆα
> στήτην, οὐδέ τί μιν προσεφώνεον οὐδ' ἐρέοντο·
> αὐτὰρ ὃ ἔγνω ᾗσιν ἐνὶ φρεσὶ φώνησέν τε·
> χαίρετε κήρυκες Διὸς ἄγγελοι ἠδὲ καὶ ἀνδρῶν,
> ἆσσον ἴτ'· οὔ τί μοι ὔμμες ἐπαίτιοι ἀλλ' Ἀγαμέμνων,
> ὃ σφῶϊ προΐει Βρισηΐδος εἵνεκα κούρης.

The man himself they found beside his shelter and his black ship
Sitting. And Achilles took no joy at all when he saw them.
These two terrified and in awe of the king stood waiting
Quietly, and did not speak a word at all nor question him.
But he understood in his mind and spoke first:
'Welcome, heralds, messengers of Zeus and of mortals.
Draw near. You are not to blame in my sight, but Agamemnon
Who sent the two of you here for the sake of the girl Briseis.'

Achilles deduces the state of mind of the two heralds from their posture
and silence.[72] Mind reading also offers an explanation for some verses in
the *Odyssey* related to Penelope's comportment. When the dead suitors
enter the Underworld, Agamemnon inquires about their fate.
Amphimedon recounts the *mnesterophonia*, claiming that Penelope con-
spired with Odysseus in the bow contest (24.167–9). Since this claim
deviates from Homer's account, it has been argued that it is a trace of an
alternative tradition in which Penelope actually was in cahoots with
Odysseus. But it is also possible and easier to explain the divergence
along different lines: seeing that Odysseus uses the bow contest to start
on his revenge, Amphimedon conjectures that Penelope colludes with
Odysseus. In this case, Homer integrates in his narrative an erroneous
act of mind reading without highlighting its mistake. If, as I have argued,
psychological plausibility is less important for the motivation of the action,
this is not so much a sign of a primitive psychology as a part of a specific
narrative logic.

At the same time, the tendency to pay more attention to the dynamics of
plot than to psychological plausibility is consonant with ancient concepts
of selfhood. In the preceding chapter, I referred to Christopher Gill's thesis
that in antiquity, character, shaped especially by moral judgement, was

---

[72] On this example, see Scodel 2014: 57–8.

more prominent than personality, which Gill defined by introspection and a Cartesian idea of selfhood.[73] While the modern focus on interiority inspires narratives which fully motivate their actions psychologically, the ancient emphasis on character seems to lean towards narrations that are more invested in plot than in character. Moral qualities that can serve as exempla come to the fore rather in actions than in reflections which render a character distinct and ultimately incomparable. It is of course possible to adduce ancient narratives that feature elements of personality, and yet, my analysis of Homeric epic suggests that Gill on the whole has managed to capture a tendency of ancient narrative.[74]

If the Homeric sense of motivation is not the expression of a primitive psychology, can it be linked to the medium itself? The medievalist Harald Haferland links retroactive motivation to oral storytelling, for here 'the attention of a narrator is mostly directed towards the further course and the goal to be reached'.[75] This thesis seems to chime with oralist explanations of inconsistencies in Homer. In *Iliad* 5, for example, Pylaemenes is killed by Menelaus (5.576). When, however, in book 13 his son dies, Pylaemenes seems to have been resurrected – he is named as part of the procession following the body (13.658). Observing parallels in South Slavic oral epic, Albert Lord made a case that this and other contradictions are a result of the thematic technique of oral composition. The theme of death and burial of a son, which 'contains in itself the detail of the mourning father',[76] takes precedence over consistency with the preceding narrative.

Lord's argument is compelling, and yet it works better for contradictions between separate scenes than for the motivation within a single scene tackled in this chapter. Note also that Lugowski's test cases are mostly products of a literate culture and therefore speak against the idea that what is described as mythical analogon is simply an oral feature. We should thus beware of the medial fallacy – explanations solely in terms of the medium often fall short of phenomena that are multifaceted. Narrative logic is certainly influenced, but not fully determined, by medium. Even if there is an affinity between retroactive motivation, thematic isolation and suspense as to how with orality, this does not exhaust their significance. They are first of all expressions of a distinct narrative logic.

---

[73] Gill 1990; 1996.
[74] I am unconvinced by Christensen's monograph on the *Odyssey*, which argues that the Homeric epic 'resonates with multiple theories about human psychology that developed during the twentieth century' (2020: 21).
[75] Haferland 2014: 71.   [76] Lord 1938: 445.

It is therefore not surprising that some of the peculiarities observed in Homeric epic also pertain to other genres and later texts. One feature is particularly conspicuous: suspense about the how looms large in ancient literature in general, particularly because many genres tap into the fountain of myth. Later epic, narrative lyric and tragedy mostly rely on stories that were well known. They also make ample use of foreshadowing that may adumbrate the outcome but has the recipient wonder about how it will come about. Even in genres with fictive subjects, suspense as to how is prominent. In New Comedy and the novel, genre conventions engender a similar effect that the familiarity of myth produces in epic and tragedy and prepare the reader for the ending.

Retroactive motivation and thematic isolation can also be traced in later literature. Even though most genres motivate their action within the narrated world, it is possible to find scenes that do not conform to what readers of the modern novels would expect. A genre that in general puts little stock in causal and psychological motivation is Old Comedy. The plots of Aristophanes' plays are not tight-woven – one of their central elements, the parabasis, even makes a point of not being fully anchored in the action and of directly addressing the audience. But also outside the parabaseis, comic purposes often get the better of a stringent course of action and a consistent portrayal of characters.[77] While it is easy to shrug off Old Comedy on the grounds that it is a genre defined by the upheaval of all sorts of conventions, tragedy offers a thought-provoking case, also because Aristotle extolled it as the exemplary genre of poetry in the *Poetics* (to which I will turn in the subsequent section). That Greek tragedy differs in the motivation of its action from naturalist drama can be gleaned from a long and intense debate on an adjacent topic: tragic character.

Inspired not least by Tycho von Wilamowitz-Moellendorff's disserta-tion on Sophocles (1917), scholars such as Dawe and Lloyd-Jones power-fully challenged the psychologizing approach that had long dominated interpretations of Greek tragedy.[78] The Greek tragedians, they claimed, did not pursue compelling character portrayals but a dramatic technique that aimed at generating the maximum dramatic effect in any scene. Inevitably, their arguments provoked counter-arguments from scholars

---

[77] Lowe 2000: 86–8 aptly discusses Old Comedy in his chapter on unclassical plots.

[78] Dawe 1963; Lloyd-Jones 1972. The different ways of referring to Tycho von Wilamowitz-Moellendorff are curious: Dawe addresses him as Tycho Wilamowitz, Lloyd-Jones speaks of Tycho (I am still waiting to see a reference to 'Hugh' in print . . .). For an early adoption of his ideas in German scholarship, see, for example, Howald 1930.

unwilling to discard the notion of character in their interpretations. Pat Easterling, for example, admitted that it 'is right to dismiss as distracting the question "What sort of a person is Agamemnon"' but insisted that 'we ought not to be depriving ourselves of full belief in Agamemnon as a real person'.[79] There is, she contended, 'human intelligibility'[80] in the characters of Greek tragedy: 'The people and events – the doing and suffering – he portrays convince us with the same kind of blind authenticity as we find in Shakespeare or George Eliot.'[81]

This is not the place for a reassessment of the debate on tragic character; let me just say that two points may help steer us toward a middle ground between the two extreme positions of either dispensing with the idea of character or denying the differences between Aeschylus and Ibsen. First, reader-response theory and cognitive approaches suggest that characters in texts be considered as something that recipients generate on the basis of textual signs, using schemata from everyday interactions as well as literary conventions.[82] Second, whether Gill fully succeeds in reconstructing ancient notions of selfhood or not, his contributions have demonstrated that characters in antiquity were viewed in moral and paradigmatic terms rather than as unique holders of interior lives. In the light of both points, it should not be difficult to accept that characters on the tragic stage fall short of the individuation that we have come to expect from literary characters but still managed to engage ancient audiences.

But it is another point that is crucial for my argument: Tycho von Wilamowitz-Moellendorff was not primarily interested in characterization; he took his cue from the inconsistencies and contradictions in tragedies that previous generations of scholars, including his famous father, had tried to solve analytically by means of textual criticism. The peculiarities from which Tycho von Wilamowitz-Moellendorff starts concern not only character portrayal, but also consistency of fact. Instead of condemning and excising them, he explains them as part of a specific dramatic technique that, in trying to make scenes as effective as possible, disregarded

---

[79] Easterling 1973: 9. See also Easterling 1977 on Sophocles.
[80] Easterling 1973: 6. Gould 1978, another important contribution to the debate, points out the problems of Easterling's notion of 'human intelligibility' and, paying particular attention to language and metaphor, stresses that tragic characters cannot be detached from the world of their plays. This approach is picked up by Goldhill 1986: 168–98. The contributions to Pelling 1990 continue the debate and extend it to other genres. As van Emde Boas 2018: 319 n. 11 notes, 'it is perhaps not too much of an exaggeration to state that little has "happened" in the debate since the collection appeared'.
[81] Easterling 1973: 7.   [82] For example, Schneider 2001.

inconsistencies with other scenes.[83] In other words, according to Tycho
von Wilamowitz-Moellendorff, thematic isolation is key in the plays of
Sophocles and, as later scholars added, also of the other tragedians.

Now, not every inconsistency detected by von Wilamowitz-
Moellendorff Jr. holds up to scrutiny. In his interpretation of *Antigone*,
for example, he considers it obscure how the heroine could remain
undetected when she buries Polyneices for the first time. However, as
Lloyd-Jones notes, 'surely it is easy for the spectator to infer that she does
so under cover of the darkness'.[84] Likewise, her return to the body is not as
inexplicable as von Wilamowitz-Moellendorff Jr. believes: 'But is one
guilty of psychologizing unreasonably if one takes it for granted that she
has heard of the desecration of the body and hastens to repair the
damage?'[85] Nonetheless, a look at scholarship suffices to see that there are
plenty more scenes which challenge modern readers looking for full causal
and psychological motivation.

A nice example that illustrates the discrepancy between the tragedians'
sense of motivation and the assumptions of modern readers is the carpet
scene in *Agamemnon*. After the third stasimon, Aeschylus has Agamemnon
enter the stage, finally returning from Troy. Clytaemnestra comes to greet
her husband, bringing crimson tapestries and asking him 'not to let your
foot touch the ground, my king, the foot/ that toppled Troy' (ἔκβαιν'
ἀπήνης τῆσδε, μὴ χαμαὶ τιθεὶς/ τὸν σὸν πόδ', ὦναξ, Ἰλίου πορθήτορα,
906–7). Agamemnon first rejects this because 'only the gods one honours
in this way./ A man who walks on fineries such as these/ walks fearfully'
(τίθει· θεούς τοι τοῖσδε τιμαλφεῖν χρεών,/ ἐν ποικίλοις δὲ θνητὸν ὄντα
κάλλεσιν/ βαίνειν ἐμοὶ μὲν οὐδαμῶς ἄνευ φόβου, 922–4). However, after
a brief stichomythia, he gives in and walks on the carpet. Why, modern
scholars have wondered, does he change his mind? Fraenkel contends that
Agamemnon is 'a great gentleman, possessed of moderation and self-
control', who is reluctant 'to get the better of a woman'. At a yet-deeper
level, he yields because 'he is tired to the utmost, worn out by the unceasing
struggle, overpowered by the slings and arrows of outrageous fortune'.[86]
The readers of the commentary of Denniston and Page encounter a very

---

[83] von Wilamowitz-Moellendorff 1917: 20: 'The dramatic effect of the individual scene thus matters
more to him than the unified analysis of the fable, and it is his calculation that the incongruence with
reference to past and minor things is not noticed because in this way what really happens in each case
is most powerful in the eyes of the spectator.' ('Die dramatische Wirkung der einzelnen Szene steht
ihm also höher als die einheitliche Analyse der Fabel, und er rechnet damit, daß, da das jedesmal vor
Augen des Zuschauers wirklich Geschehende so zur stärksten Wirkung kommt, die auf vergangene
und nebensächliche Dinge bezügliche Inkongruenz nicht bemerkt wird.')
[84] Lloyd-Jones 1972: 220.   [85] Lloyd-Jones 1972: 220.   [86] Fraenkel 1950, I: 441–2.

different Agamemnon, a haughty leader, who deep inside harbours the hybristic desire to walk on the purple, who is 'at the mercy of his own vanity and arrogance, instantly ready to do this scandalous act the moment his personal fears of divine retribution and human censure are, by whatever sophistry, allayed'.[87]

How come such outstanding philologists, intimately familiar with Aeschylus' works, offer contradictory readings? The reason is that, as Fraenkel frankly acknowledged, Aeschylus 'nowhere reveals his motives explicitly'. As in the case of Penelope, the scene is not psychologically motivated. Even Easterling in her argument against Tychoism distances herself from attempts at 'attributing motives to Agamemnon in terms of his character'.[88] It is also insufficient, if not wrong to assert that 'Agamemnon surrenders ... because it was dramatically necessary that he should do so'.[89] Agamemnon's walk on the carpet is by no means necessary for the tragedy to take its course. It is not causally linked to his death in the bathtub by the hands of Clytaemnestra. What motivates the action is a scene that is powerful in itself – Agamemnon meets Clytaemnestra and lets himself be talked into something that he knows is wrong – and highly charged with symbols, for example, the colour of the carpet, which evokes the blood that has flown and will flow.[90] The act of 'trampling with the foot' and the language used evoke other parts of the action, not least Agamemnon's decision to sacrifice his daughter at Aulis – they make the scene an intense reflection on, among others, wealth and sin, action and punishment, control and fate.[91]

As in the examination of Homer's Penelope, we can now see why this scene has intrigued scholars and provoked so many different interpretations. There is no psychological motivation in the tapestry scene – Aeschylus is not interested in what makes Agamemnon change his mind, what his thoughts or feelings are before and when he actually steps on the carpet, other than the explicitly mentioned awareness that it is transgressive. Accustomed to explaining actions in psychological terms, however, Fraenkel, Denniston and Page and others have hurried to supply Agamemnon's interior life and, since it is not provided by the text, have come up with very different interpretations that challenged those of others

[87] Denniston and Page 1957 on 931–9. For yet another view, see Lloyd-Jones 1962, who sees Atê at work in Agamemnon's decision.
[88] Easterling 1973: 15, here seconded by Heath 1987: 119–20.   [89] Dawe 1963: 50.
[90] Goheen 1955.
[91] For example, Lebeck 1971: 74–9; Easterling 1973: 17–19. On the entwinement of different temporal layers in the *Oresteia*, see Grethlein 2013a, focusing on choral odes.

and were themselves open to criticism. Among the many reasons for the continuing attraction of Greek tragedy, this may well be one: the disregard for psychological motivation, by no means in all scenes, but still in some key scenes, which stimulates the imagination of modern readers and allows for a wide range of interpretations and engaged debates. Just as in the case of Homer's Penelope, the conventions of modern literature prompt interpreters to supplement the psychological motivation that is lacking.

Thematic isolation and retroactive motivation can even be detected in the most powerful heirs of the *Odyssey*'s teleological plot design, New Comedy and Greek novel.[92] The authors of both genres take pains to couch their teleologies in actions that are also causally motivated. Indeed, it seems to be the gist of their plotting technique to create narrative universes in which every element is keyed to the tight trajectory of the plot and at the same time emerges naturally within the story-world. Nonetheless, there are cases in which the motivation at the level of the action wears so thin that the act of introducing individual elements merely for the sake of the plot reveals itself as overly transparent. Some scenes in comedies and novels are reminiscent of fairy tales, in which the prince just happens to come to the right place at the right time to fend off the dragon and wed the princess.[93] If the single steps and elements leading to such coincidences are not made fully plausible, they become a salient case of retroactive motivation and, possibly, thematic isolation.

Let me give an example from the novel discussed at more length in the preceding chapter. At the end of Heliodorus' *Ethiopica*, Charicleia has been identified as the daughter of the Ethiopian king and queen, but Theagenes is about to be sacrificed. At this very moment, an old man appears who turns out to be Charicleia's Greek stepfather. Charicles, who has come all the way from Delphi to Meroe, spots Theagenes, whom he insults as the thief of his daughter. After Charicles has been reunited with his stepdaughter, his miraculous appearance, together with other extraordinary happenings, is interpreted as sign that the gods do not wish Theagenes to be sacrificed. The entry of Charicles thus removes the last barrier that separates the plot from its telos and generates a powerful finale in which all of Charicleia's parents, both natural and surrogate, are present. Charicles had vowed to find his daughter, but his appearance in Ethiopia at this moment – he dropped from the narrator's radar after book 2 – is

---

[92] For the debt of New Comedy and Greek novel to the *Odyssey* and the trajectory of the classical plot, see Lowe 2000, which is admirable but does not notice Homer's peculiar sense of motivation that does not fit the bill of a classical plot.

[93] Compare Haferland 2014: 71–2, who draws on Lüthi's investigation of fairy tales (1975).

unprepared. There is not the kind of inconsistency that we noticed in the *Odyssey*'s portrayal of Penelope; and yet, Charicles' entry is barely motivated and simultaneously pivotal to the plot and a grand final scene, constituting a weak case of retroactive motivation and thematic isolation.[94]

As cursory as this look at Greek literature beyond Homer is, it indicates that the conventions of motivation vary from genre to genre. While, for example, New Comedy and the Greek novel indulge in tightly woven plots, the scenes in Old Comedy often lack causal links. Nonetheless, there are tendencies that distinguish the ancient sense of narrative from our view and are therefore hard to capture by approaches that take their cue from the likes of Stendhal's *The Red and the Black*. Retroactive motivation and thematic isolation is not confined to Homeric epic, and suspense about the how becomes a prominent element in a wide range of genres. Most importantly, our focus on the characters' interior lives and their uniqueness makes us expect full motivation in psychological terms – ancient narratives, on the other hand, were rather driven by the exigencies of plot and accepted inconsistencies for the launching of arresting scenes. In some ways, this discrepancy has proven fruitful in scholarship – many modern debates revolve around the psychological motivation not provided by ancient debates.

5 Motivation in Aristotle and Scholia

How does my argument about narrative logic in Homer (and later Greek literature) square with Aristotle's emphasis on motivation? The plausibility of the action is of great concern in the *Poetics* – Aristotle repeatedly stresses that events have to be either probable or necessary. However, not only is Aristotle significantly later and the literary culture of which he forms part very different from the Homeric performance culture, we also need to keep in mind the strong normative thrust of the *Poetics*. Aristotle does not necessarily give an adequate description of how tragedy and epic work. That said, if we take a closer look at Aristotle's discussion of motivation, we can see that the discrepancy with the narrative logic which we found in *Odyssey* 18 and 19 is smaller than it appears at first sight. In fact, the *Poetics* corroborates a key point of my argument.

Motivation figures prominently in Aristotle's examination of *mythos* in chapters 7 to 14. At the beginning, Aristotle stresses the importance of

---

[94] Lowe 2000: 257 observes that Charicles' intervention also fulfils Willcock's law that 'theft did not entitle one, even in comedy, to retain free possession of what had been stolen'. Theagenes can marry Charicleia only after her father, in this case Charicles, has assented to it.

unity. The definition of beginning, middle and ending implies the importance of causal links between the parts of a tragedy (1450b26–34): the beginning has no necessary connection with preceding events while triggering further events, the middle is causally connected with both what precedes and what follows and the ending ensues from earlier events, without however having something necessarily follow. In chapter 8, Aristotle stipulates that the parts of a unitary plot 'should be so constructed that the displacement or removal of any one of them will disturb and disjoint the work's wholeness. For anything whose presence or absence has no clear effect cannot be counted an integral part of the whole' (καὶ τὰ μέρη συνεστάναι τῶν πραγμάτων ὥστε μετατιθεμένου τινὸς μέρους ἢ ἀφαιρουμένου διαφέρεσθαι καὶ κινεῖσθαι τὸ ὅλον· ὃ γὰρ προσὸν ἢ μὴ προσὸν μηδὲν ποιεῖ ἐπίδηλον, οὐδὲν μόριον τοῦ ὅλου ἐστίν, 1451a32–5).

The salience of fully motivated scenes is also spotlighted in chapter 9 when Aristotle considers episodic plots the worst of all simple plots, because 'the episodes follow in a succession which is neither probable nor necessary' (λέγω δ' ἐπεισοδιώδη μῦθον ἐν ᾧ τὰ ἐπεισόδια μετ' ἄλληλα οὔτ' εἰκὸς οὔτ' ἀνάγκη εἶναι, 1451b34–5). The action becomes fearful and pitiful, on the other hand, 'when things occur contrary to expectation yet still on account of one another' (ὅταν γένηται παρὰ τὴν δόξαν δι' ἄλληλα, 1452a4). Introducing the discussion of reversal and recognition as key features of the complex plot in chapter 10, Aristotle notes that both 'should arise from the intrinsic structure of the plot, so that what results follows by either necessity or probability from the preceding events: for it makes a great difference whether things happen because of one another, or only after one another' (ταῦτα δὲ δεῖ γίνεσθαι ἐξ αὐτῆς τῆς συστάσεως τοῦ μύθου, ὥστε ἐκ τῶν προγεγενημένων συμβαίνειν ἢ ἐξ ἀνάγκης ἢ κατὰ τὸ εἰκὸς γίγνεσθαι ταῦτα· διαφέρει γὰρ πολὺ τὸ γίγνεσθαι τάδε διὰ τάδε ἢ μετὰ τάδε, 1452a18–21).

That Aristotle's ideas about motivation were stricter than the practice of the tragedians is on display when he adduces the entry of Aegeus in *Medea* as an example of an unmotivated scene in chapter 25 (1461b19–21). Aegeus' appearance in Corinth at this point is unprepared and incidental. While the Aristotelian criteria of probability or necessity are not fulfilled, the scene illustrates that motivation in tragedy does not have to be causal.[95] Structurally, the scene marks a rupture in the plot – before the encounter with Aegeus, Medea is passive and suffering, after it she becomes active. There is also a manifold thematic motivation: Aegeus' childlessness

---

[95] For a discussion of the scene with references to scholarship, see Grethlein 2003: 335–52.

spotlights the topic of parenthood, which will take on a gruesome dimension soon. When Aegeus accepts Medea's supplication and swears an oath that Athens will take her in as a refugee, he establishes a contrast with Corinth, where Jason has broken an oath and fails to heed his obligation towards Medea. Note also that the integration of Athens into the plot brings the action closer to the audience in the theatre of Dionysus – uncannily if they were familiar with the tradition that Medea, after becoming Aegeus' wife, attempted to kill his son Theseus.[96] Moreover, the Aegeus scene can be viewed as a case of retroactive motivation. Several scholars emphasize that only the security of the future asylum in Athens allows Medea to enact her revenge.[97] Seen from this perspective, the Aegeus scene is finally motivated.

While Aristotle's emphasis on causality is far from exhausting the dynamics of motivation in tragedy, the discussion of the *Poetics* is aligned with the practice of the tragedians in one important regard. Aristotle also introduces consistency as an essential aspect of well-crafted characters and points out that the criteria of probability and necessity apply to characters as well as to plot (1454a26–31);[98] and yet it is striking that he discusses motivation chiefly as an issue of plot. The psychological motivation that readers of modern realist novels are trained to expect and have come to appreciate does not play a significant role in the *Poetics*. Aristotle's infatuation with plot, on which I touched in the preceding chapter, also bears on his treatment of motivation.[99] While the causal connection of the individual events of a unified action is paramount for his theory of tragic and epic poetry, the credible emergence of actions from the interior lives of the characters is tangential. This focus corresponds to the negligence of the psychological grounding of Agamemnon's decision to step on the carpet and Penelope's comportment in *Odyssey* 18 and 19.

Aristotle's interest in motivation was, it seems, shared by many ancient critics. The scholia on Homer, tragedy and other genres frequently comment on the integration of individual scenes.[100] While lacking plausibility is a popular reason for atheteses, evidence of motivation helps save controversial passages from criticism, but it was also presented for its own sake.

---

[96] For the evidence for this tradition, see Sourvinou-Inwood 1979; Graf 1997.

[97] For example, McDermott 1989: 45 n. 9; Boedeker 1991.

[98] See also 1451b8–10 on the ramification of tragedy's engagement with the 'universal' for characterization.

[99] On Aristotle's notion of tragedy as a *mimêsis* of action and not of characters, see Jones 1962 and the works listed in Chapter 4. n. 76.

[100] See Meijering 1987: 171–220; Nünlist 2009: 27–34, with further literature in 23 n. 3 and 24 n. 7; Feddern 2021: 69–80.

The prominence of motivation in ancient criticism is tangible in the emergence of a quasi-technical term for it: *Prooikonomein* and its cognates, but also the simplex *oikonomikos*, surface frequently in the scholia.[101] The critics' fixation on motivation is also evident in interpretations that most scholars would consider forced today. Is, for example, Hector's instruction to Andromache to look after the household in *Iliad* 6 really intended to motivate the fact that she is not standing on the wall when Achilles kills Hector in book 22 (bT Il. 6.491–2)? Or what modern scholar would contend that, when Priam steps on a chariot and takes the reins in book 3, Homer 'prepares for the chariot-driving in book 24' (προοικονομεῖ τὴν ἐν τῇ Ω ἡνιοχείαν (sc. 326–7), bT Il. 3.261–2b)?

Crucially for my argument, the scholia are in line with Aristotle in their focus on matters of plot. There are also comments on psychological motivation.[102] In Euripides' *Andromache*, for example, Peleus blames Menelaus for having been quickly taken in by Helen after the fall of Troy (628–31). The scholion on 631 notes: 'This has been better presented in the verses by Ibycus (296b): for Helen flees to the temple of Aphrodite and from there talks to Menelaus. Under the sway of love he drops the sword' (ἄμεινον ᾠκονόμηται τὰ περὶ Ἴβυκον· εἰς γὰρ Ἀφροδίτης ναὸν καταλ ... εἰ ἡ Ἑλένη κἀκεῖθεν διαλέγεται τῷ Μενελάῳ, ὁ δ' ὑπ' ἔρωτος ἀφίησι τὸ ξίφος). The grammarian on whose discussion the scholion is based apparently thought that Menelaus' change of mind in Euripides was too quick to be fully convincing (bypassing the fact that the reference was a speech act intended to rebuke Menelaus).

An example from the *Iliad* can be found in the scholia on book 11. Here, Achilles sends Patroclus to Nestor in order to inquire about the wounded Greeks. The scholion notes (bT Il. 11.677–761): 'Patroclus is respectful: for, although he is in a hurry, he puts up with the old man when he is speaking for such a long time' (αἰδήμων ὁ Πάτροκλος. ἐπειγόμενος γὰρ ἀνέχεται τοῦ γέροντος μακρολογοῦντος.).[103] However, the following comment reveals the focus on causal links:

οἰκονομικῶς δὲ πέπλασται τῷ ποιητῇ ἡ μακρὰ διήγησις, ἵνα ὁ Εὐρύπυλος ἐκ τῆς μάχης φθάσας ἐλθεῖν περιτύχῃ Πατρόκλῳ, καὶ παρὰ τούτῳ ἐμβραδύνῃ περὶ τῆς τειχομαχίας· bT εἰ γὰρ ταχέως ἐπανῆλθε πρὸς Ἀχιλλέα καὶ ἐκπεμφθῆναι ἑαυτὸν ἔπεισεν εἰς τὴν μάχην, ἀνῃρέθη ἂν ἡ τειχομαχία, δι' ἣν ἐπλάσθη τὸ τεῖχος.T

---

[101] Compare Grisolia 2001.

[102] On *ethos* in the Homeric scholia, see Richardson 1980: 272–5; in tragedy, see Heath 1987: 116 n. 45.

[103] On Patroclus' gentle character, see also scholia bT Il. 11.616; 670–764; 677–8; 814; 12.1; 19.297.

The long narration is crafted economically by the poet, so that Eurypylus, who returns early from the battle encounters Patroclus, and slows down in his presence on account of the wall-fight. For if he had returned quickly to Achilles and had persuaded him to send him to the battle, the wall-fight, for which the wall has been introduced, would have been taken away.

In the eyes of the commentator, Nestor's narration and the conversation with Eurypylus serve to delay Patroclus' entry into the battle and permit the Trojans to push ahead and fight the Greeks at their wall. This wall-fight is even considered the reason for the earlier building of the wall.

Similarly, when in *Iliad* 18 Hector rejects Poulydamas' advice to return to the city and meets the approval of the army, the scholion notes first that the prospect of rich spoils prevented the soldiers from realizing the risk and then emphasizes the significance of the decision to stay in the field for the further course of the plot (bT 18.312–13b). Another scholion elaborates only on this point without touching on the soldiers' mindset (bT 18.312–13a): 'the plot economy is compelling: for had they fled to the city, the same would have happened as at the beginning, the Trojans inside the walls and a siege: and Hector would not have died and would have been prevented by the elders from stepping forward' (πιθανὴ ἡ οἰκονομία· εἰ γὰρ ἔφυγον εἰς τὴν πόλιν, ταὐτὰ τοῖς ἐν ἀρχῇ ἐγένετο, τειχήρεις οἱ Τρῶες καὶ πολιορκία. καὶ οὐδ' ἂν ὁ Ἕκτωρ ἀπώλετο, κωλυόμενος ὑπὸ τῶν δημογερόντων προελθεῖν, b(BCE3)).[104]

When Achilles returns to his tent in *Iliad* 23, he falls asleep 'for his shining limbs were grown weary / indeed, from running in chase of Hector toward windy Ilion' (νήδυμος ἀμφιχυθείς· μάλα γὰρ κάμε φαίδιμα γυῖα / Ἕκτορ' ἐπαΐσσων προτὶ Ἴλιον ἠνεμόεσσαν, 23.63–4). Achilles' ability to sleep invites speculation about his state of mind – how does he feel after killing Hector, does the sleep indicate that he has found some peace or were the strains of the past days simply too much even for Achilles? The scholion, however, instead of engaging in such psychological interpretations, emphasizes the plot function of the verse (bT Il. 23.63b): 'He [Homer] justly prepared Achilles' running, so that he is able to bring a very moving scene: for how could the distressed man be struck by such deep sleep?' (δικαίως οὖν προῳκονόμει τὸν δρόμον Ἀχιλλέως, ὅπως περιπαθὲς ἐπεισόδιον (sc. Ψ 65–107) ἐνέγκῃ· πῶς γὰρ ἂν ὁ ἔμφροντις οὕτω βαθεῖ ἐβλήθη ὕπνῳ;). The commentator was aware of the psychological implausibility of a sleeping Achilles but accepts the physical

---

[104] On the oddity of calling the *oikonomia*, not the development of the action 'compelling', see Meijering 1987: 182.

exhaustion as an explanation. His chief interest is in its significance for the plot, namely its preparation of the spectacular scene in which the dead Patroclus appears before Achilles. The scholion illustrates that ancient critics did not ignore psychological issues but were ultimately more invested with the workings of plot.

One final example: in *Iliad* 11, Odysseus finds himself alone on the battlefield and wonders whether he should flee like the other Achaeans or stand his ground. He concludes his contemplation, rendered in direct speech by Homer, with the decision to stay. Much could be said about the psychological process leading to this decision – the wavering between risk and ambition, between fear and courage – and yet the longest scholion comments on the relevance of Odysseus' decision for the further course of the action (bT 11.407–10): 'The account of Odysseus' reckoning serves the narrative economy: for the poet, because he wishes to introduce the fight at the ships, injures the best beforehand. For were they [the best] present, it would be impossible for the ships to have been burned' (χρησίμως πρὸς τὴν οἰκονομίαν ἔχει τὰ τοῦ ἐπιλογισμοῦ τῷ Ὀδυσσεῖ· ἐπειδὴ γὰρ ναυμαχίαν βούλεται εἰσάγειν ὁ ποιητής, προτιτρώσκει τοὺς ἀρίστους· ἄτοπον γὰρ ἦν παρόντων καίεσθαι τὰς ναῦς). Homer, the commentator argues, has Odysseus decide to remain, so he can be injured and, through his removal together with that of other heroes, be able to give the Trojans a chance to press on and finally reach the ships. As in the case of the wall-fight, a passage is explained as motivating a later spectacular fighting scene.

Another scholion on Odysseus' decision scene is worth quoting; it addresses Odysseus' direct speech (bT 11.403–10): 'He poetically expresses the thoughts as speech. At the same time, he gives the instruction that one ought not to rush frantically in the face of danger' (ποιητικῶς τὰ ἐνθυμηθέντα ὡς εἰρημένα διατυποῖ. ἅμα δὲ καὶ διδάσκει ὅτι οὐ μανικῶς ὁρμᾶν δεῖ εἰς τὰ δεινά). This scholion at least touches on Odysseus' thought process, but the way in which it is viewed by the scholion is revealing: instead of contemplating the emotions at work, the commentator emphasizes the moral message conveyed to the reader. Like some of the passages discussed in Chapter 4, the comment attests the preponderance in ancient criticism of evaluating over understanding.

An exploration of the ancient sense of narrative not only needs to consider developments and differences between genres, but also to take into account both ancient narrative and criticism. In this chapter, I have argued that important scenes in the Homeric epics and also passages in later works defy our criteria of motivation. Retroactive motivation, thematic isolation and suspense as to how are not what modern realist novels lead us to expect, but, with due differences, correspond to peculiarities of medieval narratives. At first sight, the importance of causal motivation in Aristotle's *Poetics* and the scholia seems to sit oddly with my argument about motivation in Homer and other ancient authors. And yet despite the differences, ancient literature and criticism share common ground in their privileging of plot over psychology. Neither is Homer unable to depict the consciousness processes of his characters nor do the scholia ignore them. However, just as Homer does not motivate Penelope's decisions psychologically but adapts them to the requirements of the plot, the commentators, on whose works the scholia are premised, seem to have paid more attention to motivation in terms of plot than of psychology.

CHAPTER 6

Ancient Texts and Postmodern Challenges

I Beyond Modern Texts and Narratology

The preceding chapters have highlighted how modern narrative theory, besides opening up new perspectives, has also narrowed our view of ancient texts. Many of its concepts were developed in view of modern realist novels, and most narratological categories were forged for the analysis of such texts as *À la recherche du temps perdu* (*In Search of Lost Time*). Classicists have eagerly grasped the opportunity to showcase the complexity of their material by demonstrating the pertinence of these concepts and categories to ancient texts. This tendency is palpable in the rhetoric of 'Homer first' – right from the beginning, Classicists note with satisfaction, Greek literature has the features that critics have spotted in the novels of Austen, James and Faulkner. I am far from denying the rich fruits of narratological studies in Classics, and I do not wish to argue against the application of Bal's and Genette's taxonomies to ancient texts. But I do think that, after taking pains to elucidate the modern qualities of ancient literature, we are well advised to try to also capture its distinct character. In this book, I have therefore delineated a perspective opposing the rhetoric of 'Homer first' – one that directs our attention to the differences between ancient and modern views of narrative.

I started my inquiries from major concepts and categories of modern narrative theory. Seeing that ancient narrative and criticism do not fully correspond to the notion of narrative derived chiefly from the study of modern realist novels, I teased out distinctive ancient views of narrative. It bears repeating that my investigation cannot claim to be exhaustive – it is rather an exploration which, without detracting from the value of the dominant approach, tries to pave the way for alternative approaches that deepen our understanding of ancient narrative. Hopefully, the argument of this book reinforces the interest in concepts of ancient criticism which do not map closely onto our modern categories and which allow us to see ancient literature in new light. While *enargeia* has attracted much attention, *ekplêxis* still awaits a full investigation, not surprisingly as it is not easily identifiable as the predecessor of an important modern category.[1] *Pathos* is another term that surfaces frequently in scholia – what exactly is its significance and how does it relate to the emotions that form the object of emotional narratology?[2] Scholars of narrative tend to be deaf to sound and rhythm, of which ancient readers were apparently highly perceptive.[3] Another dimension of narrative that, while without significance in modern narrative theory, looms large in ancient critical treatises is style.[4] Dionysius, Demetrius and other ancient critics used style as a major framework for assessing narrative as well as oratory – their taxonomies are easy to ignore when we view ancient texts through the narratological lens, but they were important for the ancient understanding of narrative.

My inquiry also suggests the fruitfulness of an extension of the comparativist field. While Homerists in particular have compared the *Iliad* and the *Odyssey* with other epic traditions, especially those of the Near East, theoretically inclined Classicists have tended to privilege modern literature as a comparandum for their material. De Jong's *Narratology & Classics: A Practical Guide* is a case in point: its discussions of narratological categories start from examples in novels by Austen and other modern authors.[5] All four case studies in this book, however, showed that comparisons with medieval narrative can shed light on aspects that set off ancient texts against modern assumptions: Medievalists encounter similar problems as Classicists in their search for the birth of fiction and have also noticed the absence of an independent narratorial instance in their material. Narratives from the Middle Ages also seem less interested in consciousness processes than modern novels and feature scenes without psychological motivation.

In the light of further parallels, it is surprising that there has not been more exchange between Classicists and Medievalists. Much has of course been written on the influence of ancient authors in the Middle Ages, but little has been done to compare the conceptions of narrative beyond such direct traditions. However, oral traditions and performances were prominent in both cultures. Scholars of Homer and scholars of *Nibelungenlied* (*The Song of the Nibelungs*) face similar questions about the genesis and form of their texts. An important difference between medieval and modern literature noted by Spearing also holds good for ancient literature:

---

[1] Brief references can be found in Nünlist 2009: 144–5; Halliwell 2021: 299 on *de subl.* 15.7–10.
[2] On *pathos*, see, for example, Munteanu 2012.
[3] Nooter 2012; 2017 and Gurd 2016 are noteworthy studies of sound in poetry. Hutchinson 2018 provides an investigation of prose rhythm in Plutarch.
[4] This is noted by Laird 2008.   [5] De Jong 2014b.

> The medieval poet characteristically does not create but recounts, *retells*, often with commentary, a pre-existing story about pre-existing characters, performing actions that have been established at least in outline in previous versions. This function of the medieval poet as a reteller and commentator marks a fundamental difference from the role of a novelist.[6]

Ancient as well as medieval authors are highly aware of literary traditions and engage in a permanent dialogue with their predecessors. At the same time, there are thought-provoking differences. What renders medieval literature so appealing for attempts at viewing ancient narratives not as providing the DNA of the modern novel is that it is a premodern literature which despite the greater temporal proximity is even further removed from modern literature in many regards. The reasons for this are manifold, one of them being the archaeology of modern literature – ancient texts had a greater impact on the emergence of the modern novel than medieval literature.

A detailed juxtaposition of ancient with medieval narratives requires the cooperation of Classicists with Medievalists, just as the further topics for the analysis of ancient narrative listed above deserve their own studies. In this epilogue, I wish to deepen the investigation of this book in a different way, by looking at postmodern literature and criticism. This may seem odd at first – why move even closer to the present in an attempt at leaving behind the modern lens of narrative theory and, as far as hermeneutically possible, approaching ancient literature on its own terms? That said, if we turn from modern novels to postmodern texts, we can detect highly instructive parallels to the features discussed in this book. The challenge that postmodern developments pose to narrative theory has been spotlighted by Brian Richardson. In several books and numerous articles, Richardson has demonstrated the insufficiency of the established narrative categories to capture what we find in such novels as Robbe-Grillet's *La Jalousie* (*Jealousy*) (1957), Martin Amis' *Time's Arrow* (1991) and Jennifer Egan's *A Visit from the Goon Squad* (2010).[7] In order to do justice to the 'unnatural' or 'anti-mimetic' narratives that have become so prominent in the past decades, Richardson and others have called for an 'unnatural narratology', punning on Fludernik's 'natural narratology'.[8]

In passing, Richardson mentions that there are premodern precedents of the phenomena he describes in contemporary literature. This epilogue will,

---

[6] Spearing 2005: 21–2.

[7] Richardson 1997b on fictional worlds; 2006 on narrators; 2019 on plot. For a programmatic article, see Richardson 2000, for a fuller presentation Richardson 2015.

[8] See Alber, Iversen, Nielsen and Richardson 2010. A substantial critique of the term and idea of 'unnatural narratology' can be found in Fludernik 2012.

on the one hand, use the material discussed in the preceding chapters to flesh out Richardson's perfunctory references to premodern parallels to features of anti-mimetic narrative. On the other hand, it will draw attention to the crucial differences ignored by Richardson. It is only at first sight that ancient and postmodern literature and criticism appear to share common ground. A closer look will reveal that the parallels are reflexive of different frames – the juxtaposition of ancient views with postmodern views will help me throw into relief their distinctive character, thereby rounding off the argument of *Ancient Greek Texts and Modern Narrative Theory*.

2   The Erasure of the Fact/Fiction Divide

Fictionality, I argued in Chapter 2, did not have to be discovered at some point, it was present from the beginning of Greek literature. However, while it is a key category of modern criticism, it was not prominent in antiquity. The issue of referentiality was far less important than the experiential quality and moral dimension of narrative. The comparatively marginal place of fictionality can be seen in light of the postmodern deconstruction of referentiality. While anticipated by reflections of Nietzsche, the postmodern challenge to representation is premised especially on Saussure's thesis that words and other signs derive their significance not from the objects they refer to but from their relations to other signs. Besides emphasizing the instability of signification in the gliding of signifiers along the chains of signifieds, post-structuralists drove home the unbridgeable gulf separating language from reality. Derrida's dictum 'there is nothing outside the text' encapsulates the postmodern belief that language is incapable of representing the world; instead, reality is seen as produced by language and subjects as generated by discourses.

The postmodern dissolution of linguistic reference manifests itself in a blurring of the boundaries between fact and fiction, on display for example in autobiographic writing. If the text cannot represent an author's life but the subject is rather a product of the text, autobiography is more or less like fiction, which creates its referent. Accordingly, *Roland Barthes par Roland Barthes* (*Roland Barthes by Roland Barthes*), a 'genuinely postmodern autobiography' as advertised by Hayden White on the cover of the English translation, begins with an epigraph: 'All this must be considered as said by a character of the novel' ('Tout ceci doit être considéré comme dit par un personnage de roman'). Besides identifying author with character and thereby anticipating the topic of my third chapter, the epigraph erases the boundary between fact and fiction. Its paradoxical quality is reinforced by its typographic setting – the claim about the fictional quality of the autobiography appears as a note handwritten by Barthes and thereby foregrounds the author and his existence.

Now Barthes was himself a major proponent of postmodern theory, but *Roland Barthes par Roland Barthes* is by no means the only instance which confounds the distinction between the factual genre of autobiography and fictional literature. Christa Wolf, one of the most prominent authors of East Germany, frames her memoir recounting her childhood in Nazi and postwar Germany with the statement: 'All characters in this book are the invention of the narrator. None is identical with any person living or dead. Neither do any of the described episodes coincide with actual events.'[9] Among the numerous other examples, Doubrovsky's *Fils* (*Threads/Son*) (1977) deserves singling out, as it coined a term that is often used to signify postmodern autobiographical writing: autofiction. Doubrovsky announces that this book, which recounts his own experiences, is 'the fiction of events and strictly real facts; if you wish, autofiction' ('fiction d'événements et de faits strictement réels; si l'on veut, autofiction'). In a later reflection, Doubrovsky contended that autofiction is ultimately a more truthful way of autobiography – the techniques of fiction permit the author to write his self more fully.[10]

The destabilization of the fact–fiction divide manifests itself not only in the transformation of autobiography and other factual genres, but also in fictional literature. A postmodern upshot of the historical novel, for example, is historiographic metafiction. *Flaubert's Parrot*, *The French Lieutenant's Woman* and similar novels narrate historical events with a high degree of reflection on their own fictionality. Linda Hutcheon, who introduced the label of historiographic metafiction, notes: 'Its theoretical self-awareness of history and fiction as human constructs (historiographic metafiction) is made the grounds for its rethinking and reworking of the form and contents of the past.'[11] If the representation of reality is beyond the means of language and all reality is a linguistic product, the reflexive use of fiction becomes a highly adequate way of approaching history.

On the surface, the postmodern inclination to blend together fact and fiction is redolent of the less than prominent role of referentiality in ancient criticism. However, the postmodern attempts to challenge the idea of fictionality as opposed to factuality are significantly different from its

[9] Wolf 1977.   [10] Doubrovsky 2013.   [11] Hutcheon 1988: 5.

marginal place in ancient reflections on narrative.[12] Deconstruction is a parasitic operation; it tackles existing concepts and tears them down by showing their inherent contradictions. However, even though demolished, the deconstructed concepts remain powerful points of reference – the deconstruction is premised on their dissection. To use an image popular with post-structuralists, terms that are erased remain visible as palimpsests. The impressive efforts to deconstruct the dichotomy of fact versus fiction has ultimately endowed it with prominence.

This is visible not only in postmodern theory which is obsessed with the idea of representation, but also in autofiction.[13] Postmodern autobiographies receive their arresting force from offering the reader two incompatible contracts, the promise of representing the author's experiences as well as the suspension of referentiality.[14] In a recent analysis, Iversen notes 'the explicit and deliberate transgressions performed by autofictive narrative', which 'relate to generic, textual and moral boundaries'.[15] The transgression, however, remains tied to the boundary it oversteps. In making the impossibility of reference its central point, postmodern autofiction continues to revolve around the issue of referentiality. It is haunted by the spectre of representation, the existence of which it takes pains to deny. My exploration of ancient texts has yielded a very different picture: while not unknown, the concept of fictionality was not a major lens for ancient views of narrative. Where postmodern authors are fixated on the idea of representation in their showcasing of its futility, ancient authors were more interested in the responses they could elicit and the moral messages they could bestow on their readers.

It is an intriguing question whether recent developments of autofiction draw closer to the ancient sense of narrative than postmodern approaches. The past two decades have seen a boom in memoir literature.[16] Such authors as Annie Ernaux, Delphine de Vigan, Emmanuele Carrère and Louis Edouard have made France a centre of memoir writing, but it is not difficult to name examples from other countries. The six volumes of Knausgård's *My Struggle* have been translated into dozens of languages. Martin Amis' *Experience* (2000) and Jeanette Winterson's *Why Be Happy When You Could Be Normal* (2011) are examples from the UK. Peter Kurzeck and Christian Haller are only two of a large group of authors

---

[12] Spearing 2005: 23 observes that medieval approaches to fictionality differ from the postmodern blurring of the boundary between fact and fiction.
[13] The alternative terms in use, all with their own nuances, include self-narration (Schmitt 2010); autobiographical fictions (Ramsay 1991); New Journalism (Wolfe and Johnson 1975).
[14] Gasparini 2004.   [15] Iversen 2020: 559.   [16] For example, Thiemann 2019: 795–9.

writing memoirs in German. An author from the United States who may be familiar to Classicists is Daniel Mendelsohn, who, beginning with *The Elusive Embrace: Desire and the Riddle of Identity* (1999), has woven elements of the memoir into his books.

Much could be said about the new wave of autobiographic writings, which encompass the accounts not only of celebrities but also of nameless individuals that nonetheless sell very well. One of the key reasons for this success is obviously the idea of authenticity.[17] The new memoirs respond to a desire of readers to hear an author's voice and to receive from it a truthful account of their lives. The ideal of unmediated access to the author's experiences is diametrically opposed to the post-structuralist emphasis on mediation. Post-structuralists decried authenticity, the currency not only of literary autofiction, but also of other kinds of medial self-fashioning, as a rhetorical effect. Jonathan Culler, for example, observes that, in order to be experienced as authentic, a memoir 'must be marked as authentic, but when it is marked as authentic it is mediated, a sign of itself, and hence lacks the authenticity of what is truly unspoiled, untouched by mediating cultural codes'.[18]

Now, the new memoirs are not void of reflections on referentiality. Carrère's recent book *Yoga* (2020) is a case in point: more or less in the middle, Carrère goes out of his way to assert truthfulness as the core tenet of his autobiographic writing but simultaneously admits that he has to lie in some places. At the end, he even confesses that entire persons are more or less invented.[19] Nonetheless, most readers will peruse *Yoga* not so much in order to meditate on the pitfalls of representational claims as to witness the author's self-exposure. Referentiality continues to be contemplated, but has ceased to be the major issue.[20] While this may remind us of its place in ancient criticism, the current focus on authenticity is not fully in line with the tendencies that I identified in antiquity. The experiential quality praised by ancient critics is nuanced differently from the authenticity for which today's readers long. While the latter are lured by the opportunity to access the unique perspective of another individual, the former rather extolled an author's capacity to make us witness actions as if we were

---

[17] For a critical assessment of the current investment in authenticity, see Schilling 2021. For other reasons, see Iversen 2020: 560. Krumrey 2015: 13–21 discusses whether it makes sense to speak of a post-postmodern form of autofiction.
[18] Culler 1988: 164.   [19] Carrère 2020: 186–7; 377.
[20] Christian Kracht's *Eurotrash* could be counted as a counter-example, which spotlights its own referentiality, but it may also be read as a pastiche of a memoir and a critique of the current boom of autobiographic writing.

present. Ancient writers also deviate from the authors of autofiction in their moral engagement. Moral issues are present in contemporary auto-biographies, but they are often concerned with conflicts between moral codes and individual perspectives. It was not only the ancient tragedians who exploited extreme cases to put to the test values and convictions; on the whole, ancient texts were more invested in the exemplary character of their subjects than modern texts that tend to stress their uniqueness.

3 Confounding Narrative Levels

My third chapter addressed narrative voice and narrative levels. Modern critics carefully distinguish the narrator from the author and envisage narrative planes that are nested into one another: the author presents their work to the reader; within this work, the narrator addresses the narratee; and in this narration, the characters communicate with one another. There is no direct contact between these levels, they are strictly separated from one another. Ancient critics, however, had no notion of an independent narratorial instance and also flagrantly ignored the separation of the narrative levels so important to us: as we saw, they ascribed utter-ances of characters to authors with a frequency that rules out negligence. The epigraph of *Roland Barthes par Roland Barthes* quoted above (p. 151) illustrates that postmodern authors also delight in crossing the boundaries between narrative levels. When Barthes frames his memoir with the claim that it should be read as presented by the character of a novel, he erases the line between author and character as well as that between fact and fiction.

An author who indulged in wittily blending together his voice with that of his narrators and characters is Nabokov. Richardson discusses several of his texts as examples of an 'unnatural' treatment of voice.[21] In *Bend Sinister* (1964), the protagonist Krug suspects that he is only a character in a novel, sensing the presence of a superior being, which Nabokov in the preface identifies as 'an anthropomorphic deity impersonated by me' (1964: xviii).[22] Krug's suspicion crosses the gulf that normally separates the narrated universe from the universe of the narration. In 'mimetic' narra-tives, characters have no awareness of being characters and belonging to the universe of fiction.

Lolita blurs the boundary between author and narrator in a more subtle way. Like other narrating characters in Nabokov's novels, John Ray advances opinions in which the author's voice breaks through:

---

[21] Richardson 2021: 1–21.   [22] Richardson 2021: 11–12.

Consider Ray's condescending reference to 'old-fashioned readers who wish to follow the destinies of "real" people beyond the "true" story' (1970, 6), or the following more tongue-in-cheek intrusion: 'The commentator may be excused for repeating what he has stressed in his own books and lectures, namely that "offensive" is frequently but a synonym for "unusual"; and a great work of art is of course always original, and thus by its very nature should come as a more or less shocking surprise' (1970, 7). These sentiments are the kind frequently found in Nabokov's critical prose and are quite beyond the reach of a middlebrow psychiatrist who is much more likely to parrot various slogans of the day or blurbs for the latest book-of-the-month club selection.[23]

In *Look at the Harlequins!* (1974), Nabokov uses the paratext to undermine the distinction between author and narrator.[24] A list of Nabokov's earlier works can be found on the first pages of his other books. In *Look at the Harlequins!*, however, there is a list of 'Books by the Narrator'. The list playfully recasts Nabokov's oeuvre, featuring both Russian and English works: *Pawn Takes Queen* (1927), for example, echoes *King, Queen, Knave*, published as *Korol', dama, valet* in 1928, and *Ardis* (1970) varies *Ada or Ardor: A Family Chronicle* (1969). The play continues in the narrative where the narrator, Vladim Vadimich, mentions his pseudonym, V. Isirin (1974: 97), which is a variation on Nabokov's own pseudonym, V. Sirin. When the narrator suddenly starts to address his beloved in the second person, we are reminded of Nabokov's memoir – in *Speak, Memory*, Nabokov directs his speech to Véra in the final chapter.[25] The striking parallels to Nabokov's factual texts as well as the playful design of the paratext undercut the distinction between author and narrator, on which our model of narrative is premised.

Nabokov's blurring of the borderlines separating the different levels of narrative is a case of metalepsis, defined by Genette as 'any intrusion by the extradiegetic narrator or narratee into the diegetic universe (or by diegetic characters into a metadiegetic universe, etc.), or the inverse'.[26] Such transgressions of the borders between narrative levels can also be found in premodern literature, but they have become particularly popular under the auspices of postmodernism:

> Its (i.e., metalepsis) core characteristics and features seem to strike a chord with contemporary thought in a way that metaphor does not, making metalepsis appear especially attuned to high postmodern sensitivities.

---

[23] Richardson 2021: 16.   [24] Richardson 2021: 17–19.
[25] On Nabokov's use of the same material in *Speak Memory* and fictional short stories, see Richardson 2021: 12–15.
[26] Genette 1980: 234–5.

Whether one thinks of postmodernism's predilection for dismantling sol-idly ordered narratives (meta- or otherwise); its democratic impulses of participatory co-construction of meaning (not by one all-powerful, but through several interacting and interdependent agents); or its joyful over-turning of ontological and epistemological one-time certainties – it is easy to see how all of these resonate strongly with the dynamics that lie at the very heart of metalepsis.[27]

Just as postmodernism deconstructs the dichotomy of fact versus fiction, it also dismantles the idea of unbridgeable narrative levels. The postmod-ern challenging of the narrator and the confounding of authors and characters has thus a very different character from the ancient tendencies with which they seem to be aligned at first sight. In Chapter 3, I concluded that the ancient model of narration is decisively unmetaleptic. The lack of a distinct narratorial instance and the repeated ascription of characters' utterances to authors make tangible an approach to narrative that, instead of distinguishing hermetically separated levels, is premised on the idea of impersonation. Authors were seen as either speaking in their own voice or as adopting the voices of characters and as mentally re-enacting the actions they were narrating. There is no 'sacred frontier'[28] that can be breached, but what modern authors view as a violation is key to the process of composition: when impersonating characters and re-enacting their deeds, the author has entered the narrated world and moves among the characters just as he or she tries to bring them as close as possible to his audience or readers. At a superficial glance, the contact between authors and characters in ancient texts resembles the metaleptic games of postmodern authors, but the ancient concept of narration gives it a rather different twist.

A comparison of metalepseis can throw into relief the difference between the postmodern and the ancient stances. Despite the unmetaleptic view of narration, it is possible to find instances in ancient literature of what we today consider metalepseis. As a result of the different understanding of narrative, however, ancient metalepseis look, by and large, different from metalepseis in postmodern texts. There are also metalepseis in contempor-ary texts that serve to pull the reader into the narrated world,[29] and yet, on the whole, the modern idea of distinct narrative levels bestows on many metalepseis the paradoxical character noted by Genette: metalepsis 'pro-duces an effect of strangeness that is either comical (when, as in Sterne or Diderot, it is presented in a joking tone) or fantastic'.[30] In particular, the

---

[27] Matzner 2020: 1.   [28] Genette 1980: 236.
[29] For example, Fludernik 2003a: 382–3; Klimek 2010.   [30] Genette 1980: 235.

breaking of the representational walls, whether the author or narrator mingles with the characters or a character turns towards the reader or narratee, tends to be anti-immersive – it reminds the reader of the mediation.[31] 'Antimimetic fiction', as Richardson puts it, 'is nonillusionistic; it flaunts rather than disguises its own fictionality.'[32]

It is possible to find abrasive metalepseis in ancient narrative,[33] but many metalepseis seem to have rather intensified the presentation. A case in point is apostrophes, one of the most striking metaleptic elements in ancient literature, especially epic. It is impossible to find a common denominator for all apostrophes, as they address a wide range of characters and occur in various contexts, but de Jong has argued that the 'sum effect of the apostrophe is to add to that vital characteristic of Homeric epic, enargeia: the events are presented in such a way that they seem to take place before the eyes of the narratees'.[34] In a later article, de Jong equated the *enargeia* of apostrophe with immersion: 'The hearers/readers of a narrative are so strongly absorbed by a narrative that they feel as if they are present themselves at the events told. They are mentally transported into the narrative world and become spectators of the events from the past.'[35]

It is odd that de Jong unqualifiedly identifies *enargeia* with immersion and claims that apostrophes help transport the audience into the narrated world. As she herself points out in a paper co-authored with Rutger Allan and Casper de Jonge, the directions envisaged in the concepts of *enargeia* and immersion are the inverse:[36] whereas immersion signifies the recipient's 'diving into' the narrated world, *enargeia* is usually described as the ability to bring the narrated action close to the recipient. Even if we leave this point aside, I wonder about the precision of de Jong's analysis. Is apostrophe really a means of making *the events told* present? The presence of narrated events requires transparency, a concealment of the mediating instance as far as that is possible (rare exceptions aside, recipients always maintain a residual awareness of the presentation).[37] The narrator's direct address, however, forcefully draws attention to the mediation; it highlights the presence of the narrator and thereby rather jolts the recipient out of the narrated action than immersing them into it. Nonetheless, it can intensify

---

[31] Compare McHale 1987: 123; Wagner 2002: 239.   [32] Richardson 2000: 37.

[33] Bing 2020: 111–14; Fulkerson 2020: 156–7.

[34] De Jong 2009: 95. Parry 1972 argues that apostrophes evoke sympathy with characters; Matthews 1980 argues that apostrophes in Homer are used *metri causa*; Mackay 2001 contends that they spotlight pivotal moments. See also Klooster 2013; Budelmann 2020; Lovatt 2020.

[35] De Jong 2020: 80.   [36] Allan, de Jong and de Jonge 2017.

[37] Compare Ryan 2001: 56–8; Wolf 2004: 340–3; Allan 2020: 19.

the presentation through the suggested closeness of the character – the address implies that narrator and characters inhabit the same plane.

It is worth revisiting in this context a scholion on a much-quoted Homeric apostrophe, the address to Patroclus right before his death: 'There, Patroclus, appeared for you the end of life' (ἔνθ' ἄρα τοι Πάτροκλε φάνη βιότοιο τελευτή, *Il.* 16.787).The bT scholion notes:

> ἡ ἀποστροφὴ σημαίνει τὸν συναχθόμενον· σοὶ γάρ, ὦ Πάτροκλε, τῷ οὕτως ὑπ' Ἀχιλλέως ἀγαπωμένῳ, τῷ πᾶν εἰς σωτηρίαν τῶν Ἑλλήνων πραγματευσαμένῳ, τῷ Νέστορος φιλοπόνως ἀνασχομένῳ, τῷ Εὐρύπυλον φιλοστόργως ἰασαμένῳ, τῷ ὑπὲρ τῶν Ἑλλήνων δακρύσαντι καὶ τὸν σκληρῶς διακείμενον Ἀχιλλέα πείσαντι, τῷ κατὰ τῆς ἑαυτοῦ ψυχῆς τὴν ἔξοδον κατορθώσαντι. ταῦτα πάντα ἔνεστιν ἐπαναφέροντας ἐπὶ τὴν ἀποστροφὴν ὁρᾶν τὸ ἐν αὐτῇ περιπαθές.

> The apostrophe signals the empathy of the poet: with you, Patroclus, who was so loved by Achilles, who did everything to save the Greeks, who diligently put up with Nestor, who affectionately cared for Eurypolus, who shed tears for the Greeks and persuaded Achilles, hardened though he was, who succeeded in bringing a resolution to events but only at the cost of his own life. If we relate all of this to the apostrophe, we can see its immense emotional force.

The commentator contemplates the apostrophe as an expression of Homer's stance. However, the fact that he joins Homer in directly addressing Patroclus and the plural in the final sentence indicate that he shares this stance and expects other readers to do so as well.[38] The intensity generated by the apostrophe according to the scholion is notably different from the immersion claimed by de Jong. It is empathy for Patroclus, not immersion in the action, that the apostrophe expresses and induces in the audience. The difference is countenanced by the references to Patroclus' deeds and Achilles' love for him. Instead of engrossing the commentator in the action, the present tide of the battle, the apostrophe prompts him to evoke earlier manifestations in Patroclus' character. The scholion can thus not be adduced as a testimony to the immersive effect of apostrophes. We should not put too much stock in the evidence of a single scholion, and yet it is a reminder that not all forms of intensity detected by ancient critics can be identified as immersion.

Although I do not agree with de Jong's interpretation of Patroclus' apostrophe as immersive, the contrast that she sees between the effects of many ancient metalepseis and postmodern cases is valid with due

---

[38] Budelmann 2020: 64–5 mentions the possibility that the scholion is 'a primarily playful imitation of Homer's literary gesture' but does not deem this very likely.

qualification: instead of disrupting the narrative as frequently as in postmodern texts, metalepseis in ancient texts tend to enthral the reader.[39] Even a metalepsis that directs our attention to the narrator alerts us not so much to the artificiality of the representation as it increases our emotional engagement.

A final example may drive home the different effects of metalepsis in ancient and postmodern narratives. When Nabokov has the narrator-character of *Lolita*, the psychiatrist John Ray, refer to his books and lectures for points that Nabokov himself was fond of making, the reader who notices the blending together of voices is stopped in their tracks and invited to chuckle about how wittily Nabokov makes his own presence felt in the utterance of a character otherwise very much unlike him. Now, the blending of voices has been identified as a form of metalepsis in ancient texts by de Jong.[40] In her analysis of Demodocus' second song in the *Odyssey*, the adultery of Ares and Aphrodite, de Jong notices that the narrator starts to present the song in indirect speech but quickly adopts direct speech. This can be explained linguistically as an instance of the 'downslip' principle: we tend to move from more complex to simpler structures, in this case from indirect to direct speech. De Jong, however, proposes that it is a conscious metaleptic move by Homer: 'Blending his own voice with that of a famous singer of the past (one of whose stories is, moreover, explicitly authenticated by the eyewitness Odysseus himself), he increases the authority of his own story and at the same time indicated that his own song is just as good as a song of the heroic past.'[41]

Further instances of this kind of metalepsis explored by de Jong are passages in epinician poetry, where Pindar switches from an indirect to a direct representation of the song of the Muses. Pindar's blending of his voice with that of the Muses endows him with authority and welds together the world of the athlete with that of the heroes. The unmarked transition from indirect to direct speech is of course a different device from putting words in the mouth of the character which are far more appropriate to the author. And yet, both devices concur in blending together the voices of author and character and thereby illustrate the different effects that ancient and postmodern metalepseis tend to have: while the latter are often, but by no means always, disruptive, many of the former either heighten the appeal of the narration or increase the author's authority.

---

[39] For this point, see also Eisen and Möllendorff 2013: 2–3; Pier 2014.   [40] De Jong 2009.
[41] De Jong 2009: 101.

Postmodern texts feature interactions of authors with characters that resemble their merging in ancient narrative and criticism, and yet the divergent effects these operations have reveal the different grounds on which they take place. Contemporary authors with a post-structuralist inflection take delight in erasing the boundaries between separate realms on which the modern idea of narration is predicated – metalepseis thus forge conflict with our expectations and flag the artificiality of the text. In antiquity, on the other hand, the presence of the narrated world was deemed an important part of composition and reception. Seen in this light, metalepseis are also though not exclusively a means of intensifying the narration.

4 Dismantled Characters

In the fourth chapter, I revisited the widely acclaimed thesis that it is essentially the opportunity to engage in mind reading which renders narrative so attractive across cultures. In the eyes of Palmer, Zunshine and their followers, the Theory of Mind is key to our response to narrative: we engage with narrative characters as with people we encounter in real life. This thesis works well for modern realist novels, in readings of which it has been mainly developed, but it is hard to sustain for ancient literature. There are of course fictional minds in ancient epic, drama, historiography and other genres; yet most ancient narratives entice readers rather through their plot than through the interior lives of their characters. Taking the arguably most complex ancient novel, the *Ethiopica*, as my test case, I analysed how Heliodorus reconfigures the narrated time in narrative time. The suspense, surprise and curiosity thereby generated shape the reading dynamics far more than the portrayal of the characters.

The approaches of Palmer, Zunshine and other cognitive scholars are based on a mimetic notion of character, the idea that literary characters are more or less like real people and therefore trigger the same kind of reactions as those we encounter in our lives. This idea had been fiercely criticized by structuralist and post-structuralist theoreticians long before it was resuscitated under the auspices of cognitivism.[42] 'How many children had Lady Macbeth?' asked Knights even before the advent of structuralism, with the purpose of ridiculing the scholarly tradition that treated literary characters like real people.[43] Wellek

---

[42] For surveys of modern theories of characters, see Phelan 1989: 1–23; Margolin 1989; Jannidis 2004: 1–10.
[43] Knights 1933.

and Warren contended that characters were only verbal constructs.[44] These approaches to characters inspired by New Criticism and its confinement to the text were taken up and radicalized by postmodern critics. In *S/Z*, Roland Barthes replaced the notion of person with that of voices: what is traditionally considered a person is only a name to which semes are attached. It is wrong to take a literary character 'off the page in order to turn him into a psychological character (endowed with motives)'.[45]

The deconstruction of the idea of character by critics was accompanied by the proliferation of characters in literature that violate the conventions of realism. Richardson observes a 'movement from the psychological novel to more impressionistic renderings of consciousness to the dissolution of consciousness into textuality'.[46] He distinguishes several forms of anti-mimetic characters.[47] 'Imperfectly human characters' are characters that have too few consistent or too many contradictory character traits to appear truly human. Edouard Manneret in Robbe-Grillet's *La maison de rendez-vous* (1965), for example, has no clear psychological profile, engages in actions that do not fit together and dies several times. Fully in tune with Barthes' approach to character, his name assembles various attributes and fulfils narrative functions without yielding a person. The other anti-mimetic forms of character discussed by Richardson are 'multiple individuals', 'parodic characters', 'fabricated entities' and 'metafictional characters', with the final ones being characters who know that they are fictional beings, similar to Krug in *Bend Sinister*.

The postmodern dismantling of the idea of coherent characters with distinct psychologies is perhaps most flagrant in theatre.[48] On the stage, there are actors – the characters are not represented by words but embodied by people in blood and flesh. When the individual actors on stage turn out not to stand for individual characters, this goes not only against the conventions of realist theatre, but also against the perception of the audience that sees individuals. Such challenges to the idea of the character were particularly popular in the 1960s and 1970s. Peter Handke's *Der Ritt über den Bodensee* (*The Ride Across Lake Constance*), for example, features eight actors but no characters. Instead of representing individuals, the actors merely voice text that is not attributed to a distinct personality.

A later example is Martin Crimp's *Attempts on Her Life: 17 Scenarios for the Theatre* (1997). This play offers a series of discourses about a woman or various versions of a woman, who is presented with different life stories: as

---

[44] Wellek and Warren 1949.   [45] Barthes 1974: 178.   [46] Richardson 2006: 13.
[47] Richardson 2020.   [48] Compare Richardson 1997a.

a scientist, as a terrorist, as a porn actress, even as a new make of car, to mention only a few. At the same time, the play 'cannot be dismissed as a mere collection of unconnected vignettes. There are several strategies, beginning with the drama's title, that invite the audience to bring many of these disparate stories into a plot and thereby partially unify its fragmented subject.'[49] A comment on one of the art performances of the woman within the play metaleptically captures Crimp's approach to character (25): 'She says she's not a real character like you get in a book or on TV, but a lack of character, an absence she calls it, doesn't she, of character.'

Like ancient texts, postmodern criticism and literature fly into the face of the assertion that mind reading is the essence of narrative. The Theory of Mind is certainly not central to how we follow Robbe-Grillet's novels or Crimp's plays. At the same time, there are glaring differences between the ancient and postmodern positions. Driven by the idea that, instead of representing reality, texts constitute reality, that subjects are ultimately constituted by discourses, postmodern authors take pains to deconstruct the very idea of character. In the most radical experiments, there is only 'a lack of character, an absence ... of character'.[50] Ancient authors, on the other hand, are far from abandoning the idea of character; their views of it, however, deviate from the modern emphasis on uniqueness and interiority. Characters in ancient texts tend to be envisaged from a third-person perspective and are seen chiefly in their social roles and relations. The ethos, which ancient authors were invested in, manifests itself in actions, as made explicit by Aristotle in the *Poetics*. Plot is therefore a central category of narrative, whereas introspection plays a minor role compared to modern novels. The salience of plot in ancient narrative and criticism throws into relief the difference from postmodern literature – besides deconstructing characters, postmodern authors also turn against the traditional idea of plot. This is tangible for example when the actors in Peter Handke's *Publikumsbeschimpfung* (*Offending the Audience*) say to the audience (9): 'We don't tell you a story. We don't perform any actions. We don't represent anything. We don't put anything on for you. We only speak.'

It is, however, possible to find closer parallels to the ancient treatment of character than postmodern experiments that ultimately dilute the very idea of character. For this, we have to venture into a vast field that most literary scholars continue to give a wide berth, the field of *paralittérature*. There are not only alternative terms for this field, each differently nuanced, such as

---

[49] Richardson 2020: 139.

[50] The challenge to readers posed by the postmodern dismantling of the idea of character is on display in Abbott's examination of unreadable minds (Abbott 2008) and Iversen's exploration of how some witness accounts of the Holocaust undermine the experientiality of narrative (Iversen 2011).

popular fiction and genre fiction, but it also encompasses a wide range of genres including romance, western, crime fiction, science fiction and adventure novels. While important differences can be noted between these genres as well as between individual works, there are features that are characteristic for many of them. In his investigation of nineteenth-century popular novels and the beginning of the *roman policier*, Couégnas extracts the following list of criteria for *paralittérature* at large: besides paratextual elements, repetition and the significance of all elements, the orientation towards plot and the rudimentary treatment of characters.[51]

Such narratives as adventure novels, crime fiction and the western have pervasive generic conventions, thrive on suspense and tend to draw on a cast of more or less stereotypical characters. They therefore parallel the ancient novel in important regards. As noted in Chapter 4, even the most complex ancient novel follows a distinct set of generic conventions, is highly invested in suspense and features characters that, while far from stock characters, do not correspond to the standards of round and indi-vidualized characters of the modern realist novel. A passage from Ian Fleming's *Casino Royale* may illustrate the parallels it shares with the *Ethiopica*. James Bond has just fallen into the hands of the evil Le Chiffre:

> He [Bond] felt thoroughly dispirited and weak in resolve as well as in his body. He had to take too much in the past twenty-four hours and now this last stroke by the enemy seemed almost too final. This time there could be no miracles. No one knew where he was and no one would miss him until well on into the morning. The wreck of his car would be found before very long, but it would take hours to trace ownership to him.[52]

Like in the scenes from the *Ethiopica* discussed in Chapter 4, it is not the hero's character and his interior life, but suspense that grips the reader. We are less interested in how Bond feels than in what is going to happen next. Bond is in general less of an individualized character than a hero, showing his qualities in a series of actions. As in Heliodorus, Fleming creates a strong tension between the present state and the end that is dictated by generic conventions. We know that Bond will triumph, and 'this last stroke *seemed almost* too final' gestures clandestinely to the solution of the tension. But how, we wonder, will he be able to turn around the situation 'this time'? As in the *Ethiopica*, it is 'suspense moyen' that tickles the reader.

[51] Couégnas 1992. For an instructive comparison of the ancient novel with *paralittérature*, see Fusillo 1996. Tagliabue 2017 is a sensitive and thought-provoking attempt to approach the peculiarities of Xenophon of Ephesus through the lens of *paralittérature*.
[52] Fleming 1954: 105.

The similarities between the *Ethiopica* and James Bond novels are admittedly limited. *Paralittérature* rarely reaches the complexity of the *Ethiopica* and lacks its self-referential sophistication, and yet they are aligned on the basis of their plot orientation. This should finally give pause to theoreticians of narrative if ancient narrative cannot stop them in their tracks. I do not risk much when I claim that Ian Fleming, Stephen King and others enjoy a far broader readership than Henry James, Virginia Woolf and William Faulkner. This could have various reasons, but it is worth noting that the narratives capitalizing on plot seem to find a larger audience than narratives that privilege the presentation of consciousness at the expense of action. For scholars who envisage mind reading as the core of narrative, this poses a serious problem. The concept of experience outlined in Chapter 4 affords an alternative framework that makes it possible to account for the dynamics of plot as well as the intricacies of character.

5 'Non-mimetic' Motivation

The *Odyssey* is an important source of the classical western plot – without direct debts to Homer, several genres and innumerous narratives deploy essential elements of its storyline. Adventure novels subject their heroes to tests and trials, romances deploy the (re)union of a couple as their telos and coming-of-age- stories follow the development of their characters, often triggered by new experiences abroad. In the modern history of criticism, Aristotle's view on the unity of plot has been arguably one of the most influential frames of reference derived from antiquity. Despite this impact of the ancient practice and theory of narrative plotting, Greek texts contain scenes that do not conform to our expectations about motivation. As we saw in Chapter 5, even the *Odyssey* continues to give modern scholars a headache: the Penelope scenes in *Odyssey* 18 and 19 have given rise to various readings that are ultimately unsatisfactory as they fail to do justice to the ancient sense of motivation.

An important reason for this gap between ancient texts and modern interpretations is the approach to characters outlined in Chapter 4. Where modern novels put a premium on the consciousness processes that render its characters unique, ancient characters are not always but often viewed from a third-person perspective and in their social relations. Psychological motivation, so central to many modern authors, is therefore less prominent. At the same time, there are other forms of motivation. In retroactive motivation, elements are justified *only* as part of the plot but do not emerge naturally within the world of the action. While retroactive motivation challenges the narrative sequence by legitimizing events through their results, thematic isolation dissolves individual scenes from their narrative context and thereby neglects the progression of the plot. Yet another manifestation of the detemporalization of plot is the tendency to replace suspense as to what by suspense as to how, which is deeply ingrained in many ancient genres.

My analysis of motivation in *Odyssey* 18 and 19 took inspiration from studies of medieval narrative. Such texts as Gottfried von Straßburg's *Tristan* jar strongly with modern ideas about plotting and have been analysed in terms that can help us appreciate features in ancient narrative that tend to be obliterated when viewed through the lens of modern realist novels. Not only medieval, but also postmodern narratives deviate from the modern ideal of a causally and psychologically motivated progression. In *A Poetics of Plot for the Twenty-First Century*, Brian Richardson discusses several anti-mimetic modes of plotting.[53] While some of these ways can complement traditional modes of sequencing, others flagrantly overthrow it. Nearly all of them can be found in Joyce's *Ulysses*. Several chapters in Joyce's *Ulysses*, for example, follow the order of the Homeric pretexts – a case of intertextual ordering. In rhetorical sequencing, the order of events serves to underline a thesis or a worldview, something that is not infrequent in ideologically charged novels. In *Ulysses*, Richardson identifies, among others, 'numerous miniature and oblique rhetorical sequences in the dialectical progression of the events in "*Scylla and Charybdis*", in which the many idealistic theses propounded by the figures in the library are followed by crassly materialistic positions of Buck Mulligan, whose entry into the room is synchronized with the model of thesis/antithesis.'[54]

Another powerful principle that can but need not run parallel to a causally and psychologically motivated plot is aesthetic ordering. In *Anna Karenina*, for example, light and dark scenes alternate; at the same time, the narrative progression is carefully motivated along causal and psychological lines. The final fifteen chapters of *Ulysses* thematize different organs of the body and simultaneously spotlight different arts and sciences. Here, the aesthetic ordering provides coherence for sequences that do not follow traditional plot conventions. 'Visual event generators' and 'verbal event generators', as they are named by Richardson, are images and words that adumbrate the material to follow: in '*Circe*', for example, the Greek nymph in the painting in Bloom's bedroom later materializes in the guise of prostitutes at Bella Cohen's brothel. Three further principles discussed by Richardson are alphabetical orderings, serial ordering and collage

---

[53] Richardson 2019: 83–98.   [54] Richardson 2019: 85.

composition. Finally, there is random ordering, hailed by Dadaists, who cut out newspaper snippets and arranged them in the order in which they were drawn from a hat.

Richardson concentrates on postmodern examples of anti-mimetic narrative progression, but he also occasionally references premodern examples. The *Chanson de Roland* (*The Song of Roland*) and *Beowulf* serve as examples for symmetrical arrangements that harness repetition, parallelism, antithesis, triadic patterns and ring composition.[55] Without further ado, Richardson lists these premodern texts together with Tom Stoppard's *Artist Descending a Staircase* (1973). This seamless alignment is ultimately at odds with his important observation:

> that many of the more vigorous non- or antiplot mechanisms of narrative sequencing presume the awareness of standard forms of emplotment, forms that these mechanisms work in a dialectical way to attenuate or negate. Thus, while the concept of plot alone cannot describe the various sequencing patterns present in many recent works of fiction, most of those patterns can be fully comprehended only in relation to plot. Even chance compositions are interesting not for any intrinsic reason but for the ways they appear to mimic or contravene the kind of order produced by emplotment.[56]

The modern ideal of plot, which postmodern authors strive to undermine, did not exist when *Beowulf* and *Chanson de Roland* (*The Song of Roland*) were composed. Medieval authors may employ similar strategies of motivation but they do not harness them in order to challenge the modern ideal of emplotment.

This is a key point that has recurred in all sections of this chapter: there are similar differences between ancient and postmodern texts, on the one hand, and modern realist novels, on the other. Like ancient narratives, the experiments of the likes of Borges and Robbe-Grillet pose problems for a narrative theory that developed its concepts and categories chiefly for modern texts such as *À la recherche du temps perdu*. However, postmodern and ancient texts are separated by a considerable gulf: the former consciously deviate from the conventions of modern narrative and even often make their violation their central concern. As Richardson stresses, 'this new practice can only be understood by reference to the mimetic aesthetic it flouts'.[57] To capture this dependence of anti-mimetic poetics on modern standards, Richardson coins the term 'Loki Principle': 'A central axiom of antimimetic poetics is what I have called the Loki Principle, which states that whenever a literary convention becomes powerful or ubiquitous,

---

[55] Richardson 2019: 87.   [56] Richardson 2019: 96–7.   [57] Richardson 2000: 30.

someone will come along and violate that convention.'[58] Ancient texts, however, do not respond to modern conventions; they are indebted to a view of narrative that is different and independent from these conventions. As in the case of other negations, the postmodern erasure of modernism remains fixated on what it erases. Ancient literature and criticism, on the other hand, operate in a very different field with their own paths and demarcations.

Richardson's view has immense merits in alerting us to the wealth of contemporary literature that flouts the standards for which many concepts of narrative theory were developed, but he does not mark the difference between pre- and postmodern texts when he claims that 'what seems to be distinctly postmodern narrative strategies often turn out to be recent manifestations of narrative constructions with a much older pedigree'.[59] In a programmatic article, he asserts without further qualification:

> I suggest that the most urgent task of narrative theory is to contrast a poetics of non-mimetic fiction that can finally do full justice to the literature of our own time. Paradoxically, by doing so we will be thereby able to recover and disclose the many premodern antecedents of strategies and techniques now identified as the most distinctly 'post-'.[60]

Just as Classicists have proudly demonstrated that the most archaic texts have the same narrative features as modern literature, Richardson adds weight to his challenge to narrative theory by enlisting premodern deviations together with postmodern challenges. Both approaches envisage ancient texts as 'antecedents' of modern and postmodern literature respectively. Such a view can help identify interesting aspects of ancient literature, but it is in danger of occluding essential features that cannot be cast as prefiguring modern conventions and postmodern experiments. The success of narratology in Classics has highlighted how modern ancient literature is in many regards – it is now time for us to become more sensitive to the distinctiveness of ancient narrative and criticism.

---

[58] Richardson 2019: 3.   [59] Richardson 2019: ix.   [60] Richardson 2000: 38.

References

Abbott, H. P. (2008) 'Unreadable minds and the captive reader', *Style*, 42/2: 448–66.

Alber, J., S. Iversen, H. S. Nielsen and B. Richardson (2010) 'Unnatural narratives, unnatural narratology: Beyond mimetic models', *Narrative*, 18/2: 113–36.

Alden, M. (2017) *Para-narratives in the Odyssey: Stories in the Frame*. Oxford.

Allan, R. J. (2020) 'Narrative immersion: Some linguistic and narratological aspects', in J. Grethlein, L. Huitink and A. Tagliabue (eds.), *Experience, Narrative, and Criticism in Ancient Greece: Under the Spell of Stories*. Oxford: 15–35.

Allan, R. J., I. J. F. de Jong and C. de Jonge (2017) 'From enargeia to immersion: The ancient roots of a modern concept', *Style*, 51/1: 34–51.

Allen, W. (1939) 'The theme of the suitors in the Odyssey', *TAPhA*, 70: 104–24.

Amis, M. (1991) *Time's Arrow*. London.

(2000) *Experience*. London.

Amory, A. (1963) 'The reunion of Odysseus and Penelope', in C. H. Taylor (ed.), *Essays on the Odyssey*. Bloomington: 100–36.

(1966) 'The gates of horn and ivory', *YClS*, 20: 3–57.

Anderson, M., D. Cairns and M. Sprevak (eds.) (2019) *Distributed Cognition in Classical Antiquity*. Edinburgh.

Arweiler, A. and M. Möller (eds.) (2008) *Vom Selbst-Verständnis in Antike und Neuzeit*. Berlin.

Auerbach, E. (2013) *Mimesis: The Representation of Reality in Western Literature*. Princeton.

Auhagen, U. (1998) 'Heu quid agat? – Erlebte Rede bei Valerius Flaccus und seinen Vorgängern', in U. Eigler and E. Lefèvre (eds.), *Ratis omnia vincet: Neue Untersuchungen zu den Argonautica des Valerius Flaccus*. Munich: 51–66.

Austin, C. and S. D. Olsen (eds.) (2004) *Aristophanes: Thesmophoriazusae*. Oxford.

Austin, N. (1975) *Archery at the Dark of the Moon: Poetic Problems in Homer's Odyssey*. Berkeley.

Avery, H. C. (1968) '"My tongue swore, but my mind is unsworn"', *TAPhA*, 99: 19–35.

Babut, D. (1974) 'Xénophane critique des poètes', *AC*, 43/1: 83–117.

Badian, E. (1993) 'Thucydides and the outbreak of the Peloponnesian War: A historian's brief', in *Plataea to Potidaea: Studies in the History and Historiography of the Pentecontaetia*. Baltimore: 125–62.

Bakker, E. J. (2009) 'Homer, Odysseus, and the narratology of performance', in J. Grethlein and A. Rengakos (eds.), *Narratology and Interpretation: The Content of Narrative Form in Ancient Literature*. Berlin: 117–36.

Bal, M. (1985) *Narratology: Introduction to the Theory of Narrative*. Toronto.

Banfield, A. (1982) *Unspeakable Sentence: Narration and Representation in the Language of Fiction*. Boston.

Baragwanath, E. (2008) *Motivation and Narrative in Herodotus*. Oxford.

Bareis, J. A. (2008) *Fiktionales Erzählen*. Gothenburg.

Barnes, J. (1984) *Flaubert's Parrot*. New York.

Baroni, R. (2007) *La tension narrative: Suspense, curiosité et surprise*. Paris.

(2009) *L'oeuvre du temps: Poétique de la discordance narrative*. Paris.

Barthes, R. (1974) *S/Z*. New York.

(1975) *Roland Barthes par Roland Barthes*. Paris.

Barwick, K. (1928) 'Die Gliederung der narratio in der rhetorischen Theorie und ihre Bedeutung für die Geschichte des antiken Romans', *Hermes*, 63/2: 261–87.

Beck, D. (2009) 'Speech act types, conversational exchange, and the speech representational spectrum in Homer', in J. Grethlein and A. Rengakos (eds.), *Narratology and Interpretation: The Content of Narrative Form in Ancient Literature*. Berlin: 137–51.

(2012) *Speech Presentation in Homeric Epic*. Austin.

Binder, G. (ed.) (1995) *Kommunikation durch Zeichen und Wort*. Trier.

Bing, P. (2020) 'Anachronism as a form of metalepsis in ancient Greek literature', in S. Matzner and G. Trimble (eds.), *Metalepsis: Ancient Texts, New Perspectives*. Oxford: 99–118.

Birke, D., E. von Contzen and K. Kukkonen (2022) 'Chrononarratology: modelling historical change for narratology', *Narrative*, 30/1: 26–46.

Blank, D. L. (ed.) (2007) *Sextus Empiricus, Against the Grammarians: Introduction, Translation, Commentary*. Oxford.

Blumenberg, H. (1979) *Arbeit am Mythos*. Frankfurt.

Boedeker, D. (1991) 'Euripides' Medea and the vanity of ΛΟΓΟΙ', *CPh*, 86/2: 95–112.

Bolens, G. (2008) *Le Style des gestes: Corporéité et kinésie dans le récit littéraire*. Lausanne.

Bona, G. (1966) *Studi sull'Odissea*. Turin.

Booth, W. C. (1961) *The Rhetoric of Fiction*. Chicago.

Bortolussi, M. (2011) 'Response to Alan Palmer's "Social Minds"', *Style*, 45/2: 283–7.

Boucher, J. (1996) 'What could possibly explain autism?', in P. Carruthers (ed.), *Theories of Theories of Mind*. Cambridge: 223–41.

Bouquet, M. and B. Méniel (eds.) (2011) *Servius et sa réception de l'Antiquité à la Renaissance*. Rennes.

Bowersock, G. W. (1994) *Fiction as History: Nero to Julian*. Berkeley.

Bowie, E. (1993) 'Lies, fiction and slander in early Greek poetry', in C. Gill and T. P. Wiseman (eds.), *Lies and Fiction in the Ancient World*. Exeter: 1–37.

(1994) 'The readership of the Greek novels in the ancient world', in J. Tatum (ed.), *The Search for the Ancient Novel*. Baltimore: 435–59.

Boyd, B. (2006) 'Fiction and theory of mind', *Ph&Lit*, 30/2: 590–600.

(2017) 'Does Austen need narrators? Does anyone?', *NLH*, 48/2: 285–308.

Bremer, J. M., I. de Jong and J. Kalff (eds.) (1987) *Homer, beyond Oral Poetry: Recent Trends in Homeric Interpretation*. Amsterdam.

Bremond, C. (1973) *Logique du récit*. Paris.

Büchner, W. (1940) 'Die Penelopeszenen in der Odyssee', *Hermes*, 75: 129–67.

Budelmann, F. (2020) 'Metalepsis and readerly investment in fictional characters', in S. Matzner and G. Trimble (eds.), *Metalepsis: Ancient Texts, New Perspectives*. Oxford: 59–78.

Budelmann, F. and P. Easterling (2010) 'Reading minds in Greek tragedy', *G&R*, 57: 289–303.

Budelmann, F. and I. Sluiter (eds.) (2023) *Minds on Stage. Greek Tragedy and Cognition*. Oxford.

Bühler, W. (1976) 'Das Element des Visuellen in der Eingangsszene von Heliodors Aithiopika', *WS*, 10: 177–85.

Byre, C. S. (1988) 'Penelope and the suitors before Odysseus. *Odyssey* 18.158–303', *AJPh*, 109/2: 159–73.

Cairns, D. L. and R. Scodel (eds.) (2014) *Defining Greek Narrative*. Edinburgh.

Calame, C. (1999) 'Performative aspects of the choral voice in Greek tragedy', in S. Goldhill and R. Osborne (eds.), *Performance Culture and Athenian Democracy*. Cambridge: 125–53.

Calboli, G. (ed.) (1993) *Cornifici Rhetorica ad C. Herennium: Introduzione, testo critico, commento*. Bologna.

Carrère, E. (2020) *Yoga*. Paris.

Casali, S. and F. Stok (2008) *Servius: Exegetical Stratifications and Cultural Models*. Brussels.

Cassin, B. (1995) *L'effet sophistique*. Paris.

Cave, T. (2016) *Thinking with Literature: Towards a Cognitive Criticism*. Oxford.

Chatman, S. B. (1978) *Story and Discourse: Narrative Structure in Fiction and Film*. Ithaca.

Chekhov, A. P. (1974) *Literary and Theatrical Reminiscences*. New York.

Christensen, J. (2020) *The Many-Minded Man: The Odyssey, Psychology, and the Therapy of Epic*. Ithaca.

Clarke, M. (2019) *Achilles Beside Gilgamesh: Mortality and Wisdom in Early Epic Poetry*. Cambridge.

Clay, D. (1998) 'The theory of the literary persona in antiquity', *Materiali e discussioni per l'analisi dei testi classici*, 40: 9–40.

Cohn, D. (1999) *The Distinction of Fiction*. Baltimore.

Collard, C. (1975) *Euripides: Supplices*. I–II. Groningen.

Couégnas, D. (1992) *Introduction à la paralittérature*. Paris.

Crimp, M. (1997) *Attempts on Her Life: 17 Scenarios for the Theatre*. London.

Culler, J. D. (1988) *Framing the Sign: Criticism and Its Institutions*. Oxford.

Currie, B. (2016) *Homer's Allusive Art*. Oxford.

Currie, G. (2010) *Narratives and Narrators: A Philosophy of Stories*. Oxford.

Dachs, H. (1913) *Die lysis ek tou prosopou: Ein exegetischer und kritischer Grundsatz Aristarchs und seine Neuanwendung auf* Ilias *und* Odyssee. Erlangen.

Dawe, R. D. (1963) 'Inconsistency of plot and character in Aeschylus', *Proceedings of the Cambridge Philological Society*, 9: 21–62.

de Jong, I. J. F. (1987) *Narrators and Focalizers: The Presentation of the Story in the* Iliad. Amsterdam.

(2001) *A Narratological Commentary on the Odyssey*. Cambridge.

(2005) 'Aristotle on the Homeric narrator', *Classical Quarterly*, 55: 616–21.

(2009) 'Metalepsis in ancient Greek literature', in J. Grethlein and A. Rengakos (eds.), *Narratology and Interpretation: The Content of Narrative Form in Ancient Literature*. Berlin: 87–116.

(2014a) 'The anonymous traveller in European literature: A Greek meme?', in D. L Cairns and R. Scodel (eds.), *Defining Greek Narrative*. Edinburgh: 314–33.

(2014b) *Narratology and Classics: A Practical Guide*. Oxford.

(2020) 'Metalepsis and the apostrophe of Heroes in Pindar', in S. Matzner and G. Trimble (eds.), *Metalepsis: Ancient Texts, New Perspectives*. Oxford: 79–98.

de Jong, I. J. F. and R. Nünlist (eds.) (2007) *Time in Ancient Greek Literature: Studies in Ancient Greek Narrative, Vol. 2*. Leiden.

de Jong, I. J. F., R. Nünlist and A. Bowie (eds.) (2004) *Narrators, Narratees, and Narratives in Ancient Greek Literature. Studies in Ancient Greek Narrative, Vol. 1*. Leiden.

De Temmerman, K. (2014) *Crafting Characters: Heroes and Heroines in the Ancient Greek Novel*. Oxford.

De Temmerman, K. and E. van Emde Boas (eds.) (2018a) *Characterization in Ancient Greek Literature*. Leiden.

De Temmerman, K. and E. van Emde Boas (2018b) 'An Introduction', in K. De Temmermann and E. van Emde Boas (eds.), *Characterization in Ancient Greek Literature*. Leiden: 1–26.

Denniston, J. D. and D. L. Page (eds.) (1957) *Aeschylus: Agamemnon*. Oxford.

Derrida, J. and H.-G. Gadamer (1989) *Dialogue and Deconstruction: The Gadamer–Derrida Encounter*, ed. D. P. Michelfelder and R. E. Palmer. Albany.

Dickey, E. (2007) *Ancient Greek Scholarship: A Guide to Finding, Reading, and Understanding Scholia, Commentaries, Lexica, and Grammatical Treatises, from Their Beginnings to the Byzantine Period*. Oxford.

Dillon, M. (1995) 'By gods, tongues, and dogs: The use of oaths in Aristophanic comedy', *G&R*, 42: 135–51.

Doležel, L. (1998) *Heterocosmica: Fiction and Possible Worlds*. Baltimore.

Doubrovsky, S. (1977) *Fils*. Paris.

(2013) 'Autofiction', *Auto/Fiction*, 1/1: 1–3.

Dover, K. J. (1964) 'The poetry of Archilochus', in J. Pouilloux (ed.), *Archiloque: 7 exposés et discussions; Vandoeuvres-Genève, 26 aôut–3 septembre 1963*. Geneva: 181–212.

Duff, T. E. (2005) *Plutarch's Lives: Exploring Virtue and Vice*. Oxford.

Easterling, P. E. (1973) 'Presentation of character in Aeschylus', *G&R*, 20/1: 3–19.

(1977) 'Character in Sophocles', *G&R*, 24/2: 121–9.

Edwards, M. W. (1987) *Homer: Poet of the Iliad*. Baltimore.

Effe, B. (1975) 'Entstehung und Funktion "personaler" Erzählweisen in der Erzählliteratur der Antike', *Poetica*, 7/2: 135–57.

Egan, J. (2010) *A Visit from the Goon Squad*. New York.

Egger, B. (1994) 'Women and marriage in the Greek novels. The boundaries of romance', in J. Tatum (ed.), *The Search for the Ancient Novel*. Baltimore: 260–80.

Eisen, U. and P. von Möllendorff (eds.) (2013) *Über die Grenze: Metalepse in Text- und Bildmedien des Altertums*. Berlin.

Elmer, D. F. (2008) 'Heliodoros's "sources". Intertextuality, paternity, and the Nile River in the *Aithiopika*', *TAPhA*, 138/2: 411–50.

Else, G. F. (1972) *The Structure and Date of Book 10 of Plato's Republic*. Heidelberg.

Elsner, J. (2023) 'Visual epitome in late antique art', in M. Formisano and P. Sacchi (eds.), *Epitomic Writing in Late Antiquity and Beyond: Forms of Unabridged Writing*. London: 202–29.

Emlyn-Jones, C. (1984) 'The reunion of Penelope and Odysseus', *G&R*, 31/1: 1–18.

Erbse, H. (1972) *Beiträge zum Verständnis der Odyssee*. Berlin.

Farrell, J. (2016) 'Ancient commentaries on Theocritus' *Idylls* and Virgil's *Eclogues*', in C. Kraus and C. Stray (eds.), *Classical Commentaries: Explorations in a Scholarly Genre*. Oxford: 397–418.

Feddern, S. (2018) *Der antike Fiktionalitätsdiskurs*. Berlin.

(2021) *Elemente der antiken Erzähltheorie*. Berlin.

Feeney, D. C. (1993) 'Epilogue. Towards an account of the ancient world's concepts of fictive belief', in C. Gill and T. P. Wiseman (eds.), *Lies and Fiction in the Ancient World*. Exeter: 230–44.

(1995) 'Criticism ancient and modern', in D. Innes, H. Hines and C. Pelling (eds.), *Ethics and Rhetoric*. Oxford: 301–10.

(2008) 'Review: Irene J. F. de Jong, René Nünlist, *Time in Ancient Greek Literature*', *BMCR*, 20080724.

Felski, R. (2015) *The Limits of Critique*. Chicago.

Felson-Rubin, N. (1987) 'Penelope's perspective: Character from plot', in J. M. Bremer, I. de Jong and J. Kalff (eds.), *Homer, beyond Oral Poetry: Recent Trends in Homeric Interpretation*. Amsterdam: 61–83.

(1994) *Regarding Penelope: From Character to Poetics*. Princeton.

Fenik, B. (1974) *Studies in the Odyssey*. Wiesbaden.

Finkelberg, M. (1998) *The Birth of Literary Fiction in Ancient Greece*. Oxford.

Fleming, I. (1954) *Casino Royale*. London.

Fludernik, M. (1996) *Towards a 'Natural' Narratology*. London.

(2003a) 'Scene shift, metalepsis, and the metaleptic mode', *Style*, 37/4: 382–400.

(2003b) 'The diachronization of narratology', *Narrative*, 11/3: 331–48.

(2012) 'How natural is "unnatural narratology"; or, What is unnatural about unnatural narratology?', *Narrative*, 203: 357–70.

(2015) 'Plotting experience: A comment on Jonas Grethlein's "Heliodorus Against Palmer, Zunshine & Co."', *Style*, 49/3: 288–93.

Fludernik, M., N. Falkenhayner and J. Steiner (eds.) (2015) *Interdisziplinäre Perspektiven. Faktuales und fiktionales Erzählen* 1. Würzburg.

Fludernik, M. and M.-L. Ryan (eds.) (2020) *Narrative Factuality: A Handbook.* Berlin.

Foley, H. (2001) *Female Acts in Greek Tragedy.* Princeton.

Ford, A. L. (2002) *The Origins of Criticism: Literary Culture and Poetic Theory in Classical Greece.* Princeton.

Formisano, M. and P. Sacchi (eds.) (2023) *Epitomic Writing in Late Antiquity and Beyond: Forms of Unabridged Writing.* London.

Forster, E. M. (1993 [1927]) *Aspects of the Novel.* London.

Fowler, D. (1990) 'Deviant focalisation in Virgil's Aeneid', *PCPhS*, 36: 42–63.

(2001) 'Narrative: Introduction', in S. Harrison (ed.), *Texts, Ideas and the Classics. Scholarship, Theory and Classical Literature.* Oxford: 65–9.

Fowles, J. (1969) *The French Lieutenant's Woman.* London.

Fraenkel, E. (ed.) (1950) *Aeschylus:* Agamemnon, *Vol. 1.* Oxford.

Frank, J. (1945) 'Spatial form in modern literature: An essay in two parts', *The Sewanee Review*, 53/2: 221–40.

(1991) *The Idea of Spatial Form.* New Brunswick.

Fränkel, H. (1993) *Dichtung und Philosophie des frühen Griechentums: Eine Geschichte der griechischen Epik, Lyrik und Prosa bis zur Mitte des fünften Jahrhunderts*, 4th ed. Munich.

Franz, M. (1991) 'Fiktionalität und Wahrheit in der Sicht des Gorgias und des Aristoteles', *Philologus*, 135/2: 240–8.

Frege, G. (1960 [1892]) 'On sense and reference', in M. Black and P. T. Geach (eds.), *Translations from the Philosophical Writings of Gottlob Frege.* Oxford: 56–78.

Fuhrer, T. (2015) 'Teichoskopia: Female figures looking on battles', in J. Fabre-Serris and A. Keith (eds.), *Women and War in Antiquity.* Baltimore: 52–70.

Fuhrmann, M. (ed.) (1976) *Aristoteles:* Poetik. Munich.

Fuhrmann, M. (1992) *Die Dichtungstheorie der Antike: Aristoteles, Horaz, Longin. Eine Einführung.* Darmstadt.

Fulkerson, L. (2020) 'Close encounters: Divine epiphanies on the fringes of Latin love elegy', in S. Matzner and G. Trimble (eds.), *Metalepsis: Ancient Texts, New Perspectives.* Oxford: 147–66.

Fusillo, M. (1985) *Il tempo delle Argonautiche: Un'analisi del racconto in Apollonio Rodio.* Rome.

(1989) *Il romanzo greco: Polifonia ed eros.* Venice.

(1996) 'Il romanzo antico come paraletteratura? Il topos del racconto di ricapitolazione', in O. Pecere and A. Stramaglia (eds.), *La letteratura di consumo nel mondo greco-latino.* Cassino: 49–67.

Gadamer, H.-G. (1990) *Wahrheit und Methode: Grundzüge einer philosophischen Hermeneutik.* 6th ed. Tübingen.

(2004 [1960]) *Truth and Method.* London.

Gagné, R. and M. Hopman (eds.) (2013) *Choral Mediations in Greek Tragedy.* Cambridge.

Gaifman, M. and V. Platt (eds.) (2018) 'Special issue: The embodied body in antiquity', *Art History* 41/3.

Gallagher, C. (2006) 'The rise of fictionality', in F. Moretti (ed.), *The Novel, Vol. 1: History, Geography and Culture.* Princeton: 336–63.

(2011) 'What would Napoleon do? Historical, fictional, and counterfactual characters', *NLH*, 42/2: 315–36.

Gallagher, S. (2001) 'The practice of mind: Theory, simulation or primary interaction?', *Journal of Consciousness Studies*, 8/5–7: 83–108.

(2005) *How the Body Shapes the Mind.* Oxford.

Garcea, A., M.-K. Lhommé and D. Vallat (eds.) (2016) *Fragments d'érudition.* Hildesheim.

Gasparini, P. (2004) *Est-il je? Roman autobiographique et autofiction.* Paris.

Genette, G. (1966) 'Frontières du récit', *Communications*, 8: 152–63.

(1972) *Figures* III. Paris.

(1980) *Narrative Discourse.* Ithaca.

(1983) *Nouveau discourse du récit.* Paris.

(1993) *Fiction and Diction.* Ithaca.

Gill, C. (1983) 'The question of character-development: Plutarch and Tacitus', *CQ*, 33/2: 469–87.

(1984) 'The ethos/pathos distinction in rhetorical and literary criticism', *CQ*, 34, 1: 149–66.

(1986) 'The question of character and personality in Greek tragedy', *Poetics Today*, 7/2: 251–73.

(1990) 'The character-personality distinction', in C. Pelling (ed.), *Characterization and Individuality in Greek Literature.* Oxford: 1–31.

(1993) 'Plato on falsehood – not fiction', in C. Gill and T. P. Wiseman (eds.), *Lies and Fiction in the Ancient World.* Exeter: 38–87.

(1996) *Personality in Greek Epic, Tragedy, and Philosophy: The Self in Dialogue.* Oxford.

(2006) *The Structured Self in Hellenistic and Roman Thought.* Oxford.

(2008) 'The ancient self: Issues and approaches', in P. Remes and J. Sihvola (eds.), *Ancient Philosophy of the Self.* New York: 35–56.

Glauch, S. (2009) *An der Schwelle zur Literatur: Elemente einer Poetik des höfischen Erzählens. Studien zur historischen Poetik* 1. Heidelberg.

(2010) 'Ich-Erzähler ohne Stimme: Zur Andersartigkeit mittelalterlichen Erzählens zwischen Narratologie und Mediengeschichte', in H. Haferland and M. Meyer (eds.), *Historische Narratologie – mediävistische Perspektiven: Tagung an der Universität Osnabrück vom 22. bis zum 25. November 2007.* Berlin: 149–86.

Goheen, R. F. (1955) 'Aspects of dramatic symbolism: Three studies in the *Oresteia*', *AJP*, 76/2: 113–37.

Goldhill, S. (1986) *Reading Greek Tragedy.* Cambridge.

(1990) *The Poet's Voice: Essays on Poetics and Greek Literature.* Cambridge.

(1995) *Foucault's Virginity: Ancient Erotic Fiction and the History of Sexuality.* Cambridge.

(2015) 'A guide to narratology. I.J.F. de Jong, *Narratology and Classics. A Practical Guide*', *CR*, 65/2: 327–9.

Goldman, A. I. (2006) *Simulating Minds: The Philosophy, Psychology, and Neuroscience of Mindreading.* Oxford.

Gould, J. (1978) 'Dramatic character and "human intelligibility" in Greek tragedy', *PCPhS*, 24: 43–67.

Graf, F. (1997) 'Medea, the enchantress from afar: Remarks on a well-known myth', in J. J. Clauss and S. I. Johnston (eds.), *Medea: Essays on Medea in Myth, Literature, Philosophy and Art.* Princeton: 21–43.

Green, D. H. (2002) *The Beginnings of Medieval Romance.* Cambridge.

Greimas, A. J. (1966) *Sémantique structurale: Recherche de méthode.* Paris.

Grethlein, J. (2003) *Asyl und Athen: Die Konstruktion kollektiver Identität in der griechischen Tragödie.* Stuttgart.

(2006) *Das Geschichtsbild der Ilias: Eine Untersuchung aus phänomenologischer und narratologischer Perspektive.* Göttingen.

(2010) 'The narrative reconfiguration of time beyond Ricœur', *Poetics Today*, 31/2: 313–29.

(2011a) 'Die Fabel', in B. Zimmermann (ed.), *Handbuch der Altertumswissenschaften. Griechische Literatur. Vol. 1: Die Literatur der archaischen und klassischen Zeit.* Munich: 321–5.

(2011b) 'Review of R. Scodel, *Epic Facework. Self-presentation and Social Interaction in Homer*', *Mnemosyne*, 64/3: 481–5.

(2012a) 'Review of Irene J. F. de Jong, *Space in Ancient Greek Literature. Studies in Ancient Greek Narrative 3*', *BMCRev*, 20120918.

(2012b) 'Xenophon's *Anabasis* from character to narrator', *JHS*, 132: 23–40.

(2013a) 'Choral intertemporality in the *Oresteia*', in R. Gagné and M. Hopman (eds.), *Choral Mediations in Greek Tragedy.* Cambridge: 78–99.

(2013b) *Experience and Teleology in Ancient Historiography. 'Futures Past' from Herodotus to Augustine.* Cambridge.

(2015) 'Aesthetic experiences, ancient and modern', *New Literary History*, 46/2: 309–33.

(2017a) *Die* Odyssee: *Homer und die Kunst des Erzählens.* Munich.

(2017b) *Aesthetic Experiences and Classical Antiquity: The Content of Form in Narratives and Pictures.* Cambridge.

(2018) 'More than minds: Experience, narrative, and plot', *Partial Answers*, 16/2: 279–90.

(2019) '"Stories embroidered beyond truth": Reading Herodotus and Thucydides in light of Pindar's *Olympian* 1', in J. Baines, H. van der Blom, Y. S. Chen and T. Rood (eds.), *Historical Consciousness and the Use of the Past in the Ancient World.* Sheffield: 313–29.

(2020) 'Plato in therapy: A cognitivist reassessment of the *Republic*'s idea of mimesis', *The Journal of Aesthetics and Art Criticism*, 78/2: 157–70.

(2021) *The Ancient Aesthetics of Deception. The Ethics of Enchantment from Gorgias to Heliodorus.* Cambridge.

(2022) 'Für Interpretation', *Merkur* 76/881: 75–82.

Grethlein, J. and L. Huitink (2017) 'Homer's vividness: An enactive approach', *JHS*, 137: 67–91.

Grethlein, J., L. Huitink and A. Tagliabue (eds.) (2019) *Experience, Narrative and Criticism in Ancient Greece: Under the Spell of Stories.* Oxford.

Grethlein, J. and A. Rengakos (eds.) (2009) *Narratology and Interpretation: The Content of Narrative Form in Ancient Literature.* Berlin.

Griffin, J. (1980) *Homer on Life and Death.* Oxford.

Grisolia, R. (2001) *Oikonomia: Struttura e tecnica drammatica negli scoli antichi ai testi drammatici.* Naples.

Gurd, S. A. (2016) *Dissonance: Auditory Aesthetics in Ancient Greece.* New York.

Gutzwiller, K. J. (2010) 'Literary criticism', in J. J. Clauss and M. Cuypers (eds.), *A Companion to Hellenistic Literature.* Chichester: 337–65.

Haferland, H. (2014) '"Motivation von hinten": Durchschaubarkeit des Erzählens und Finalität in der Geschichte des Erzählens', *Diegesis* 3/2: 66–95.

Haferland, H. and M. Meyer (eds.) (2010) *Historische Narratologie – Mediävistische Perspektiven.* Berlin.

Halliwell, S. (1986) *Aristotle's* Poetics*: A Study of Philosophical Criticism.* London.

(1987) *The* Poetics *of Aristotle: Translation and Commentary.* Chapel Hill.

(2002) *The Aesthetics of Mimesis: Ancient Texts and Modern Problems.* Princeton.

(2011) *Between Ecstasy and Truth: Interpretations of Greek Poetics from Homer to Longinus.* Oxford.

(2014) 'Diegesis – Mimesis', in P. Hühn (ed.), *The Living Handbook of Narratology.* Hamburg.

(2014) 'Laughter', in M. Revermann (ed.), *The Cambridge Companion to Greek Comedy.* Cambridge: 189–205.

(2015) 'Fiction', in P. Destrée and P. Murray (eds.), *A Companion to Ancient Aesthetics.* Chichester: 341–53.

Halliwell, S. (ed.) (2021) *Sul Sublime – On the Sublime.* Milan.

Hamburger, K. (1993 [1957]) *The Logic of Literature.* Bloomington.

Handke, P. (1971) *Der Ritt über den Bodensee.* Frankfurt am Main.

(2019 [1966]) *Publikumsbeschimpfung und andere Sprechstücke.* Frankfurt am Main.

Harris, W. V. (1989) *Ancient Literacy.* Cambridge, MA.

Harrison, S. (2001) 'General introduction: Working together', in S. Harrison (ed.), *Texts, Ideas and the Classics: Scholarship, Theory and Classical Literature.* Oxford: 1–25.

Harsh, P. W. (1950) 'Penelope and Odysseus in *Odyssey* xix', *AJPh*, 71/1: 1–21.

Hau, L. I. (2016) *Moral History from Herodotus to Diodorus Siculus.* Edinburgh.

Haubold, J. (2013) *Greece and Mesopotamia: Dialogues in Literature.* Cambridge.

(2014) 'Beyond Auerbach: Homeric narrative and the *Epic of Gilgamesh*', in D. L. Cairns and R. Scodel (eds.), *Defining Greek Narrative.* Edinburgh: 13–28.

Havelock, E. A. (1963) *Preface to Plato*. Oxford.

Haynes, K. (2003) *Fashioning the Feminine in the Greek Novel*. New York.

Heath, M. (1987) *The Poetics of Greek Tragedy*. London.

Heitman, R. (2005) *Taking Her Seriously: Penelope and the Plot of Homer's Odyssey*. Ann Arbor.

Hempfer, K. W. (1990) 'Zu einigen Problemen einer Fiktionstheorie', *ZFSL*, 100: 109–37.

Herman, D. (ed.) (2011a) *The Emergence of Mind: Representations of Consciousness in Narrative Discourse in English*. Lincoln.

Herman, D. (2011b) 'Introduction', in D. Herman (ed.) *The Emergence of Mind: Representations of Consciousness in Narrative Discourse in English*. Lincoln: 1–40.

Hogan, P. C. (2011) 'Palmer's anti-cognitivist challenge', *Style*, 45/2: 244–8.

Holmes, B. (2010) *The Symptom and the Subject: The Emergence of the Physical Body in Ancient Greece*. Princeton.

Hölscher, U. (1967) 'Penelope vor den Freiern', in H. Meller and H.-J. Zimmermann (eds.), *Lebende Antike: Symposion für Rudolf Sühnel*. Berlin: 27–33.

Horkheimer, M. and T. W. Adorno (1969) *Dialektik der Aufklärung: Philosophische Fragmente*. Frankfurt.

Hornblower, S. (ed.) (1994) *Greek Historiography*. Oxford.

Horsfall, N. (1995) 'Rome without spectacles', *G&R*, 42/1: 49–56.

Hose, M. (1996) 'Fiktionalität und Lüge. Über einen Unterschied zwischen römischer und griechischer Terminologie', *Poetica*, 28/3–4: 257–74.

Howald, E. (1930) *Die griechische Tragödie*. Munich.

Howie, J. G. (1984) 'The revision of myth in Pindar *Olympian* 1', *ARCA*, 11: 277–313.

Hunter, R. L. (2009) *Critical Moments in Classical Literature: Studies in the Ancient View of Literature and Its Uses*. Cambridge.

Hunter, R. and D. Russell (eds.) (2011) *Plutarch: How To Study Poetry (de audiendis poetis)*. Cambridge.

Hutcheon, L. (1988) *A Poetics of Postmodernism: History, Theory, Fiction*. New York.

Hutchinson, G. O. (2018) *Plutarch's Rhythmic Prose*. New York.

Hutto, D. D. (2007) 'Folk psychology without theory or simulation', in D. D. Hutto and M. Ratcliffe (eds.), *Folk Psychology Re-assessed*. Dordrecht: 115–35.

(2008) *Folk Psychological Narratives: The Sociocultural Basis of Understanding Reasons*. Cambridge.

Ioli, R. (2018) *Il felice inganno: Poesia, finzione e verità nel mondo antico*. Milan.

Iser, W. (1991) *Das Fiktive und das Imaginäre: Perspektiven literarischer Anthropologie*. Frankfurt am Main.

Iversen, S. (2011) '"In flaming flames": Crises of experientiality in non-fictional narratives', in J. Alber and R. Heinze (eds.), *Unnatural Narratives – Unnatural Narratology*. Berlin: 89–103.

(2020) 'Transgressive narration: The case of autofiction', in M. Fludernik and M.-L. Ryan (eds.), *Narrative Factuality: A Handbook*. Berlin: 555–64.

Jacobson, H. (1974) *Ovid's* Heroides. Princeton.

Jaeger, W. (1943) *Paideia: The Ideals of Greek Culture, Vol. 2. In Search of the Divine Centre*. New York.

Jahn, M. (2011) 'Mind = mind + social mind? A response to Alan Palmer's target essay', *Style*, 45/2: 249–53.

Jajdelska, E. (2007) *Silent Reading and the Birth of the Narrator*. Toronto.

Janko, R. (ed.) (2011) *Philodemus* On Poems Books 3–4 *with the Fragments of* Aristotle On Poets: *Introduction, Translation, Commentary*. Oxford.

Jannidis, F. (2004) *Figur und Person: Beitrag zu einer historischen Narratologie*. Berlin.

Johnson, W. A. and H. Parker (eds.) (2009) *Ancient Literacies: The Culture of Reading in Greece and Rome*. Oxford.

Johnson, W. A. (2010) *Readers and Reading Culture in the High Roman Empire: A Study of Elite Communities*. Oxford.

Jones, J. (1962) *On Aristotle and Greek Tragedy*. London.

Jones, M. (2012) *Playing the Man: Performing Masculinities in the Ancient Greek Novel*. Oxford.

Joyce, J. (1922) *Ulysses*. Paris.

Kablitz, A. (2008) 'Literatur, Fiktion und Erzählung – nebst einem Nachruf auf den Erzähler', in I. Rajewski and U. Schneider (eds.), *Im Zeichen der Fiktion: Aspekte fiktionaler Rede aus historischer und systematischer Sicht*. Stuttgart: 13–44.

Kafalenos, E. (2006) *Narrative Causalities*. Columbus.

Kania, A. (2005) 'Against the ubiquity of fictional narrators', *The Journal of Aesthetics and Art Criticism*, 63/1: 47–54.

Kannicht, R. (1980) 'Der alte Streit zwischen Philosophie und Dichtung', *AU*, 23/6: 6–36.

Kant, I. (1929 [1781/7]) *Critique of Pure Reason*. London.

Karnes, M. (2020) 'The Possibilities of Medieval Fiction', *NHL*, 51/1: 209–28.

Kassel, R. (1991) *Kleine Schriften*. Berlin.

Katz, M. (1991) *Penelope's Renown: Meaning and Indeterminacy in Homer's* Odyssey. Princeton.

Kelly, A. (2012) 'The audience expects: Odysseus and Penelope', in E. Minchin (ed.), *Orality and Literacy in the Ancient World*. Leiden: 3–24.

(2014) 'Homeric battle narrative and the ancient Near East', in D. L. Cairns and R. Scodel (eds.), *Defining Greek Narrative*. Edinburgh: 29–54.

Kim, L. Y. (2010) *Homer Between History and Fiction in Imperial Greek Literature*. Cambridge.

Kirk, G. (1962) *The Songs of Homer*. Cambridge.

(1985) *The* Iliad: *A Commentary. Volume 1: Books 1–4*. Cambridge.

Klauk, T. and T. Köppe (2014) 'Bausteine einer Theorie der Fiktionalität', in T. Klauk and T. Klöppe (eds.), *Fiktionalität: Ein interdisziplinäres Handbuch*. Berlin: 3–32.

Klimek, S. (2010) *Paradoxes Erzählen: Die Metalepse in der phantastischen Literatur*. Paderborn.

Klooster, J. (2013) 'Apostrophe in Homer, Apollonius and Callimachus', in U. E. Eisen and P. von Moellendorff (eds.), *Über die Grenze: Metalepse in Text- und Bildmedien des Altertums [Transferring Borders. Metalepsis in Texts and Artifacts of Antiquity]*. Berlin: 151–73.

Knights, L. C. (1933). *How Many Children Had Lady Macbeth? An Essay in the Theory and Practice of Shakespeare Criticism*. Cambridge.

Köhnken, A. (1974) 'Pindar as innovator: Poseidon Hippios and the relevance of the Pelops story in *Olympian 1*', CQ, 24/2: 199–206.

Konstan, D. (1994) *Sexual Symmetry. Love in the Ancient Novel and Related Genres*. Princeton.

(2004) '"The Birth of the Reader". Plutarch as a literary critic', *Scholia*, 13/1: 3–27.

Köppe, T. (2014) 'Die Institution Fiktionalität', in T. Klauk and T. Klöppe (eds.), *Fiktionalität: Ein interdisziplinäres Handbuch*. Berlin: 35–49.

Köppe, T. and J. Stühring (2011) 'Against pan-narrator theories', *Journal of Literary Semantics*, 40/1: 59–80.

Kracht, C. (2021) *Eurotrash*. Cologne.

Kragl, F. (2019) 'Autor und Erzähler – Mittelalter', in E. von Contzen and S. Tilg (eds.), *Handbuch historische Narratologie*. Berlin: 82–93.

Krieter-Spiro, M. (2009) *Homers Ilias. Dritter Gesang (G). Fasz. 2, Kommentar*. Berlin.

Krumrey, B. (2015) *Der Autor in seinem Text: Autofiktion in der deutschsprachigen Gegenwartsliteratur als (post-)postmodernes Phänomen*. Göttingen.

Kukkonen, K. (2014) 'Presence and prediction: The embodied reader's cascades of cognition', *Style*, 48/3: 367–84.

Kuzmičová, A. (2012) 'Presence in the reading of literary narrative: A case for motor enactment', *Semiotica*, 189/1: 23–48.

(2013) *Mental Imagery in the Experience of Literary Narrative: Views from Embodied Cognition*. Stockholm.

Laird, A. (2008) 'Approaching style and rhetoric', in T. Whitmarsh (ed.), *The Cambridge Companion to the Greek and Roman Novel*. Cambridge: 201–17.

Lamarque, P. and S. H. Olsen (eds.) (1994) *Truth, Fiction, and Literature: A Philosophical Perspective*. Oxford.

Lateiner, D. (1989) *The Historical Method of Herodotus*. Toronto.

Lather, A. (2021) *Materiality and Aesthetics in Archaic and Classical Poetry*. Edinburgh.

Lattmann, C. (2005) 'Die Dichtungsklassifikation des Aristoteles', *Philologus*, 149/1: 28–51.

Lauwers, J., H. Schwall and J. Opsomer (eds.) (2018) *Psychology and the Classics: A Dialogue of Disciplines*. Berlin.

Lavocat, F. (2016) *Fait et fiction: Pour une frontière*. Paris.

Lebeck, A. (1971) *The* Oresteia*: A Study in Language and Structure*. Cambridge.

Leudar, I. and A. Costall (eds.) (2009a) *Against Theory of Mind*. Houndmills.

Leudar, I. and A. Costall (2009b) 'Introduction: Against "Theory of Mind"', in I. Leudar and A. Costall (eds.), *Against Theory of Mind*. Houndmills: 1–16.

Leverage, P., H. Mancing, R. Schweickert and J. M. William (eds.) (2011) *Theory of Mind and Literature*. West Lafayette.

Levine, D. B. (1983) 'Penelope's laugh: *Odyssey* 18.163', *AJPh*, 104/2: 172–8.

Lieberg, G. (1982) *Poeta creator: Studien zu einer Figur der antiken Dichtung*. Amsterdam.

Liebert, R. S. (2017) *Tragic Pleasure from Homer to Plato*. Cambridge.

Liveley, G. (2019) *Narratology*. Oxford.

Lloyd-Jones, H. (1962) 'The guilt of Agamemnon', *CQ*, 12/2: 187–99.

    (1972) 'Tycho von Wilamowitz-Moellendorff on the dramatic technique of Sophocles', *CQ*, 22/2: 214–28.

    (1982) *Classical Survivals: The Classics in the Modern World*. London.

Lord, A. B. (1938) 'Homer and Huso II: Narrative inconsistencies in Homer and oral poetry', *TAPhA*, 69: 439–45.

Lotman, R. V. (1977) *The Structure of the Artistic Text*. Ann Arbor.

Lovatt, H. (2020) 'Metalepsis, grief, and narrative in *Aeneid* 2', in S. Matzner and G. Trimble (eds.), *Metalepsis: Ancient Texts, New Perspectives*. Oxford: 167–94.

Lowe, N. J. (2000) *The Classical Plot and the Invention of Western Narrative*. Cambridge.

Lucas, D. W. (1968) *Aristoteles:* Poetics. Oxford.

Lugowski, C. (1976 [1932]) *Die Form der Individualität im Roman: Studien zur inneren Struktur der frühen deutschen Prosaerzählung*. Frankfurt.

Lüthi, M. (1975) *Das Volksmärchen als Dichtung: Ästhetik und Anthropologie, Vol. 1*. Düsseldorf.

Mackay, E. A. (2001) 'The frontal face and "you": Narrative disjunction in early Greek poetry and painting', *Acta Classica*, 44: 5–34.

Manieri, A. (1998) *L'immagine poetica nella teoria degli antichi: Phantasia ed enargeia*. Pisa.

Mar, R., Djikic, M. and Oatley, K. (2008) 'Effects of reading on knowledge, social abilities, and selfhood: Theory and empirical studies', in S. Zyngier, S., M. Bortolussi, A. Chesnokova and J. Auracher (eds.), *Directions in Empirical Literary Studies: In Honor of Willie van Peer*. Amsterdam: 127–37.

Margolin, U. (1989) 'Structuralist approaches to character in narrative: The state of the art', *Semiotica*, 75: 1–24.

Mariani, A. J. (1978) 'The Forged Feature: Created Identity in Homer's *Odyssey*'. PhD diss, Yale University.

Martínez, M. (1996) *Formaler Mythos: Skizze einer ästhetischen Theorie*. Paderborn.

Martínez, M. and M. Scheffel (1999) *Einführung in die Erzähltheorie*. Munich.

Matthews, V. J. (1980) 'Metrical reasons for apostrophe in Homer', *LCM*, 5: 93–9.

Matzner, S. (2020) 'By way of introduction. Back to the future: Problems and potentials of metalepsis avant Genette', in S. Matzner and G. Trimble (eds.), *Metalepsis: Ancient Texts, New Perspectives*. Oxford: 1–24.

Matzner, S. and G. Trimble (eds.) (2020) *Metalepsis: Ancient Texts, New Perspectives*. Oxford.

Mayer, R. G. (2003) 'Persona<l> problems. The literary persona in antiquity revisited', *Materiali e discussioni*, 50: 55–80.

McDermott, E. A. (1989) *Euripides' 'Medea': The Incarnation of Disorder*. University Park.

McHale, B. (1983) 'Unspeakable sentences, unnatural acts. Linguistics and poetics revisited', *Poetics Today*, 4/1: 17–45.

  (1987) *Postmodernist Fiction*. New York.

Meijering, R. (1987) *Literary and Rhetorical Theories in Greek Scholia*. Groningen.

Meineck, P., W. M. Short and J. Devereaux (eds.) (2019) *The Routledge Handbook of Classics and Cognitive Theory*. London.

Mendelsohn, D. (2000) *The Elusive Embrace: Desire and the Riddle of Identity*. New York.

Merkelbach, R. (1951) *Untersuchungen zur* Odyssee. Munich.

Mikalson, J. D. (1991) *Honor Thy Gods: Popular Religion in Greek Tragedy*. Chapel Hill.

Mind and Language (1992) 7/1–2.

Montanari, F. (ed.) (2015) *Brill's Companion to Ancient Greek Scholarship*. Leiden.

Montanari, F. (ed.) (2020) *History of Ancient Greek Scholarship: From the Beginnings to the End of the Byzantine Age*. Leiden.

Morgan, J. R. (1989) 'A sense of the ending: The conclusion of Heliodoros' *Aithiopika*', *TAPhA*, 119: 299–320.

  (1991) 'Reader and audiences in the *Aithiopika* of Heliodoros', in E. Forsten (ed.), *Groningen Colloquia on the Novel 4*. Groningen: 85–103.

  (1993) 'Make-believe and make believe: The fictionality of the Greek novels', in C. Gill and T. P. Wiseman (eds.), *Lies and Fiction in the Ancient World*. Exeter: 175–229.

  (1999) 'The story of Knemon in Heliodoros' *Aithiopika*', in S. Swain (ed.), *Oxford Readings in the Greek Novel*. Oxford: 259–85.

  (2018) 'Heliodorus', in K. D. Temmerman and E. van Emde Boas (eds.), *Characterization in Ancient Greek Literature*. Leiden: 628–49.

Morrison, J. V. (1992) *Homeric Misdirection: False Predictions in the* Iliad. Ann Arbor.

Muecke, F. (1982) 'A portrait of the artist as a young woman', *CQ*, 32/1: 41–55.

Müller, M. (1966) *Athene als göttliche Helferin in der* Odyssee: *Untersuchungen zur Form der epischen Aristie*. Heidelberg.

Munteanu, D. L. (2012) *Tragic Pathos: Pity and Fear in Greek Philosophy and Tragedy*. Cambridge.

Murnaghan, S. (1987) *Disguise and Recognition in the* Odyssey. Princeton.

Nabokov, V. V. (1928) *Korol', dama, valet*. Berlin.

  (1951) *Speak, Memory*. London.

  (1955) *Lolita*. Paris.

  (1964 [1947]) *Bend Sinister*. New York.

  (1974) *Look at the Harlequins!* New York.

Nannini, S. (1986) *Omero e il suo pubblico nel pensiero dei commentatori antichi.* Rome.

Narrative (2015) Special Issue 'Social Minds in Factual and Fictional Narration', 23/2.

Ní Mheallaigh, K. (2014) *Reading Fiction with Lucian.* Cambridge.

Nielsen, H. S., J. Phelan and R. Walsh (2015) 'Ten theses about fictionality', *Narrative*, 23/1: 61–73.

Nightingale, A. W. (2006) 'Mimesis: Ancient Greek literary theory', in P. Waugh (ed.), *Literary Theory and Criticism.* Oxford: 37–47.

Noë, A. (2004) *Action in Perception.* Cambridge, MA.

Nooter, S. (2012) *When Heroes Sing: Sophocles and the Shifting Soundscape of Tragedy.* Cambridge.

(2017) *The Mortal Voice in the Tragedies of Aeschylus.* Cambridge.

Nünlist, R. (2009) *The Ancient Critic at Work: Terms and Concepts of Literary Criticism in Greek Scholia.* Cambridge.

Oatley, K. (2009) 'Changing our minds', *Greater Good*, 5/3.

Onea, E. (2014) 'Fiktionalität und Sprechakte', in T. Klauk and T. Klöppe (eds.), *Fiktionalität: Ein interdisziplinäres Handbuch.* Berlin: 68–96.

Orlemanski, J. (2019) 'Who has fiction? Modernity, fictionality, and the Middle Ages', *NLH*, 50/2: 145–70.

Otto, N. (2009) *Enargeia: Untersuchung zur Charakteristik alexandrinischer Dichtung.* Stuttgart.

Pagan, N. O. (2014) *Theory of Mind and Science Fiction.* Basingstoke.

Page, D. L. (1955) *The Homeric* Odyssey: *The Mary Flexner Lectures Delivered at Bryn Mawr College, Pennsylvania.* Oxford.

Paige, N. D. (2011) *Before Fiction: The ancien régime of the Novel.* Philadelphia.

Palmer, A. (2004) *Fictional Minds.* Lincoln, NE.

(2010) *Social Minds in the Novel.* Columbus.

(2015) 'Response to Jonas Grethlein's essay "Is narrative 'the description of fictional mental functioning'? Heliodorus Against Palmer, Zunshine & Co."', *Style*, 49/3: 285–88.

Parry, A. (1972) 'Language and characterization in Homer', *HSPh*, 76: 1–22.

Patron, S. (2009) *Le narrateur: Introduction à la théorie narrative.* Paris.

Pavel, T. G. (2003) *La pensée du roman.* Paris.

Payne, M. (2007) *Theocritus and the Invention of Fiction.* Cambridge.

Pelling, C. (ed.) (1990) *Characterization and Individuality in Greek Literature.* Oxford.

(2013) 'Xenophon's and Caesar's third-person narratives – or are they?', in A. Marmodoro (ed.), *The Author's Voice in Classical and Late Antiquity.* Oxford: 39–76.

Peponi, A.-E. (2012) *Frontiers of Pleasure: Models of Aesthetic Response in Archaic and Classical Greek Thought.* Oxford.

Phelan, J. (1989) *Reading People, Reading Plots: Character, Progression, and the Interpretation of Narrative.* Chicago.

Pier, J. (2014) 'Metalepsis', in P. Hühn, J. C. Meister, J. Pier and W. Schmid (eds.), *Handbook of Narratology.* Berlin: 326–43.

Pinheiro, M. P. F. (1998) 'Time and narrative technique in Heliodorus' "Aethiopica"', *ANRW* II 34/4: 3148–73.

Pitcher, L. (2012) 'Themistogenes', in I. Worthington (ed.), *Brill's New Jacoby*. Leiden.

Plotke, S. (2017) *Die Stimme des Erzählens: Mittelalterliche Buchkultur und moderne Narratologie*. Göttingen.

Pratt, L. H. (1993) *Lying and Poetry from Homer to Pindar: Falsehood and Deception in Archaic Greek Poetics*. Ann Arbor.

Premack, D. and G. Woodruff (1978) 'Does the chimpanzee have a Theory of Mind?', *The Behavioral and Brain Sciences*, 1.4: 515–26.

Primavesi, O. (2009) 'Zum Problem der epischen Fiktion in der vorplatonischen Poetik', in U. Peters and R. Warning (eds.), *Fiktion und Fiktionalität in den Literaturen des Mittelalters*. Munich: 105–20.

Privitera, S. (2018) '*Odyssey* 20 and cognitive science: A case study', in J. Lauwers, H. Schwall and J. Opsomer (eds.), *Psychology and the Classics*. Berlin: 32–45.

Propp, V. J. (1968) *Morphology of the Folktale*. Austin.

Proust, M. (1913) *À la recherche du temps perdu*. Paris.

Puelma, M. (1989) 'Der Dichter und die Wahrheit in der griechischen Poetik von Homer bis Aristoteles', *MH*, 46/2: 65–100.

Purves, A. (2015) 'Ajax and other objects: Homer's vibrant materialism', *Ramus*, 44: 75–94.

Raaflaub, K. (2010) 'Ulterior motives in ancient historiography: What exactly, and why?', in L. Foxhall, H.-J. Gehrke and N. Luraghi (eds.), *Intentional History: Spinning Time in Ancient Greece*. Stuttgart: 189–210.

Rabel, R. J. (1997) *Plot and Point of View in the* Iliad. Ann Arbor.

Raffa, M. (2011) 'Il canto di Achille (Ps. Plut. *De mus.* 40, 1145d–f', *QUCC*, 99: 165–76.

Rajewski, I. (2020) 'Theories of fictionality and their real other', in M. Fludernik and M.-L. Ryan (eds.), *Narrative Factuality: A Handbook*. Berlin: 29–50.

Ramsay, R. (1991) 'Autobiographical fictions: Duras, Sarraute, Simon, Robbe-Grillet. Re-writing history, story, self', *The International Fiction Review*, 18: 25–33.

Richardson, B. (1997a) 'Beyond poststructuralism: Theory of character, the personae of modern drama, and the antinomies of Critical Theory', *Modern Drama*, 40/1: 86–99.

(1997b) *Unlikely Stories: Causality and the Nature of Modern Narrative*. Newark.

(2000) 'Narrative poetics and postmodern transgression: Theorizing the collapse of time, voice, and frame', *Narrative*, 8/1: 23–42.

(2006) *Unnatural Voices: Extreme Narration in Modern and Contemporary Fiction*. Columbus.

(2015) *Unnatural Narrative: Theory, History, and Practice*. Columbus.

(2019) *A Poetics of Plot for the Twenty-First Century: Theorizing Unruly Narratives*. Columbus.

(2020) 'Transcending humanistic and cognitive models: Unnatural characters in fiction, drama, and popular culture', in J. Alber and B. Richardson (eds.),

Unnatural Narratology: Extensions, Revisions, and Challenges. Columbus: 135–64.

(2021) *Essays in Narrative and Fictionality: Reassessing Nine Central Concepts.* Cambridge.

Richardson, N. J. (1980) 'Literary criticism in the exegetical scholia to the *Iliad*: A sketch', *CQ*, 30/2: 265–87.

(1986) 'Pindar and later literary criticism in antiquity', *ARCA*, 19: 383–401.

Rimmon-Kenan, S. (1983) *Narrative Fiction: Contemporary Poetics.* London.

Rispoli, G. M. (1988) *Lo spazio del verisimile: Il racconto, la storia e il mito.* Naples.

Robbe-Grillet, A. (1957) *La jalousie.* Paris.

(1965) *La maison de rendez-vous.* Paris.

Rohde, E. (1914) *Der griechische Roman und seine Vorläufer.* Leipzig.

Rood, T. (1998) *Thucydides: Narrative and Explanation.* Oxford.

(2015) 'Review of D. Cairns and R. Scodel (eds.), *Defining Greek Narrative*', *CR*, 65/2: 329–30.

Rosen, R. M. (2007) *Making Mockery: The Poetics of Ancient Satire.* Oxford.

Rösler, W. (1980) 'Die Entdeckung der Fiktionalität in der Antike', *Poetica*, 12/3–4: 283–319.

(1985) 'Persona reale o persona poetica? L'interpretazione dell'"io" nella lirica greca arcaica', *QUCC*, 19/1: 131–44.

Ruffell, I. A. (2011) *Politics and Anti-Realism in Athenian Old Comedy: The Art of the Impossible.* Oxford.

Russell, B. (2005 [1905]) 'On denoting', *Mind*, 114/456: 873–87.

Russell, D. A. (1981) *Criticism in Antiquity.* London.

Russo, J. (1982) 'Interview and aftermath: Dream, fantasy, and intuition in *Odyssey* 19 and 20', *AJPh*, 103/1: 4–18.

Rutherford, R. B. (1992) *Homer:* Odyssey *Books* XIX *and* XX. Cambridge.

Ryan, M.-L. (1991) *Possible Worlds, Artificial Intelligence and Narrative Theory.* Bloomington.

(2001) *Narrative as Virtual Reality: Immersion and Interactivity in Literature and Electronic Media.* Baltimore.

(2010) 'Narratology and cognitive science: A problematic relation', *Style*, 44/4: 469–95.

(2015) 'Response to Jonas Grethlein's "Is narrative 'the description of fictional mental functioning'? Heliodorus Against Palmer, Zunshine & Co."', *Style*, 49/3: 293–8.

Sandnes, K. O. (2009) *The Challenge of Homer: School, Pagan Poets and Early Christianity.* London.

Sandy, G. N. (1982) *Heliodorus.* Boston.

Santini, C. and F. Stok (eds.) (2004) *Hinc italae gentes: Geopolitica ed etnografia dell'Italia nel commento di Servio all'Eneide.* Pisa.

Savarese, R. J. and L. Zunshine (2014) 'The critic as neurocosmopolite; or, what cognitive approaches to literature can learn from disability studies: Lisa Zunshine in conversation with Ralph James Savarese', *Narrative*, 22/1: 17–44.

Schaefer, U. (2004) 'Die Funktion des Erzählers zwischen Mündlichkeit und Schriftlichkeit', in W. Haubrichs, E. Lutz and K. Ridder (eds.), *Erzähltechnik und Erzählstrategien in der deutschen Literatur des Mittelalters: Saarbrücker Kolloquium 2002, Wolfram-Studien* XVIII. Berlin: 83–98.

Schaeffer, J.-M. (1999) *Pourquoi la fiction?* Paris.

  (2014) 'Fictional vs. factual narration', in P. Hühn, J. C. Meister, J. Pier and W. Schmid (eds.), *Handbook of Narratology*. Berlin: 98–114.

Schein, S. (2019) 'Homerus ethicus', in L. Grace Canevaro and O. Rourke (eds.), *Didactic Poetry of Greece, Rome, and Beyond: Knowledge, Power, Tradition*. Swansea: 75–95.

Schilling, E. (2021) *Authentizität: Karriere einer Sehnsucht*. Munich.

Schirren, T. (2005) *Philosophos Bios: Die antike Philosophenbiographie als symbolische Form. Studien zur* Vita Apollonii *des Philostrat*. Heidelberg.

Schlaffer, H. (1990) *Poesie und Wissen: Die Entstehung des ästhetischen Bewusstseins und der philologischen Erkenntnis*. Frankfurt am Main.

Schlemm, A. (1893) *De Fontibus Plutarchi Commentationum de Audiendis Poetis et de Fortuna*. Göttingen.

Schlunk, R. (1974) *The Homeric Scholia and the* Aeneid*: A Study of the Influence of the Ancient Homeric Literary Criticism on Vergil*. Ann Arbor.

Schmedt, H. (2020) *Antonius Diogenes, "Die unglaublichen Dinge jenseits von Thule": Edition, Übersetzung, Kommentar*. Berlin.

Schmid, W. (2010) *Narratology: An Introduction*. Berlin.

Schmitt, A. (ed.) (2008) *Aristoteles:* Poetik. Darmstadt.

Schmitt, A. (2010) 'Making the case for self-narration against autofiction', *Auto/Biography Studies*, 25/1: 122–37.

Schmitz, T. A. (1997) *Bildung und Macht: Zur sozialen und politischen Funktion der zweiten Sophistik in der griechischen Welt der Kaiserzeit*. Munich.

  (2015) 'Review of Irene J. F. Jong, Narratology and classics: A practical guide', *Mnemosyne*, 69/4: 707–10.

Schneider, C. (2019) 'Handlung und Handlungslogik – Mittelalter', in E. von Contzen and S. Tilg (eds.), *Handbuch Historische Narratologie*. Stuttgart: 249–61.

Schneider, R. (2001) 'Toward a cognitive theory of literary character: The dynamics of mental-model construction", *Style*, 35/4: 607–39.

Schollmeyer, J. (2021) *Gorgias' Lobrede auf Helena: Literaturgeschichtliche Untersuchungen und Kommentar*. Berlin.

Schwartz, E. (1924) *Die* Odyssee. Munich.

Scodel, R. (1997) 'Teichoscopia, catalogue, and the female spectator in Euripides', *Colby Quarterly*, 33/1: 76–93.

  (2005) 'Review of I. J. F. de Jong, R. Nünlist, A. M. Bowie, *Narrators, Narratees, and Narratives in Ancient Greek Literature. Studies in Ancient Greek Narrative, Vol. 1*', *BMCRev*, 20050748.

  (2008) *Epic Facework: Self-Presentation and Social Interaction in Homer*. Swansea.

(2012) 'ἦ and Theory of Mind in the *Iliad*', in M. Meier-Brügger (ed.), *Homer, gedeutet durch ein großes Lexikon*. Berlin: 319–34.

(2014a) 'Introduction', in D. L. Cairns and R. Scodel (eds.), *Defining Greek Narrative*. Edinburgh: 1–10.

(2014b) 'Narrative focus and elusive thought in Homer', in D. L. Cairns and R. Scodel (eds.), *Defining Greek Narrative*. Edinburgh: 55–74.

Schulz, A. (2012) *Erzähltheorie in mediävistischer Perspektive*. Berlin.

Searle, J. R. (1979) 'The logical status of fictional discourse', in *Expression and Meaning*. Cambridge: 58–75.

Segal, C. P. (1962) 'Gorgias and the psychology of the logos', *HSCPh*, 66: 99–155.

Sheppard, A. (2014) *The Poetics of Phantasia: Imagination in Ancient Aesthetics*. New York.

Snell, B. (1993) *Die Entdeckung des Geistes*, 7th ed. Hamburg.

Sommerstein, A. (1994) *Aristophanes:* Thesmophoriazusae. Warminster.

Sorabji, R. (2006) *Self: Ancient and Modern Insights about Individuality, Life and Death*. Chicago.

(2008) 'Greco-Roman varieties of self', in P. Remes and J. Sihvola (eds.), *Ancient Philosophy of the Self*. New York: 13–34.

Sourvinou-Inwood, C. (1979) *Theseus as Son and Stepson: A Tentative Illustration of Greek Mythological Mentality*. London.

Spearing, A. C. (2005) *Textual Subjectivity: The Encoding of Subjectivity in Medieval Narratives and Lyrics*. Oxford.

(2012) *Medieval Autographies: The 'I' of the Text*. Notre Dame, IN.

Starr, R. J. (1991) 'Reading aloud: Lectores and Roman reading', *CJ*, 86/4: 337–43.

Steiner, D. (2010) *Homer* Odyssey: *Books* XVII *and* XVIII. Cambridge.

Stenger, J. R. (2016) 'Athens and/or Jerusalem? Basil's and Chrysostom's views on the didactic use of literature and stories', in P. Gemeinhardt, L. v. Hoof and P. van Nuffelen (eds.), *Education and Religion in Late Antique Christianity*. London: 86–99.

Sternberg, M. (1978) *Expositional Modes and Temporal Ordering in Fiction*. Baltimore.

(1992a) 'Telling in time (I)', *Poetics Today*, 11/4: 901–48.

(1992b) 'Telling in time (II)', *Poetics Today*, 13/3: 463–541.

Stoppard, T. (1973) *Artist Descending a Staircase*. London.

Struck, P. T. (2016) *Divination and Human Nature: A Cognitive History of Intuition in Classical Antiquity*. Princeton.

Stürmer, F. (1921) *Die Rhapsodien der* Odyssee. Würzburg.

Style (2011) Special Issue 'Social Minds', 45/2.

Swain, S. (1996) *Hellenism and Empire: Language, Classicism, and Power in the Greek World,* AD *50–250*. Oxford.

Tagliabue, A. (2015) 'Heliodorus's *Aethiopica* and the Odyssean *Mnesterophonia*: An intermedial reading', *TAPhA*, 145/2: 445–68.

(2017) *Xenophon's* Ephesiaca: *A Paraliterary Love-Story from the Ancient World*. Groningen.

Telò, M. (2011) 'The eagle's gaze in the opening of Heliodorus' "Aethiopica"', *AJPh*, 132/4: 581–613.

Thalmann, W. (2014) 'Review of Irene J.F. de Jong (ed.), *Space in Ancient Greek Literature. Studies in Ancient Greek Narrative 3*', *JHS*, 134: 175–6.

Thiemann, A. (2019) 'Postmodernity', in M. Wagner-Egelhaaf (ed.), *Handbook of Autobiography/Autofiction*. Berlin: 778–804.

Tilg, S. (2014) *Apuleius' Metamorphoses: A Study in Roman Fiction*. Oxford.

   (2017) 'Eine Gattung ohne Namen, Theorie und feste Form: Der griechische Roman als literaturgeschichtliche Herausforderung', in J. Grethlein and A. Rengakos (eds.), *Griechische Literaturgeschichtsschreibung: Traditionen, Probleme und Konzepte*. Berlin: 83–101.

   (2019) 'Autor und Erzähler – Antike', in E. von Contzen and S. Tilg (eds.), *Handbuch historische Narratologie*. Berlin: 69–81.

Troscianko, E. T. (2014) *Kafka's Cognitive Realism*. New York.

Turolla, E. (1930) *Saggio sulla poesia d'Omero*. Bari.

Valette-Cagnac, E. (1997) *La lecture à Rome: Rites et pratiques*. Paris.

van Emde Boas, E. (2018) 'Aeschylus', in K. de Temmermann and E. van Emde Boas (eds.), *Characterization in Ancient Greek Literature*. Leiden: 317–36.

van Nortwick, T. (1979) 'Penelope and Nausicaa', *TAPhA*, 109: 269–76.

Vester, H. (1968) 'Das 19. Buch der *Odyssee*', *Gymnasium*, 75: 417–34.

Veyne, P. (1988) *Did the Greeks Believe in Their Myths? An Essay on the Constitutive Imagination*. Chicago.

Vlahos, J. B. (2011) 'Homer's *Odyssey*: Penelope and the case for early recognition', *College Literature*, 38: 1–75.

Vogt-Spira, G. (2020) 'Review of S. Feddern, *Der antike Fiktionalitätsdiskurs*', *Anzeiger für die Altertumswissenschaft*, 73/1: 8–18.

   (2022) '*Secundum verum fingere*: Wirklichkeitsnachahmung, Imagination und Fiktionalität. Epistemologische Überlegungen zur hellenistisch-römischen Literaturkonzeption', in *Studien zur römischen Anthropologie*. Freiburg: 95–118.

von Contzen, E. (2014) 'Why we need a medieval narratology: A manifesto', *Diegesis*, 3/2: 1–21.

   (2015) 'Why medieval literature does not need the concept of social minds: Exemplarity and collective experience', *Narrative*, 23: 140–54.

   (2018) 'Diachrone Narratologie und historische Erzählforschung: Eine Bestandsaufnahme und ein Plädoyer', *Beiträge zur mediävistischen Erzählforschung*, 1: 18–38.

von Contzen, E. and S. Tilg (2020) 'Fictionality before fictionality? Historicizing a modern concept', in M. Fludernik and H. S. Nielsen (eds.), *Traveling Concepts: New Fictionality Studies*. Berlin: 91–114.

von Contzen, E. and S. Tilg (eds.) (2019) *Handbuch Historische Narratologie*. Berlin.

von Wilamowitz-Moellendorff, T. (1917) *Die dramatische Technik des Sophokles*. Berlin.

von Wilamowitz-Moellendorff, U. (1927) *Die Heimkehr des Odysseus: Neue homerische Untersuchungen.* Berlin.

Wagner, F. (2002) 'Glissements et déphasages: Note sur la métalepse narrative', *Poétique*, 130: 235–53.

Walker, A. D. (1993) '*Enargeia* and the spectator in Greek historiography', *TAPhA*, 123: 353–77.

Walsh, G. B. (1984) *The Varieties of Enchantment: Early Greek Views of the Nature and Function of Poetry.* Chapel Hill.

Walsh, R. (1997) 'Who is the narrator?', *Poetics Today*, 18/4: 495–513.

 (2007) *The Rhetoric of Fictionality: Narrative Theory and the Idea of Fiction.* Columbus.

Walton, K. L. (1990) *Mimesis as Make-Believe: On the Foundations of the Representational Arts.* Cambridge, MA.

Wardy, R. (1996) *The Birth of Rhetoric: Gorgias, Plato and their Successors.* London.

Webb, R. (2009) *Ekphrasis, Imagination and Persuasion in Ancient Rhetorical Theory and Practice.* Farnham.

 (2016) 'Sight and insight: Theorizing vision, emotion and imagination in ancient rhetoric', in M. Squire (ed.), *Sight and the Ancient Senses.* London: 205–19.

Wellek, R., Warren, A. (1949) *Theory of Literature.* New York.

West, M. L. (ed.) (1966) *Hesiodus:* Theogony. Oxford.

White, H. (1975) *Metahistory: The Historical Imagination in Nineteenth-Century Europe.* Baltimore.

Whitman, C. H. (1958) *Homer and the Heroic Tradition.* Cambridge.

Whitmarsh, T. (2001) *Greek Literature and the Roman Empire: The Politics of Imitation.* Oxford.

 (2011) *Narrative and Identity in the Ancient Greek Novel: Returning Romance.* Cambridge.

 (2013) 'An I for an I: Reading fictional autobiography', in A. Marmodoro and J. Hill (eds.), *The Author's Voice in Classical and Late Antiquity.* Oxford: 233–47.

Winkler, J. J. (1985) *Auctor & Actor: A Narratological Reading of Apuleius's* Golden Ass. Berkeley.

 (1990) *The Constraints of Desire: The Anthropology of Sex and Gender in Ancient Greece.* New York.

 (1999) 'The mendacity of Kalasiris and the narrative strategy of Heliodoros' *Aithiopika*', in S. Swain (ed.), *Oxford Readings in the Greek Novel.* Oxford: 286–350.

Winterson, J. (2011) *Why Be Happy When You Could Be Normal.* New York.

Wolf, C. (1977) *Kindheitsmuster.* Darmstadt.

Wolf, W. (1993) *Ästhetische Illusion und Illusionsdurchbrechung in der Erzählkunst. Theorie und Geschichte mit Schwerpunkt auf englischem illusionsstörenden Erzählen. Anglia* XXXII. Tübingen.

 (2004) 'Aesthetic illusion as an effect on fiction', *Style*, 38/3: 325–50.

(2008) 'Is aesthetic illusion "illusion référentielle"? "Immersion" in (narrative) representations and its relationship to fictionality and factuality', *Journal of Literary Theory*, 2/1: 99–126.

Wolfe, T. and E. W. Johnson (1975) *The New Journalism*. London.

Woodhouse, W. J. (1930) *The Composition of Homer's* Odyssey. Oxford.

Wright, D. H. (1993) *Der Vergilius Vaticanus: Ein Meisterwerk spätantiker Kunst*. Graz.

Wyatt, W. F. (1989/90) 'Homeric transitions', *Archaiognosia*, 6: 11–23.

Zanker, G. (1981) '*Enargeia* in the ancient criticism of poetry', *RhM*, 124/3–4: 297–311.

Zeitlin, F. I. (1991) 'Introduction', in J.-P. Vernant. and F. I. Zeitlin (eds.), *Mortals and Immortals: Collected Essays*. Princeton: 3–26.

Zipfel, F. (2001) *Fiktion, Fiktivität, Fiktionalität: Analysen zur Fiktion in der Literatur und zum Fiktionsbegriff in der Literaturwissenschaft*. Berlin.

Zlatev, J., T. P. Racine, C. Sinha and E. Itkonen (eds.) (2008) *The Shared Mind: Perspectives on Intersubjectivity*. Amsterdam.

Zunshine, L. (2006) *Why We Read Fiction: Theory of Mind and the Novel*. Columbus.

(2011) '1700–1775: Theory of Mind, social hierarchy, and the emergence of narrative subjectivity', in D. Herman (ed.), *The Emergence of Mind: Representations of Consciousness in Narrative Discourse in English*. Lincoln, NE: 161–86.

Zwaan, R. A. (2004) 'The immersed experiencer: Toward an embodied theory of language comprehension', in B. H. Ross (ed.), *The Psychology of Learning and Motivation 44*. New York: 35–62.

(2014) 'Embodiment and language comprehension: Reframing the discussion', *Trends in Cognitive Sciences*, 18/5: 229–34.

Index Locorum

Aeschylus
Agamemnon
    906–7: 138
    922–4: 138
Anonymus Seguerianus
    96: 94
Apuleius
Metamorphoses
    11.27.9: 68
Archilochus
    fr. 172–181 W: 30
    fr. 185–7 W: 30
    fr. 5 W: 54
Aristophanes
Frogs
    13–15: 73–4
Thesmophoriazusae
    148–52: 73
    275–6: 57
Aristotle
Poetics
    1448a21–2: 65
    1450a15–23: 104
    1450a23–38: 104
    1450a38–1450b4: 104
    1450b26–34: 142
    1451a16–17: 35
    1451a32–4: 35
    1451a32–5: 142
    1451a36–7: 35
    1451a36–8: 34
    1451b29–32: 35
    1451b34–5: 142
    1451b4–5: 34
    1451b5–11: 36
    1452a18–21: 142
    1452a4: 142
    1454a16–19: 105
    1454a22–6: 105
    1454a26–31: 143

    1455a22–6: 36
    1455a22–32: 72
    1461b19–21: 57, 142
Rhetoric
    1416a28–31: 57-8
Athenaeus
    12.551 = Hermippus fr. 36 KA: 59
Augustine
de civitate Dei
    18.18: 55

Cassius Dio
    2.30–1: 109
Choricius
    21.2: 66–7
Critias
    88 B 44 DK = Ael. *VH* 10.13: 54

Demetrius
de elocutione
    216: 101
Diomedes Grammaticus
    Keil, *Grammatici Latini* 1, p. 491
        31
Dionysius of Halicarnassus
On Lysias
    7: 94

Eratosthenes
    1 A 14 Berger: 46
    1 A 17 Berger: 46
    1 A 19 Berger: 46
    1 A 4 Berger: 46
    Strabo 1.1.10: 44
Eupolis
    fr. 155 KA = Plut. Vit. *Per.* 3.7: 58–9
    fr. 269 KA = Poll. *Onom.* 9.102: 59
Euripides
Andromache
    628–31: 144

General Index

Achilles, 108–10, 134, 144, 145, 159
Aegeus, 142
Aeschylus, 44, 138–40
  carpet scene in *Agamemnon*,
    138–40
affordances, 78
Agamemnon, 138
Agathon, 73
agōn, 101
ainos, 30
Allen, Walter, 123
Amis, Martin, 153
Amory, Anne, 119
Amphimedon, 134
anachronies, 3, 127
aoidē, 14
apatē, 38, 42
apostrophe, 158–60
Apuleius, 32, 67, 80
  Golden Ass, 32
Archilochus, 30, 80
argumentum, 30, 49, 50
Aristarchus, 47, 60
Aristophanes, 31, 57, 74
  Frogs, 44
  Thesmophoriazusae, 73
Aristotle, 17, 19, 22, 45, 49, 57, 60, 65–6, 71, 107,
    116, 136, 163, 165
  discussion of fiction(ality)?, 34–6
  on motivation, 141–4
  on narrative modes, 65
  on plot and character, 103–5
  Poetics, 18, 22, 26, 36, 42, 50, 72,
    103–8
Asclepiades of Myrlea, 23, 48
Athenaeus, 59
Auerbach, Erich, 12
Augustine, 22, 67–8, 69
  de civitate dei, 54–5
  on Apuleius, 54–5, 67
Austin, Norman, 119

author
  and characters in ancient criticism, 53–80
  described as doing what characters are
    doing, 73–5
  implied, 80
  relation to narrated world unmetaleptic in
    ancient criticism, 75–6
  seen as impersonating characters, 63–8
autism
  and Theory of Mind, 86
autofiction, 152, 153–5

Badian, Ernst, 3
Bakhtin, Michail, 1
Bal, Mieke, 2, 21, 148
Banfield, Ann, 23, 80
Baron-Cohen, Simon, 84
Baroni, Raphaël, 103
Barthes, Roland, 1, 2, 151–2, 155, 162
Basil
  ad adulescentes, 45
Beowulf, 167
Birke, Dorothee, 8, 9
Boccaccio, 126
Bond, James, 164
Brémond, Claude, 115
bucolic poetry, 31
Budelmann, Felix, 81

Cairns, Douglas, 7
Calasiris, 89, 99–100
Carrère, Emmanuel, 153, 154
character
  and author in ancient criticism, 53–80
  and plot in ancient criticism, 103–11
  in ancient novels, 87
  in postmodern texts, 161–5
  in tragedy, 136–40
  utterances of ascribed to author in ancient
    criticism, 57–60
  vs. personality, 87, 90, 134